DOMINANT LANGUAGES:
LANGUAGE AND HIERARCHY
IN BRITAIN AND FRANCE

DOMINANT LANGUAGES

Language and Hierarchy
in Britain and France

R. D. GRILLO

University of Sussex

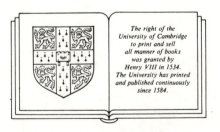

The right of the
University of Cambridge
to print and sell
all manner of books
was granted by
Henry VIII in 1534.
The University has printed
and published continuously
since 1584.

CAMBRIDGE UNIVERSITY PRESS

CAMBRIDGE

NEW YORK   PORT CHESTER   MELBOURNE   SYDNEY

Published by the Press Syndicate of the University of Cambridge
The Pitt Building, Trumpington Street, Cambridge CB2 IRP
40 West 20th Street, New York, NY 10011, USA
10 Stamford Road, Oakleigh, Melbourne 3166, Australia

First published 1989

Printed in Great Britain by the University Press, Cambridge

British Library cataloguing in publication data

Grillo, R. (Ralph D.)
Dominant languages: language and hierarchy
in Britain and France
1. French language. Social aspects of usage
2. English language. Social aspects of
usage
1. Title
428

Library of Congress cataloguing in publication data

Grillo, R. D.
Dominant languages: language and hierarchy in Britain and France
R. D. Grillo.
    p.   cm.
Bibliography.
Includes index.
ISBN 0-521-36540-6
1 Sociolinguistics – Great Britain.   2. Sociolinguistics – France.
3. Great Britain – Languages – Political aspects.   4. France –
Languages – Political aspects.   1. Title
P40.45.G7G75   1989
401'.9'0941 – dc19   89-509   CIP

ISBN 0521 36540 6

CONTENTS

v

PREFACE

THIS book has been a long time in writing. In 1975–6 I undertook fieldwork in Lyons, France, on relations between the personnel of the French institutional system (social workers, teachers and so on) and immigrants and their families in an industrial city. That research led to a range of theoretical and analytical problems concerned with language in society which in a monograph on Lyons (Grillo 1985) I had to leave aside. Later (1977–80) I participated in a seminar on anthropological research in Western Europe (supported by the then Social Science Research Council) from which emerged à collection of papers taking as their focus the concepts of 'nation' and 'state' (Grillo 1980). A second was planned, linking contributions on 'Ideologies and social movements' and 'Dominant languages', which it was hoped would further the exploration of the nation-state framework by focusing on the relationship between language and power. Unfortunately this collection was never published, but stimulated by the seminar proceedings I drafted an introduction which guided my own later reading and writing, and generated the title of the present book. Many of the questions explored here thus derived from anthropological fieldwork, and discussions between anthropologists who had located similar issues in their own research. One aim in writing this book, then, has been to show how and why the study of language is particularly important for an anthropology of Europe, given the discipline's long-standing interest in language as a social phenomenon and in differentiation as a central feature of social structure. This is undertaken through a comparative account of 'dominant languages', and the politics of language in two European countries (Britain and France).

The book also has implicit objectives of a methodological and theoretical kind. Its stance has been shaped by participation, from 1982 onwards, in a joint Anthropology/Linguistics Workshop at the University of Sussex. This Workshop brings together faculty and postgraduates from those two disciplines and others to explore orientations towards the study of language in society – what I shall call 'social linguistics'. The Workshop forced me to consider much more fully than I had previously what form an anthropological contribution to the investigation of language in European society might take. They also made me aware of the limitations of existing models of language found in mainstream linguistics, and of the models of language in society which some linguists had formulated in an effort to break free of them.

The emphasis throughout is on an interdisciplinary perspective. Language in society is a phenomenon of great importance for many disciplines: linguistics, of course, sociology, if a distinction may be drawn between it and anthropology, psychology, social history, geography in some of its manifestations, political science, education, international relations, and in recent years the study of language and literature. The topic's theoretical and practical importance for all these disciplines has emerged very clearly in the last twenty years or so in debates about the connection between language and class, language and race, language and gender, and literature and politics. Nevertheless I hope to demonstrate that an anthropological perspective is especially valuable for a field which by nature and practice is an interdisciplinary one, *inter alia* enabling linkages between the contributions which come from other disciplines. However, to make that contribution effective anthropology must go beyond its traditional approach.

Non-anthropologists may think this reveals an unnecessary concern for one's own discipline, or perhaps a kind of imperialism, but anthropology is especially helpful because it offers ways of handling the complex social data which constitute the evidence for linguistic inequality, providing means of analysing in processual terms how that inequality operates. Anthropology's emphasis on the need to take into account, and understand, the continuity between what occurs at the 'micro' level of the small-scale, the local and the interpersonal, and at what is usually conceived as the 'macro' level of large-scale, general, social and cultural processes is particularly relevant. One of anthropology's strengths is in the location of 'pivotal' or 'nodal' relationships, phenomena which enable the continuity between 'levels' to be conceptualised and understood (see Grillo 1980: 5). Of equal importance is the insistence on making analytically central the dialectical relationship between 'social structure' (the principal forces shaping social existence) and 'social construction' (what a society's members themselves make of it). The nature of the anthropological contribution, actual or potential, to the study of language in society relates to another implicit objective of this book, to explore the theoretical foundations of a field which may be described by the very broad term 'social linguistics'. Other labels – 'sociolinguistics', 'sociology of language', 'anthropological linguistics', 'linguistic anthro-

pology', 'ethnography of speaking', 'discourse analysis', to name but a few –
are best employed to describe particular schools of thought within, or
approaches to, that field (cf. Edwards, J. R. 1985:4). It is beyond the scope
of this volume to set out in detail the theoretical problems involved in
constituting a satisfactory account of language in society: what form such an
account might take, the barriers to its formulation, how they might be
overcome etc., though I do suggest what some of the difficulties are, and
outline an approach which may be found useful (see also Grillo, Pratt and
Street 1987).

A large number of people have contributed to the development of this
book. At the University of Sussex, I have found considerable stimulus in the
work of fellow anthropologists, especially that of Jeffrey Pratt, and Brian
Street. Their work, together with that of other, non-anthropological,
colleagues such as Margaret Deuchar, Jim McGiveny, Ulrike Meinhof and
Trevor Pateman, has meant that the University provided a most stimulating
environment in which to think about the issues raised by this book. Richard
Burton has once again proved to be a mine of information on nineteenth-
century French thought, and I would like to thank him for his ever helpful
advice. I have also been aided by frequent discussions with anthropology
postgraduates at Sussex (in particular Andrea Caspari, Lucy Rushton,
Susanna Rostas, and Crispin Shore) whose research in various ways touched
on linguistic issues. Undergraduate students taking various courses
concerned with language in European society have more than once been
crucial in helping me formulate, defend, and modify a particular point of
view. Outside Sussex, a number of people have over the years generously
shared views and criticisms, and here I wish to acknowledge my particular
indebtedness to Professor Lorraine Baric, of the University of Salford, Dr
Verity Saifullah Khan, formerly of the Linguistic Minorities Project,
Institute of Education, and Dr Gill Seidel of the University of Bradford. I
owe a great deal to my wife, Bron Grillo, who undertook most of the
translation of the texts by Grégoire, Barère and Talleyrand used extensively
in chapter 2 and elsewhere in the book. A Personal Research Grant awarded
by the Economic and Social Research Council allowed a period of
concentrated effort during the first half of 1985 and enabled me to complete
a large part of a manuscript exploring these issues.

Social linguistics employs a large technical vocabulary which I have tried
to keep to a minimum. Where it is unavoidable I will explain the meaning
when a term is first used.

I

INTRODUCTION:
THE POLITICS
OF COMMUNICATIVE PRACTICE

THE POLITICS OF LANGUAGE IN BRITAIN AND FRANCE

EVERY European society is, and has always been, 'multilingual'. In each there co-exist what are conventionally thought of as different languages (e.g. French/Breton, English/Welsh), and different regional or local forms of these languages (e.g. English dialects). There are also many different 'ways of speaking' (called variously 'registers', 'styles', 'codes' or 'discourses') sometimes associated with particular languages or regional forms. It is also the case that in every European society languages and their speakers are usually of unequal status, power and authority, and there is commonly a hierarchical ordering of languages, dialects and ways of speaking. How (and why) do linguistic inequality and linguistic hierarchy manifest themselves, and with what consequences? How has this kind of inequality been conceptualised? And how does it mesh with the other kinds of inequality? To provide a systematic review of these critical issues this book compares two European nation-states (Britain and France) where language in all its forms has not only been a significant element in social differentiation, but also a major site of political conflict. The study traces aspects of that conflict from the Late Middle Ages onwards. Reviewing anthropological writing on Europe (Grillo 1980), I suggested that to go beyond the limitations of existing research anthropologists could employ a heuristic definition of 'Europe' as a social, economic, political and cultural system comprising a set of processes and a set of 'real' societies which the processes in part constituted. Three processes in particular command attention: the emergence of supra-local identities and the incorporation of localities within wider entities such as the nation; the growth of powerful institutions within the public domain (the state); and the development of an 'economy' with organisational features characteristic of what are usually called industrial societies (capitalist and non-capitalist).

This framework, which provided an entrée to the study of 'nation' and 'state' (in Grillo 1980), also offers a way into the study of relationships of super- and subordination generally. Linguistic inequality, and the connection between language and power, are central to such a project. This is because it is impossible to discuss a European 'system' without reference to linguistic differentiation. Language has been a major element in the organisation of European society, and of the construction of 'difference' both within and between the countries of Europe, especially over the last 200 years. ('Difference' is the way in which social differentiation is perceived and conceived by social actors, the subjective aspect of differentiation.) Language is, for example, one differentiating criterion, enmeshed with others in complex ways, in the formation of nation-states, and as such has been the subject of intense ideological speculation and the site of intense political struggle.

The political history of language in Britain and France shows that when in the Early Modern period language was a matter of state it had only a specific, limited importance. Britain and France in, say, the sixteenth or seventeenth centuries, had many of the characteristics of what Gellner (1983) calls 'agro-literate' polities. It was necessary for several reasons that the state, and critically the courts, employed a single tongue (the 'King's language'), and inevitably that language was the language of the Court. Competence in the language of court and Court became a necessary skill for anyone (such as the gentry) aspiring to participate in those circles. But it was rarely a matter of state policy that this should be so, and in neither Britain nor France was anyone really interested in what the great mass of people actually spoke.

By the eighteenth century, the 'standardized language-of-state' (Anderson 1983), which by then had become the standardised language of élite literature and of printing, was employed much more widely as an essential element of commerce. But it was not until the end of the eighteenth century in France, perhaps even later in England, that this language became in any significant way a matter of state concern. Then, however, what the mass of people spoke *did* become an issue. Linguistic homogeneity became critical, and the chosen, indeed inevitable, vehicle for achieving it was education.

The material from Britain and France illustrates an important point made by the historian Jonathan Steinberg in a recent brief but thought-provoking paper. Steinberg argues that the *questione della lingua*, the 'language question', 'flickers in and out of the constant interplay between culture and power' (1987:206), in Italy, for example, appearing now in one form, then in another. There do, however, appear to have been certain historic moments, not only in Italy but in Europe as a whole, when the language question has assumed extreme importance. As Steinberg acknowledges, our own age appears to be one such period. How and why this happens, and with what consequences for essentially pluralistic systems, are some of the principal issues which need to be addressed.

DOMINANT LANGUAGES

The title of this book ('Dominant languages') points towards a particular way of regarding the connection between the linguistic and the political. The focus throughout is on the hierarchical ordering of languages and their speakers. By this I refer to two closely related phenomena: the placing of those speaking different languages in higher or lower statuses and positions of power and authority; and the ranking of the languages themselves as inferior or superior. There is thus on the one hand social differentiation which incorporates a linguistic dimension, and on the other an ideology of linguistic hierarchy which stems from and reflects a social hierarchy based partly at least on linguistic criteria.

Two types of linguistic hierarchy are considered in this book. One is associated with what is usually, and roughly, called 'ethnicity', the other with what is generally, and again roughly, termed 'class'.

Linguistic hierarchy of the ethnic type appears in two kinds of situation typical of the 'core' countries of Western Europe.

(a)   Where nation-states have united in a single polity speakers of different languages and dialects under the hegemony of speakers of one language or dialect, i.e. where that language has become a 'standard'.

(b)   Where mass labour migration has brought into a polity speakers of languages other than those of the 'receiving' (or 'host') society, and immigrant or 'guest' language speakers occupy subordinate social, cultural, economic and usually political statuses.

Both entail what linguists have called *diglossia*. Ferguson (1959) originally applied this term to societies where two varieties of a language (e.g. a standard language and a dialect) were spoken by members of the same 'speech community', with each variety having its own function and situationally defined range of usage. One variety he terms 'H(igh)', the other 'L(ow)' by reference to the generally perceived status of the variety's functions. For example the H language may be used for education, the L for family conversation. Fishman (1976a:290 ff.) extended this to cover all cases where languages – and not just varieties of the same language – co-existed, and noted differences between situations in which diglossia occurred with, and without, bilingualism (where two or more languages were widely spoken by many members of the society, and where they were not). It is diglossia in Fishman's sense that characterises situations (a) and (b), and the first part of the book is concerned with the processes which bring about and shape it. The book is thus about the 'politics of diglossia'.

To speak of 'dominant languages', however, is to imply more than a static hierarchical order. Another technical term, one closely associated with the school of 'sociologists of language' of which Fishman was a founder member, is 'domain' or ('demesne' as Mackinnon, 1977, would have it). This refers to groups or classes of social situation, or 'spheres of activity' which are 'under the sway of one language or variety' (Fishman 1972a:439). The concept fits readily with that of diglossia, in that the latter is associated with a division of social life into sets of domains in which, generally, one language (say the H variety) is expected or appropriate or obligatory.

At the descriptive level the concept of domain has proved useful, even if, as Fishman recognises, the identification of *a* domain is often a matter of the analyst's intuition (1972a:449). Although I would disagree with Fishman that 'domains . . . *reveal* the links that exist between micro- and macrosociolinguistics' (p. 451, my emphasis), I nonetheless accept that some such notion must have a central role in the analysis of those linkages. Frequently, however, domain is used in an ahistorical, aprocessual and apolitical way merely to describe in a summary fashion the result of a sociolinguistic investigation showing that statistically the H language tends to be spoken here, the L language tends to be spoken there (cf. the Kingman Report (1988) with its rough identification of 'home', 'street', 'school' and 'work' as the domains in which different varieties of English are spoken). But that the H language is usually to be identified with the state and state power, the L language with hearth and home, and the 'community', requires that we consider the process by which this condition has been reached, and thus give an account of how the domains of one language can be extended, those of another limited. A subordinate language may indeed be *defined* as one restricted to domains from which power in general societal terms is absent (cf. Calvet 1974:79, Edwards J. R. 1985:94, Williams, Glyn 1987:86). Hence 'domain limitation' and 'domain extension', both dynamic social and political processes, are an important part of diglossia.

4

Critical here is the concept of legitimacy.

'Domination' is the English word chosen by Matthews (in Runciman 1978:38) to translate Weber's term *Herrschaft* – 'the probability that a command will be obeyed' (Weber 1964:153 – awkwardly glossed by Parsons as 'imperative control'). Weber himself distinguished *Herrschaft* from *Macht* ('power') – 'Every possibility within a social relationship of imposing one's own will, even against opposition' (Runciman 1978:38). To avoid confusion, I should state that here 'dominant' is employed with reference to *Herrschaft*. What is conventionally called 'authority' is in Weber's terminology a particular type of *Herrschaft*, *Legitime Herrschaft*, legitimate domination. For Weber a key issue was how power was exercised, how authority achieved, without recourse to force. Authority does not, normally, in most societies, stem openly and explicitly from the gun barrel. Weber's problem was in this respect similar to one which troubled the Italian Marxist Antonio Gramsci who found it necessary to distinguish between what he called (confusingly from our point of view) 'domination', power exercised through force alone, and 'hegemony', leadership exercised by other means (Gramsci 1971:55, Williams, R. 1977:108). Pateman's contrast (1980:83) between 'oppressive' and 'repressive' relationships is similar.

The study of dominant languages therefore entails, *inter alia*, the study of language as an integral part of the relationship between those groups who dominate in Weber's sense (or have in Gramsci's terms hegemonic status) and those who are dominated. As the earlier discussion of 'domain' has suggested, domination, and its corollary subordination should be conceived as a *process of hierarchical ordering*. If we call a language 'dominant' it means that it stands at one point on the spectrum of powerful–powerless. Domination is an end result. Robert Lafont, referring to the situation of subordinate languages and regions in France, would describe the process which leads to this result as one of 'alienation', a consequence of which is that 'a national existence sees its autonomous destiny blocked off, and finds itself invited to espouse the destiny of the one which forces it to submit' (Lafont 1968:35–6). Such alienated societies may also, in Bourdieu's terms, be described as victims of 'symbolic violence', through which legitimate meanings are imposed 'by concealing the power relations' of the force which imposes them (Bourdieu and Passeron 1977:4). This, therefore, leads us to examine how, precisely, language is associated with the processes which generate a particular distribution of authority and enable certain groups to exercise domination/hegemony, and the relationship between language and their exercise of power. That subordination is an end result also means that linguistic hierarchy normally entails struggle. Domination has to be achieved, and may be avoided or evaded. Political struggle may occur over ownership and control of the means of production, distribution and exchange, but it is obviously important for this book that it is frequently also over culture and the possibility of producing culture – ideas, beliefs, values, knowledge, personality, language, the possibility of conceptualising one's own domination.

This latter theme emerges principally in the second half of the book which is also concerned with diglossia, albeit in a form closer to that which Ferguson envisaged, in that it deals with the distribution through the class system of dialects of the dominant languages (English and French). What has been happening to language in the formation of Britain and France as nation-states? In later chapters I refer to what I call a 'double development' involving two linked social linguistic processes, both deeply embroiled in the politics of language. First, there was increasing separation of the language into class and status-based varieties, with a parallel incorporation of speakers of the regional *patois* (and of the unrelated languages) into the speech community on a class basis. Secondly, there emerged at the highest levels a specialised version of the élite variety which was the *written* language of state and of literature. In many respects it is this latter development which has been the most important. It is that language – or rather that set of linguistic and communicative practices – which has been the principal concern of proponents of homogeneity and universalisation. And it was the implementation of that language through the education system – at once both unificatory and divisive – which has posed the most serious problems.

A distinctive feature of this language is the ideology surrounding it through which it makes a claim to be *the* rational language and the language *of* rationality. It is partly through this claim that I see this language constituting a class-related, institutionally-based set of communicative practices. But it is class-related in a way different from that in which certain dialects of French and English (e.g. upper class English spoken with Received Pronunciation) are class-related. Nor do I see the language as exclusively an adjunct, or effect, of the capitalist system, but rather as a consequence of, and perhaps an integral component of science and technology-based production systems. It happens, for historical reasons, that this language is actualised in French and English in a form of speech which is derived ultimately from particular class dialects, but it is in no simple way to be identified with them.

VARIETIES OF THE POLITICS OF LANGUAGE

Situations in which speakers of different languages occupy different positions in social hierarchies are widely distributed in Europe and elsewhere, and have been the subject of varied comment (see Calvet 1974, Fishman 1972a, Halliday 1978, Haugen 1972, 1981, Hymes 1975, Kelman 1972, Lafont *et al.* 1982, Lorwin 1972, Ross 1979, Rundle 1946, Stephens 1976, Weinreich 1967 for a variety of treatments). However, as a number of recent studies have sought to make clear, any study of linguistic dominance, linguistic hierarchy and linguistic inequality is inevitably a political study (for example Kramerae *et al.* eds. 1984, *Language and power*, and Wolfson and Manes (eds.) 1985, *Language of inequality*, or Olivia Smith's excellent and detailed book on England, *The politics of language, 1791–1819*). A review of the literature suggests, however, that there are at least six ways in which the relationship between language, power and politics has been analytically constructed. (Some of this discussion is developed further in Grillo 1989.)

The first might be termed 'Language *and* politics'. In this approach, which itself consists of a variety of approaches, language is constituted as an *object* of political or governmental action (cf. O'Barr 1976:4). Language is treated as an attribute of, or a property belonging to, a defined human group which becomes political when, as attribute or property, it becomes the object of policy, and hence of conflict. The field of investigation which takes this view is a well-developed one in two areas: the study of language and nationalism, and, related to it, the study of language planning, especially in the Third World.

When language and politics in the sense defined have been discussed in a European context, there has been a stress on ideology, on the history of ideas about language, in particular within the Romantic tradition, and with the impact of that tradition on the mobilisation of nationalism and the formation of nation-states (see Smith 1981:46, and for examples, Anderson 1983, Gellner 1964, 1983, Kedourie 1960, Kohn 1944, 1946, 1967, Seton-Watson 1977, Smith 1976). Notwithstanding the importance of such studies, and indeed of the issues which they address (see in this book chapters 3 and 5 especially), the approach needs to be complemented by one which treats as fundamental the political and economic processes in which linguistic differentiation and incorporation occur. To some extent, such a treatment is to be found in the work of the 'sociologists of language', notably Fishman (e.g. 1973) and Haugen (e.g. 1972) whose studies provide a more specifically linguistic focus than those dealing mainly with the nationalist element in linguistic ideologies. As in the example of 'domain', however, the sociology

7

of language is descriptive rather than analytical, and often lacks a sense of the dynamic aspects of the politics of language.

A second approach, which is a distinct variant of the first, does claim to offer a strong, dynamic, theoretical and political framework. This, the 'Political economy of language', may be found in different ways in the work of Hechter (1975), Glyn Williams (1978), and Nairn (1977) on the British Isles, and, again in different ways, in that of Lafont (in numerous publications) and Renée Balibar (1974) on France. Here the politics of language is treated as a function of regionalism which in turn is treated as a function of the economic system, in particular of the economic, and political, relationship between core centres and dependent peripheries. This approach has much to offer (see Rokkan and Urwin 1982) but it is sometimes misleading because of its ultimate reductionism, its dismissal of ideology as mere rhetoric, and the simplistically macroscopic perspective it adopts (cf. Nairn 1977:201, Williams, Gwyn 1982). Above all there is a tendency to treat language as entirely epiphenomenal.

This is not always true, of course. Depending partly on how thorough-going a materialist perspective is adopted, language is seen as being of greater or lesser importance to the political process. Thus Robert Lafont, for example, in his writing on 'Occitanie', the region of Southern France in which the *langue d'Oc* was historically spoken, sees the way in which that region was incorporated economically and politically into 'France', under the hegemony of a French-speaking centre, as crucially involving language. The economic and political imperialism of France in Lafont's view entailed a cultural, and hence linguistic, imperialism. This perspective has, since World War II, been one widely shared by proponents of minority languages, whether or not they would accept the economic and political assumptions underlying the core–periphery model of national–regional relations.

In both these approaches the political is defined as pertaining to large-scale, inter and intra-national relationships. In a third approach, the 'Micropolitics of language', it is seen as something which inheres in interpersonal relationships. Here the focus is not on major institutional formations but on small groups and the interaction between individuals, and there is a strong theoretical orientation to methodological individualism. The political, if that term is ever employed, is identified with the power that one person can exercise over another (what Weber called *Macht*). Much of the social psychology of language (for example the work of Howard Giles) is ultimately concerned with this, as is what linguists call 'pragmatics'. Or rather, in so far as pragmatics deals with politics and power, it is with politics and power of this micro-level kind. Conventional 'discourse analysis' (what

I later call 'Discourse I') is also concerned with the micro-political in this sense. Though not denying the importance of the socio-psychological or interpersonal dimensions, I do not believe that such an orientation can provide a satisfactory account of the politics of language. The personal may be a *site* of the political, as for example feminists would argue, but this does not mean that the political can be defined, or adequately understood, as a function of interpersonal relations.

A fourth approach is also sometimes linked to perspectives from within the methodological individualism which characterises the 'Micropolitics of language'. This, the 'Language *of* politics', may be identified with what O'Barr calls a focus on how language affects the political process. Language is thought of as 'a resource in the political process . . . used to control, manipulate, and achieve political ends' (O'Barr 1976:7). The emphasis is on linguistic form, and the messages which form signals, as for example in some of Gumperz's writing (e.g. 1982a and 1982b). O'Barr in his account of legal language argues: 'Form is communication; variations in form communicate different messages; and speakers manipulate form, but not always consciously, to achieve beneficial results' (O'Barr 1982:11). Thus the control of form becomes crucial.

It is this perspective which underlies much of the discussion in a recent paper by Parkin (1984, see Parkin 1975). There is, however, another aspect which Parkin also discusses under the rubric 'Political language', and I will use that term to designate a distinct fifth approach which has, by and large, been the principal contribution of social anthropologists to the politics of language in general. This approach is concerned less with form than with content, and with the political power of different ways of encoding language. It is thus frequently concerned with rhetoric, in the classical sense, and with the persuasive nature of rhetorical devices such as metaphor. It appeals to anthropologists partly because of their traditional concern with indigenous concepts and conceptual systems. This is obviously important, but there is a danger that an emphasis on the conceptual leads to an excessively intellectualist orientation, treating conceptual systems as intellectual and philosophical systems existing apart from any framework of social action. This happens, to an extent, in the work of the late Edwin Ardener and his associates at Oxford (e.g. Chapman 1978). In recent years this has sometimes led anthropologists towards semantic accounts of language which have ignored the political dimension entirely. Bloch's edited collection on *Political language and oratory in traditional societies* stands virtually alone in attempting to explore the connection between linguistic, conceptual and political domains at both macro and micro levels, albeit mainly in a non-European context (but see Seidel 1975).

The 'political language' approach sometimes come close to a sixth: 'language/discourse as politics' (see Grillo, Pratt and Street 1987). There is a crucial difference, however, in the latter's treatment of the individual as 'subject', and in its identification of the political with power relations stemming from the dominant mode of production (i.e. capitalism), and thence with its servant, the dominant ideology.

Once again there are several strands and variants. In its most reductionist form, as perhaps in the work of Michel Pêcheux (1982), there is little examination of what comes between 'ideology' (all too often seen as an unproblematic adjunct of the dominant mode of production), and the 'subject', constructed in and through that ideology. This ignores the existence of a middle level where we find a multiplicity of class-relatable phenomena (I specifically do not say class correlated), not all of which are constituted wholly and exclusively in and through the dominant ideology. It also ignores the fact that it is at this level that language is often a crucial site of struggle. On the other hand, in the work of writers such as Gill Seidel or Olivia Smith this approach becomes an extremely powerful, indeed essential, tool for any study of the politics of language in modern society.

DOMINANT LANGUAGES: THE MEANING OF LANGUAGE

Later I say more about this last approach, but first it is necessary to consider what is meant by language. A focus on linguistic inequality and the politics of language is a response to Dell Hymes's concern with the 'sources and consequences of linguistic inequality' (1975:64) which Hymes considers a question of central importance inadequately treated by linguistics. It is also to take seriously Noam Chomsky's point that 'Questions of language are basically questions of power' (1979:191, cf. Haugen 1981:100ff.). But what features of language, intrinsic or extrinsic, may be connected to the holding of power and the exercise of hegemony?

Language, as the word is used in this book, refers to any one of several ways in which linguistic variety is constituted. This follows normal everyday English practice in which we refer on the one hand to instituted varieties such as 'the English language' or 'French' and those associated with particular groups or circles – 'You're talking my language', 'the language of the gutter', 'the language of politics'. This usage conflates several phenomena which are sometimes distinguished. In French and Italian, for example, *langue/lingua* and *langage/linguaggio* may be used to distinguish between two types of speech. *Langue/lingua* may refer to discrete entities usually associated with a particular nation or culture sometimes seen as species-like (e.g. 'French', 'Italian'). *Langage/linguaggio* may mean any sort of language variety of the kind suggested by the examples cited above. Adopting, but ultimately dissolving, this continental distinction, I will for the moment refer to the distinction as one between language and 'language'. (*Langage/linguaggio* may also refer to 'language in general', the human faculty of language. This is not a sense employed here. I am grateful to Margaret Deuchar for clarifying some of the points of usage discussed in this section.)

Social linguistics has a wide range of terms to describe varieties of language and 'language', some applied to one or the other, some to both. Thus 'dialect' generally refers to a language variety, while varieties of 'language' are usually described as 'styles', 'codes' or 'registers' (cf. Bell 1976, Halliday 1978, Haugen 1972, Hudson 1980, Labov 1972b, Robinson 1972). However, as Haugen (1972:240) remarks, 'dialect' was once used in English for 'any specialised variety of the language', e.g. 'lawyer's dialect'. 'Register' may also point in two directions, being conceived sometimes as a variety of 'language' used in defined situations (Bell 1976:27, Halliday 1978:32, 111, 157, Hudson 1980:48, Robinson 1972:35), sometimes as the property of a social group, and thereby entangled with 'dialect' (cf. Rickard 1974:128 on French). Thus Halliday refers to the bureaucratic 'register' which 'demand(s) the "standard" (national) dialect . . . Hence the dialect comes to symbolise the register' (1978:186). There are, however, likely to be situational varieties (registers) within the bureaucratic register ('language' variety) which may itself be associated with a dialect (language variety).

'Code' is also used in this context, but it is a dangerously ambiguous term. Halliday makes a distinction in the index to his 1978 book – it does not occur in the text – between 'code (i)' and 'code (ii)'. We come to 'code (i)' in a moment. 'Code (ii)' is sometimes a synonym for 'style' or stylistic variation, but Halliday, referring to the work of Gumperz (1971), Labov (1972a, cf. Labov 1972b), and Haugen (1972:250), identifies code in this sense with any 'language or language variety coexisting with other languages or language varieties in a (multilingual and multidialectal) society' (1978:65). It thus encompasses both dialect and register, and what Gumperz calls the 'code matrix' (1971:208–9) in a given community may include both language and 'language' varieties. This leads Bell (1976:110) to conclude that inter- and intra-language switching differ only in degree (cf. Calvet 1974:65, Hudson 1980:56, Milroy and Milroy 1985:125 ff.).

Language (without inverted commas) is perhaps preferable to one or other of the more specialised terms which are difficult to employ precisely and often used indiscriminately (cf. Ervin-Tripp 1976:44 ff., 1976:227).

'Dominant language' would therefore refer to a variety characteristically employed by those occupying superordinate positions: it is the language – in all senses – of the powerful. Thus the study of linguistic domination concerns the distribution through the social hierarchy and the power structure of what are usually thought of as several kinds of speech (and indeed writing).

'Code (i)', what Dittmar (1976:10) calls a 'speech code', introduces a different dimension. In the work of Basil Bernstein, as interpreted by Hasan (1973) and Halliday, code is a 'principle of semiotic organisation' (Halliday 1978:69, 111) which is 'actualized in language through register', and thereby connected with, or more often confused with, 'code (ii)'. As it will be necessary later to comment on Bernstein's ideas, it is useful here to point out that his 'codes' are at a 'more general level than that of language variety' (Hasan 1973:258). This is certainly true of his later writing where codes are described as 'dominant principles of interpretation' and 'dominant cultural principles' (Bernstein 1975:24, cf. 30).

This brings us to 'discourse', another term employed in a variety of senses, at least five, though for convenience I will reduce them to two: 'Discourse I' and 'Discourse II'.

In conventional linguistics discourse refers to verbal exchanges, to the flow of speech in conversations. This usage is of long standing in English, for example Samuel Pepys normally uses 'discourse' in his diaries to describe what we would call 'conversation' or 'discussion'. This is what 'discourse analysis' studies (Bell 1976:204–5, Coulthard 1977, Hudson 1980:131, Labov 1976:206, Trew 1979b:219, and Halliday 1978:108 on 'text'). This is 'Discourse I'.

Discourse may also refer, secondly, to a wide range of higher order linguistic practices (i.e. above the level of the phrase) of which conversation is but one example. (In linguistics, discourse has, in theory, this primary meaning). Thirdly, it is sometimes a synonym for 'register' (cf. Halliday, 1973:343, on the 'bureaucratic mode of discourse', and Cameron 1985:152). Fourthly it may mean a metalanguage – e.g. 'a discourse on method', or 'a discourse on language', 'talk about talk'. Discourse in these three senses may be interconnected in complex ways. For example, code (i) might be thought of as underlying discourse in both the second and third senses (higher order linguistic formations and 'register'), and may 'appear', implicitly, in the fourth, the talk about talk. Some people in fact argue that the 'elaborated' version of code (i) *is* a metalanguage (see Atkinson 1985:106–7).

The fifth sense (e.g. in Touraine 1977:193, 284, 290, Seidel 1979, Trew 1979b:154 and many others) stems principally from the writings of a number of French scholars, among whom Michel Foucault has been especially influential. For Foucault, discourse designates a 'group of statements in so far as they belong to the same discursive formation' (1972: 117). Statements are 'groups of verbal performances . . . linked at the statement level' (p. 115). That level is identified by the way that a statement is linked to a 'referential' (p. 91), which consists of 'laws of possibility, rules of existence for the objects that are named, designated or described within it, and for the relations that are affirmed or denied in it' (*ibid.*). In this sense discourse bears a family resemblance to Kuhn's modified concept of 'paradigm' (Kuhn 1970: 182 ff.). What I call 'Discourse II' is based principally on this conception of Foucault's, though it also contains elements of the second, third and fourth usages. And occasionally when, as in later chapters, I discuss something called 'elaborated discourse' the term signals all of these aspects simultaneously.

Although the theoretical perspective usually associated with Discourse II goes far beyond what the preceding paragraph suggests to provide a total conception of how society constitutes its members, and of the role of language in that process, it is not my purpose to address that issue here. Nor is that purpose simply to demonstrate the confusion surrounding the terminology of social linguistics, but to indicate a range of connected phenomena that a discussion of the concept of dominant language has to encompass. It also shows that within the framework of a discussion of language variety one is very rapidly led, via concepts such as dialect, register, code (ii), Discourse II, paradigm and code (i) to the question of ideology. Trew puts it thus: 'Concepts in a discourse are related as a system, they are part of a theory or ideology, that is a system of concepts and images which are a way of seeing and grasping things and interpreting what is seen or heard or read' (1979a: 95). The study of language (and its varieties) and of ideology are therefore inextricably intertwined (cf. Coward and Ellis 1977: 78, 92, Hodge, Kress and Jones 1979: 81, Kress and Hodge 1979: 6, Williams, R. 1977), and as Thompson (1984: 4) has remarked, 'to study ideology . . . is to study the ways in which meaning (or signification) serves to sustain relations of domination'.

LANGUAGE IN SOCIETY: LEVELS OF INVESTIGATION

The question 'what is language?' has, however, another side to it. What *aspects* of language are we to take into account? And what levels of linguistic phenomena are relevant to the understanding of linguistic – and ideological – domination?

For those familiar with the kind of linguistics with which he is associated, it may seem strange to cite Chomsky in support of the study pursued here. In fact, in the reference cited earlier, Chomsky distinguishes between the subject matter of linguistics, which for him is 'grammar', and that of sociolinguistics which: 'is presumably concerned not with grammars . . . but rather with concepts of a different sort, among them, perhaps, "language", *if such a notion can become an object of serious study*' (Chomsky 1979:190, my emphasis). The sting is in the tail. Chomsky and many other linguists have developed a view of language in which it is studied as an abstract system which for both theoretical and practical reasons is treated as isolatable from any social or cultural context. I will not, here, develop the case against this theory of an 'autonomous linguistics', as it is sometimes called, but will say only that I share the opinion of those who have quite fundamental difficulties with the view of the nature of language which it entails. More important for this book is the fact that a number of social scientists, trying to break out of this tradition, nevertheless bring to the study of language in society a definition of language close to that employed by Chomsky. The accounts which are generated are only of partial value from a sociological point of view as discussion in chapters 8–10 of sociolinguistic findings on language and class will show.

One problem is that especially, but not exclusively, in what is called 'correlational sociolinguistics', language is circumscribed extremely narrowly. Briefly, and perhaps unfairly, linguistics – sociolinguistics often included – frequently confines the study of language to certain features of grammar and pronunciation (and the 'rules' governing their use) through which the lexicon (sometimes seen as little more than a pack of blank cards) is manipulated to produce 'utterances'. This focus is microstructural in that it deals only with phonology and grammar at the phrase level. The principal macrostructural concepts include the several ways of labelling varieties of language – *a* language, dialect, register, etc. These are obviously important, but to focus on the one hand on the minutiae of the phrase, and on the other on the large-scale language or language variety, is to omit from consideration the huge middle area of higher order language use (i.e. the way in which language is ordered above the level of the phrase). Yet it is at this level that one finds some of the most interesting aspects of language and the social operationalisation of language. Perhaps what is meant by this will emerge from the following.

A positive way of studying language in society is to begin not with language (whatever we mean by that) but with what have been called *linguistic practices*, though following Hymes it is preferable to use the broader term *communicative* practices, since we may wish to include activities such as *silence* (as for example in O'Barr 1982:98–110, and in a more complex way Ardener, E. 1975).

Briefly, I construe communicative practices as a multifocal concept referring to:

(a) The social activities through which language or communication are produced.

(b) The way in which these activities are embedded in institutions, settings or domains which in turn are implicated in other, wider, social, economic, political and cultural processes.

(c) The organisation of the practices themselves, including their labelling.

(d) The ideologies, which may be linguistic or other, which guide processes of communicative production. (This is close to what Bourdieu calls 'relation to language'.)

(e) The outcome – utterances and sequences of utterances, texts and sequences of texts.

What such a concept entails is illustrated by Brian Street's book *Literacy in theory and practice*. For although Street does not accord the notion any thoroughgoing theoretical or methodological treatment, it is and remains throughout central to his conception of the field as his opening sentence shows: 'I shall use the term "literacy" as shorthand for the social practices and conceptions of reading and writing' (1984:1). Literacy is seen as one type of communicative practice. Another example is Cameron (1985) which is as valuable for the direction it implicitly gives to the study of language in society as a whole as for what it explicitly says about language and gender.

The concept of communicative practice at once forces attention on higher orders of linguistic organisation such as discourse, in both the narrower and broader senses defined above, enabling us to see that linguistic stratification in Britain and in France often entails a hierarchy of practices of which the language used (e.g. French, Breton, English, Urdu, 'standard', 'non-standard') is but one element. Furthermore, the politics of language is frequently, though not always, concerned with the legitimacy of one kind of practice as against another. In short, there are competing discourses (Discourse II) of communicative practice which are constantly in conflict.

The perspective has the further advantage of providing us with a tool through which to make sense of, and demonstrate the continuity between, what occurs at the micro-level of small-scale, local, personal relations (for example in the schoolroom), and what may be characterised as the macro-level of society-wide social, economic and political processes. It also imposes an obligation to take into account the fact that practices change, and forces us towards a socio-historical linguistics of a kind which is almost totally lacking in Britain (with certain important exceptions) but which in various forms has been long-established in France. It also has a bearing on what may constitute relevant data. What are conventionally called secondary sources may also be primary in that they have, directly or indirectly, contributed to the politics of language or because they themselves illustrate a particular discourse of communicative practice. For example, Ferdinand Brunot's magnificent multi-volume *Histoire de la langue française*, or the work of Basil Bernstein, are primary in both these senses. Thus secondary writing on language – including of course that of linguists themselves – inevitably becomes part of the datum of inquiry.

The concept of linguistic practice is, of course, not novel, nor does it offer a magic wand. The term itself is used by Renée Balibar in her discussion of primary and secondary education in France, and also by Bourdieu; there is some relationship between it and 'speech act' as that term is used in the ethnography of speaking (and, more problematically, as used in 'speech act theory'); it appears in the work of Bernstein (e.g. 1985a, 1985b), and it is implied in some of the work of Harold Rosen, and in that of Gill Seidel (especially the notion of 'discursive strategy'); and conventional 'discourse analysis' (Discourse I) is certainly concerned with mid-range linguistic organisation. Unfortunately, where mid-range phenomena of this kind are discussed by linguists, and 'discourse analysis' is a good example, the underlying interactionist model of social relations frequently employed does not enable any serious attack to be made, for example, on the issue of language and class. The point perhaps is that the failure is not in identifying phenomena, but in knowing what to do with them, which is to return to the more general issue of how the relationship between the linguistic and the political may be formulated.

THE ORGANISATION OF THE BOOK

I have been able to do little more than sketch various approaches and suggest something about their respective strengths and weaknesses. Rigorous versions of each serve to highlight their differences and what may seem to be their incompatible theoretical assumptions about the nature of language and of politics. Nevertheless, despite their incompatibilities, these different approaches (which in practice often overlap) each point to important aspects of the politics of language which cannot be ignored. To that extent the perspective adopted here will tend to one of what might be called 'conditional eclecticism'. That is, it draws inspiration from a variety of schools of thought, provided that what they offer is consistent with the following basic assumptions.

First, and providing the principal framework of investigation, is the assumption that language is intertwined with the political, economic and organisational orders of European society. The politics of language cannot exist without reference to the interrelationship of nation, state, economy, and mode of organisation. Secondly, and following from this, that language has become an 'object' within this framework is an important social fact which needs to be explained. Thirdly, it is a contested object. The politics of language is about conflict and struggle. Fourthly, it is so in a wide variety of ways and at many different levels of both society and language. In understanding the politics of language, the linkage between levels is crucial. Especially important for this analysis is what I have termed communicative practices. However, fifthly, communicative practices are both object of, and vehicle for, the politics of language. Thus language is doubly implicated in the political, and the politics of language incorporates a multiple struggle on the one terrain – about language, in language, for language.

The way in which the politics of communicative practice appear in this volume is as follows. Chapters 2 to 5 deal with language and nation in France and Britain. Chapter 2 opens with discussion of two contrasting views of the place of language in the construction of national identity, one linked to ideas associated with the Enlightenment, the other to the perspective known as Romanticism. It continues with an account of a debate about language during the French Revolution, and with a Report by the Abbé Grégoire on the 'Annihilation of the patois and the universalisation of French' (1794). Linguistic ideas of the period led one dominant group of Revolutionaries to stress the liberalising and liberating quality of the French language and of certain linguistic practices which they then proposed to 'universalise' throughout France, and indeed elsewhere. The language policy of the Revolution, which sought a kind of uniformity, is compared with that which prevailed under the Ancien Régime, and both in turn with actual practice, with what actually happened as the process by which French spread throughout the country accelerated.

Chapter 3 is concerned with Britain, and with comparable processes of linguistic incorporation in the British Isles. Ethnographic accounts of rural Wales, Scotland and Ireland, coupled with recently published historical research, enable us to put together a detailed picture of language change and indicate its source in other factors. Chapters 4 and 5 complement these 'views from the centre' with two 'views from the periphery'. Chapter 4 assesses the response to the penetration of French and to other changes seen as emanating from incorporation into a centralised state. The historical and ethnographic evidence which is discussed comes mainly from the southern half of France, an area which has been called 'Occitanie'. The chapter includes a history of the South, as seen through the eyes of 'Occitanian' historians, linguists and other activists, and then deals with the nineteenth-century Romantic-influenced Félibrige movement associated with the poet Frédéric Mistral, and with the 'Occitanian' movement as it developed after World War II. Here the writing of Robert Lafont is examined in some depth. A final section provides an assessment of the 'Political economy' approach to the study of regional languages (i.e. that which sees regions as dependent peripheries, internal colonies, etc.). Chapter 5 returns to Britain, considering the political response to England in Wales, Scotland and Ireland, and examining the relative importance of language for the three nationalist movements. A comparison is made between Mistral and the Welsh nationalist Saunders Lewis.

Chapters 6 and 7 are about immigrants and language in both Britain and France. Chapter 6 is linked directly with earlier chapters in that the issue of the 'mother tongue' (maintenance, preservation), of great current concern, raises in another arena the problems of cultural and linguistic diversity which are also posed by processes of centralisation. The publication of the Swann Report (1985) provides an opportunity to review current research and thinking in the two countries (including, for example, the work of the Linguistic Minorities Project), and also set the issues in a wider socio-historical perspective. The problems posed for European societies by the presence of immigrant ethnic minorities and those posed by ethnically and linguistically different regional minorities are directly related in that both raise serious questions about cultural homogeneity in contemporary societies, and the prospects for cultural and social pluralism.

Chapter 7 continues the discussion of pluralism focusing this time on 'competence' in the dominant language and what lack of it entails. 'Competence' is used here in the sense proposed by the American linguistic anthropologist Dell Hymes rather than in that associated with the linguist Noam Chomsky. This survey leads to an assessment of recent socio-linguistic research in Britain, France and Germany on the relationship between language and educational under-achievement on the part of youngsters of West Indian, Algerian and Turkish origin. This anticipates some of the discussion in chapters 9 and 10.

Chapters 8 to 10 are generally to do with language and class, and thus with another form of linguistic stratification (see Fishman 1976:292). Chapter 8 examines the conventional sociolinguistic and socio-historical evidence for linguistic stratification in Britain and France from the fifteenth century onwards, i.e. the association of certain ways of speaking with distinct strata of the population. Chapter 9 takes up a further point about hierarchy. Over a long period both subordinate regional languages and non-elite dialects have been despised as more or less inadequate forms of communication. Until well into the nineteenth century, and in some respects later, there prevailed a discourse within which the 'barbarity' of such languages and dialects (the term 'barbarous' was a frequent epithet in both Britain and France) was compared with 'cultivated' speech, and with writing. At a deeper level what was in contrast were two modes of communicative practice, and in the twentieth century a very similar kind of contrast (even to points of detail) emerges in a discourse which sees speakers of subordinate languages as 'deficient'. The dominant model of language emphasises 'rationality', and ascribes rationality to its own linguistic practices. The two themes of chapters 8 and 9 come together in chapter 10 which looks at language, class and education. That education has been a major battleground of the politics of language will have been made abundantly clear in previous chapters on language and nation and on immigrants and language. Chapter 10 considers the dominant languages (English and French) as mother tongues employed in and through the educational curriculum. It looks on the one hand at dialect, social standing and achievement, and on the other at the discursive practices of education. This provides two ways of looking at language and class, one of which seeks correlations between two sorts of categories ('language speakers', 'class'), the other of which broadens the discussion to encompass institutionally powerful types of linguistic practice.

Addressing the politics of language through the connections between language and nation, language and state, and language and the economic order means that certain issues which are less directly relatable to the principal themes have not been treated as fully and as systematically as they deserve.

First, a major omission, the difference, if any, between the linguistic practices of men and women, and/or the ways in which a particular set of practices differentiates between them. These have been the subject of considerable discussion in recent years, not all satisfactory, some quite excellent. Language and gender is obviously a subject of the greatest importance, and one which is by no means ignored in this book. However, to tackle it systematically would have entailed engaging with analytical and theoretical problems which are otherwise beyond the book's scope. I do not imply by this that language and gender do not form a significant site of linguistic struggle, nor that that struggle is unrelated to those concerned with nation, state and class. I do not mean to exclude gender from the politics of language, even from the types of politics discussed here. It is simply that the integration of these issues would have been very difficult to achieve within the compass of this book, and in any case I felt unable to improve on what has been said in a number of recent publications (notably in Britain by Cameron 1985, Coates 1986).[1]

Secondly, the politics of English or French *outside* Britain or France, their past and present roles as dominant *international* languages, and as the languages of major colonising powers. This again is an important subject in its own right, and one better documented than most. The high international status of French or English, in different ways and at different times, has clearly affected the development of the languages internally, that is within their countries of origin (and perhaps vice versa), but to do justice to this subject would have extended the scope of this book beyond acceptable limits.

Thirdly, the relationship between religious and linguistic practices. There was in the past, and in certain situations still, a very important connection here on which a large amount of scattered information is available, though no one, so far as I know, has produced a full-scale account of it. In this book the connection in Britain, where the link between religion, nationalism and language in Wales, Scotland and Ireland is relatively well documented, is treated more fully than that in France. There the precise relationship between the practices of the Catholic Church at different levels of the hierarchy and in different regions and the universalisation of French (or alternatively the maintenance of the patois) remains to be documented and is currently unclear.

Fourthly, differences between urban and rural linguistic practices, and the consequences of urbanisation and urbanism. The recent work of F. Furet and J. Ozouf (1982) which examines the spread of one kind of practice, i.e. literacy, indicates what can be said in this domain, but their analysis needs to be extended to other aspects of language. In any event this theme cannot be developed systematically here. Fifthly, the relationship between language and control, and between language, ideology and power. I earlier suggested ways in which the discussion in this book inevitably led to these issues. Once again, the theme cannot be explored here, though I hope to deal with it elsewhere. (See Grillo 1987).

Finally, the relationship between the politics of language and the somewhat different traditions of writing about language to be found in Britain and France. Although initially I thought that the politics of language was different in the two countries, it is clear that there are in fact great similarities. The terrain of linguistic conflict (for example, the development

---

[1] It is interesting and instructive that despite what has been written on language and gender the recent Kingman Report (1988) on the teaching of English in Britain has not one word to say on the matter.

of national standard languages and their relationship to regional minority languages, 'non-standard' dialects, and the languages of immigrants), its form and outcome, and its connection with processes such as centralisation and state formation are in both cases closely comparable. There are indeed differences, such as the greater explicit ideological salience accorded language in France as compared with Britain (illustrated in the different traditions of writing about language in the two countries), but more in what is said than in what is done.

None of these is in any sense a residual problem. Each emerges directly from the material actually considered in this book, and any theoretical or analytical framework must attempt to encompass them. They simply cannot be tackled here.

2

THE VIEW FROM THE CENTRE:
FRANCE

La force des choses le commande.

TALLEYRAND

TWO CONCEPTIONS OF LANGUAGE AND NATION

HENRY PEYRE begins his study *La royauté et les langues provinciales* (1933) by citing a view of nation and the relationship between nation and language found in the writing of the sixteenth-century French chancellor, Michel de l'Hôpital. In Hôpital's opinion, which Peyre believes was typical of his period, linguistic divisions were no danger to the kingdom since under the monarchy the factors of unity were 'one faith, one law, one king' (Peyre 1933: 10).

Peyre also cites the nineteenth-century moralist, Ernest Renan (1823–92), who in his 1882 address *Qu'est-ce qu'une nation* declared, in a much quoted phrase: 'It is not speaking the same language that makes a nation, it is having done great things together in the past, and wishing to do so again in the future.'

Although the 'nation' which Hôpital and Renan had in mind was very different, their understanding of the place of language in a sixteenth-century kingdom and a nineteenth-century nation-state was surprisingly similar. I will term this perspective 'nation as association'. It is in strong contrast, says Peyre, with another view in which language, so far from being a contingent element in the definition of the body politic, was quite crucial to it. I will call that 'nation as community'.

The two correspond roughly with 'will' and 'culture' which Gellner (1983: 53) has described as 'two promising candidates for the construction of a theory of nationality'. 'Community' and 'association' are the usual

22

translation of the German *Gemeinschaft* and *Gesellschaft*, terms found in the work of Ferdinand Tönnies, and used by him to refer to two great classes of social relationship and social organisation which the English nineteenth-century historian of jurisprudence, Sir Henry Maine, distinguished as those based on 'status' and those based on 'contract'. They are generically related to Durkheim's contrast between societies bound together by 'mechanical' solidarity (deriving from the similarity of the elements which constitute the social entity), and those where solidarity is 'organic' (deriving from the dissimilarity, hence interdependence, of the elements). They address the same problem which underlies Max Weber's distinction between 'traditional' and 'rational–legal' (bureaucratic) types of authority.

For Tönnies, *Gemeinschaft* is characteristic of small-scale and local units of organisation. It signifies relationships derived from likeness, from communalities of blood and locality, kinship and affinity. The home and the farm are typically, for Tönnies, examples of *Gemeinschaft*-like social entities. These are 'traditional' institutions based on natural will: sentiment or emotion. *Gesellschaft* relationships, on the other hand, are typical of town and industry. They are based on exchange and on rational will. Larger units, such as nations and states, are *Gesellschaft*-like.

This view of nation as a *Gesellschaft* was represented in the eighteenth century by the *Encyclopédie*, by Sieyès and by Rousseau of the *Social contract*, and is linked to one of the great intellectual movements of the era: the Enlightenment. The nation was a body of *citizens* brought together by a shared set of governmental institutions. The state is a rational–legal enterprise created by what Rousseau calls 'an act of association'. But what Rousseau called 'the general will', embodied by the state, is more than this, and requires more than common agreement to sustain it (Cohler 1970). Hence uniformity of language may be essential for the actualisation of the practices of association, as the Revolutionaries argued ('Words being the bonds which hold society together', as Grégoire put it). Hence the demands for what Fishman (1973:24 ff.) calls the 'state–nation process', and for what I have called the 'ethnicisation of the polity' (cf. Calvet 1974:169, for a similar formulation). This chapter looks at a detailed instance of this conception of the nation and of the place of language within it.

THE GRÉGOIRE REPORT

On the 16th Prairial, Year II of the French Republic, One and Indivisible (6 June 1794), the Abbé Grégoire presented a report to the National Convention on 'The need and the means to eradicate the patois and to universalise the use of the French language.'[1] Estimating that some thirty 'patois' were spoken in France, with names (Bas-Breton, Picard, Bourguignon, Bressan, Béarnais and so on) recalling the provinces of the Old Régime, he argued:

It is no exaggeration to say that at least six million Frenchmen, particularly in the countryside, do not speak the national language; that an equal number are more or less incapable of sustaining a coherent conversation; that as a result, the number of true speakers does not exceed three million, and that the number of those who write it correctly is probably even smaller.

Although many of the patois were related dialects of French, the state of communications in the country meant that they were often understood only with difficulty even a few miles from where they were spoken.

With thirty different local dialects, we are still, as regards language, at the Tower of Babel, whilst as regards liberty we form the avant-garde of nations. (We must) make uniform the language of a great nation, so that all its citizens can without hindrance communicate their thoughts to each other. Such a project, which no nation has yet fully accomplished, is a worthy one for the French people, who are in the process of centralising all branches of social organisation and who should be concerned, in a Republic one and indivisible, to establish as soon as possible the language of liberty as the one and only language . . . Unity of language is an integral part of the Revolution. If we are ever to banish superstition and bring men closer to the truth, to develop talent and encourage virtue, to mould all citizens into a national whole, to simplify the mechanism of the political machine and make it function more smoothly, we must have a common language.

The Abbé Grégoire (1750–1831) was a Catholic priest and Revolutionary who supported many of the liberal causes of his day: the reform of the Church, the emancipation of slaves, the rights of Jews to full French citizenship, the development of a compulsory, free, system of public primary education, and the universalisation of the French language. Although his report of 1794 was far from being the only contribution to a debate then taking place, and possibly not even the most significant, it was undoubtedly an important one, and has become more so in retrospect.

Its publication history is not without interest. In the nineteenth century examples were so rare that when in 1880 Gazier produced an edition he did so because 'one of the foremost scholars of our era has been reduced to asking me for a copy' (Gazier 1969:290). In the 1890s it was also made available in Guillaume's edition of the proceedings of the 'Education Committee' of the National Convention (vol. IV). In 1930 the report figured

---

[1] The French text of Grégoire's Report may be found in de Certeau *et al.* 1975: 300 ff., and in Gazier 1969: 290 ff. The Barère text, discussed later, is also in de Certeau *et al.* (p. 291 ff.). The translation here is by Bron Grillo.

prominently in Volume IX, Part I of Ferdinand Brunot's history of the French language (Brunot 1967, see also Brun 1927), but again it seems to have dropped from view. Although it is mentioned by a number of writers who were familiar with Brunot (including Dauzat), it does not occur in Godechot's authoritative study (1968) of Revolutionary institutions. Indeed Godechot has nothing to say about language, and relatively little about education. Grégoire's biographer, Necheles, in an otherwise full account of his life, is silent on this report and does not record it in an extensive bibliography, though she does make a passing reference to Grégoire's interest in language and national identity (Necheles 1971:29, 47).

In the 1960s and 1970s, however, perhaps for reasons connected with the rise of interest in regional languages and regional movements, the relationship between Revolutionary ideals and French language policy began to be discussed seriously. In 1962, Gershoy published a life of Barère, another major contributor to the Revolutionary language debate. In 1967 the relevant volume of Brunot was republished and in 1969 a facsimile of Gazier's edition was issued. Since then a veritable Grégoire industry has developed (see Balibar and Laporte 1974, Calvet 1974, de Certeau *et al.* 1975, Gordon 1978, Higonnet 1980, Kohn 1967, Lafont 1968, Marcellesi 1975, 1979, Rickard 1974). Before setting Grégoire's report in the context of the contemporary debate on language, national unity, national identity and education, let us look at the linguistic state of France as recorded by Grégoire himself and by others.

Grégoire's observation that 'six million people in France do not speak French' is one he repeated elsewhere. His precise figures must be treated with caution,[2] nonetheless he provides a reasonable estimate of the proportions of the population in various linguistic categories, and of the dimension of what from his point of view was a serious problem.

A survey by Coquebert de Monbret gave the breakdown of the population within the politically extended boundaries of France in 1807 as French 27,926,000, Italian 4,079,000, German 2,705,000, Flemish 2,277,000, Breton 967,000, Basque 108,000 (Brunot 1967:598–9). The political extension of France in 1807 had considerably increased the numbers of Italians, German and Flemish speakers within the country. There were perhaps 2 million (8% of the population) within the frontiers of 1794. The speakers of Breton were nearly a million, or 4% of the total,

---

[2] Grégoire must have been aware of the census available by 1794 which revealed a population of some 26 million within the frontiers of 1789. (Reinhard 1961:26–8, Toutain 1963). His own figures add to 15 million: 6 million do not speak French, 6 speak it inadequately, 3 correctly. Does the first 6 million include only speakers of the idioms (Germans, Basque, etc.), or does it include some speakers of dialect? And what of the other 11 million? Eugen Weber, relating Grégoire's figures to the census (cf. Dauzat 1930:548) has him reporting 'three quarters of the population speak some French', and comments that this seems an 'optimistic view' (Weber 1976:71). Curiously, the record of Barère's speech of 8 Pluviôse has him refer to 600,000 Frenchmen 'completely ignorant of the national language'. A simple error?

forming 70% of the inhabitants of the three departments of Finistère, Côtes-du-Nord, Morbihan. The Basques, though relatively fewer in number, constituted some 30% of the population of the Basses-Pyrénées. In addition there were the millions of French patois speakers who, as Grégoire says, could not hold a conversation in 'the national language', still less write or read it. 'In only about fifteen departments of the Interior, [i.e. out of 83] is French the sole language spoken; and even there it is noticeably altered, either in pronunciation or by the use of unsuitable and outdated terms.' Besides differences of language and dialect there were also differences of register, as for example in German and French between the written and spoken languages.

It is not always clear when Grégoire is referring only to the patois (dialects of French or at any rate French-like languages), and when he means to include all languages such as German, Breton and Basque, generally regarded as completely different. The distinction was not always easy to make. For example, the Catalan spoken in southern France was sometimes thought of as a distinct language, sometimes as a dialect of the *langue d'Oc*. Moreover, various terms were used to classify languages which were not always used consistently (cf. de Certeau *et al.* 1975: chapter 2). Besides *dialecte* and *patois* there were *idiome*, and *jargon*, which could also be used as a modern linguist would employ 'register' ('lawyer's jargon', for example). All of these words, including 'patois', were pejorative, though the really abusive term was *baragouin* ('jabber' – possibly of Breton origin, Dauzat 1946:207–9). Brunot (1967:6) cites the administrators of Sauveterre d'Aveyron complaining in 1792 of their 'accursed idiom . . . this unhappy jargon which stifles the development of our ideas'. As for patois, the *Encyclopédie* of 1788 (cited in de Certeau *et al.* 1975:51) defined it as 'corrupted language (*langage*) which is spoken in almost all the provinces. The language (*langue*) is only spoken in the capital.' Brunot gets round the terminological confusion by using 'dialect' to mean the spoken varieties of the *langue d'Oc* and *langue d'Oïl*, and reserves 'idiom' for the rest. This has some analytical value. But if the two were confused in speech, as they sometimes were, it may have been because genealogical and historical difference was less important than similarity of status. 'The language is only spoken in the capital.'

Another difference which excited opinion was that between the language of the court and aristocracy and that of the people. Grégoire again:

They used to say of Quinault that he had made the language *spineless* by his use of all that was most effeminate in polite conversation, and all that was most abject in flattery. I have already remarked that the French language was cowed into slavery when the corrupt courtiers imposed their rules on it. It was the jargon of (court) cliques and the vilest passions. The exaggeration of the discourse always falls short of or overshoots the truth. Instead of being *sorry* or *pleased* one had to be *despairing* or *delighted*. Soon there would have been nothing left in nature that was beautiful or ugly; there would have been only the *execrable* or the *divine*. It is time for this deceitful style with its servile formulae to disappear. It is time for the language throughout to display that character of truth and laconic pride which is the outstanding virtue of Republicans . . . 'There is in our language', said a royalist, 'a hierarchy of style because words are put into classes like the subjects of a monarch.' This admission is illuminating for anyone who thinks about the subject. By comparing inequality of style to inequality of (social) condition one can draw conclusions which prove the importance of my project in a democracy.

A similar point was made earlier (8 Pluviôse, Year II – 27 January 1794) by Bertrand Barère:

Our enemies made the French language the language of the courts. They debased it . . . Still it appeared to belong only to certain classes of society. It was tainted by usages distinctive of the nobility. The courtier, not content to distinguish himself by his vice and depravity, sought to set himself apart from others in the same country by using another language. You would have said there were several nations in one.

'Several nations in one', a polity divided and stratified linguistically and socially. 'Citizens', said Barère, 'the language of a free people should be one and the same for all!' What led Revolutionaries such as Barère and Grégoire to such a conclusion? And what did they propose to do about it?

SEVERAL NATIONS IN ONE

Under the monarchy France was what Strayer calls a 'mosaic state' (1963:23, cf. Soboul 1977), a patchwork of provinces joined to the kingdom at various times by conquest and diplomacy. Henry Peyre (1933) suggests that in the sixteenth century the consequent linguistic diversity posed few problems. 'What the king demanded above all was loyalty . . . It mattered little then, up to a certain point, that custom and usage differed from one province to another' (Peyre 1933:16). 'One king, one law, one faith.' The principal linguistic question concerned the conflict between the 'vulgar' language and *Latin* as languages of literature and of the state. In the thirteenth century, Dante in *De vulgari eloquentia* (see Welliver 1981) had urged the virtues of the vernacular language – the spoken language of Italian society, but in France the debate between French and Latin was not resolved until at least the sixteenth century when writers such as Du Bellay and Henri Estienne (1896 edition:29) successfully argued that French was a

27

legitimate vehicle for literary expression, capable not only of standing alongside Latin or Italian, but of surpassing them. It was against Latin, too, Peyre argues, that the famous edict of François I in 1539, known as the Ordonnance of Villers-Cotteret, was directed. Article III of the Ordonnance said:

And because such things [doubts and uncertainties] frequently occurred in connection with the interpretation of Latin words contained in the said decrees, we wish that henceforth all judgements, together with all other proceedings, whether of our sovereign courts and other subordinate and inferior courts, or accounts, inquiries, contracts, warrants, wills and any other acts and processes of justice or such as result from them, be pronounced, recorded and issued to the parties in the French mother tongue (*langage maternel françois*), and in no other way.

There has been considerable discussion of the significance of this edict, and of the meaning of *langage maternel françois* (see Peyre 1933). Some have interpreted it as signalling a linguistic policy through which the French nation would be united. According to Peyre, however, such a policy did not emerge until much later under the monarchy, if indeed the monarchs ever had a linguistic policy in a modern (post-Revolutionary) sense of the term. Peyre's view is that the monarchy generally adopted a liberal stance towards the languages of the peoples who made up the French kingdom. Certainly by the seventeenth century French was promoted as the language of state, but Peyre suggests that the fundamental view of the Ancien Régime was that 'The existence of a unique administrative language is an element favourable to the organisation of a state which has attained a certain level of centralisation, but linguistic unity is not to be imposed on peoples speaking different languages who live under the same sovereign' (1933:217). Even later edicts which enforced the use of French in the courts were applied with caution, and a large measure of bilingualism tolerated. The prevalence of interpreters, says Peyre, 'doubled the agents of the royal administration in the provinces where there was a bilingual régime' (1933:244).

The Ancien Régime appears to have followed policies typical of rulers of what Gellner has called 'agro-literate' societies where 'the state is interested in extracting taxes, maintaining the peace, and not much else, and has no interest in promoting lateral communication between its subject communities' (1983:10). Although Gellner is not concerned specifically with monarchies of the French kind, Anderson makes a similar point with regard to language choice in dynastic régimes of the absolutist type. In the case of France and others that he cites, 'the "choice" of language appears as a gradual, unself-conscious, pragmatic, not to say haphazard development' (1983:45). He adds: 'For essentially administrative purposes these dynasties

... settled on certain print-vernaculars as languages of state – with the "choice" of language essentially a matter of unself-conscious inheritance or convenience' (p. 81).

Although there was no *policy* of linguistic unification under the Ancien Régime, French was the dominant language, the language of the powerful, of the king and Court, and gradually infiltrated many areas of public life. Brunot (1927) shows how in the sixteenth and seventeenth centuries French penetrated literature, medical sciences, philosophy, and through the various attempts to formulate a French grammar the study of language itself. A standard language was in formation guided *inter alia* by Malherbe's insistence on the principle of 'good usage' which Vaugelas (1647) identified with 'the way of speaking of the soundest element of the Court' (in Brunot 1930:27). (Grévisse's widely used student guide to French usage is called *Le bon usage*.) The Académie Française, which began as an informal circle of learned friends, was, on the initiative of Richelieu, formally instituted in 1635 and charged with the task of regulating the language and pronouncing on vocabulary and grammar. It was this language (cf. Dauzat 1930:545) which slowly spread via the upper classes to the provinces, particularly the towns. In the countryside, and among most of the other classes, the patois and idioms remained the predominant medium of communication, and 'in those provinces which had for long been part of the kingdom and which did not speak French, the administration seemed little concerned to impose its language' (Brunot 1947:104).

If there was, by the Revolution, a well-formed idea of a national language – and the term appears several times in the Barère and Grégoire texts, and in the speeches of Talleyrand – it was a conception of the French language as a language of state and literature, at the centre and of the upper classes. In the seventeenth and eighteenth centuries 'nation' often referred to the 'conscious and active part of society' (Kohn 1944:580–1). It was a self-description of the bourgeois elements of society (Guiomar 1974:28–9). The rest were 'the people' (cf. Smith 1983:191). The Revolutionaries appropriated that language, and attributed to it a national identity in their sense of the term 'nation'. Moreover, what had previously been 'tendencies' on the part of François I and Richelieu became state doctrine: 'the language must be national and form one of the essential elements of nationality' (Brunot 1967:420). Nation, state and language became identified, and there was a demand for the 'ethnicisation' of the polity (Grillo 1980). The state had to become a nation.

Fundamental here is the changing concept of nation. Under the Ancien Régime, the coherence of the polity was created in and through the kingship: sovereignty resided in the sovereign (cf. Guiomar 1974:85). Godechot

(1968:4) cites Louis XV: 'Sovereign power resides in my person . . . public order in its entirety emanates from me.' In 1789, however, the third article of the Declaration of Rights resolved that sovereignty resided not in the kingship, but in the nation: 'La nation est la maîtresse de toute autorité.' In the view of the constitutional philosopher Sieyès the nation was 'prior to everything . . . the source of everything' (Sieyès 1963:124), and only natural law was above it. Henceforth the nation would give coherence to the polity. A 'citizen' would be a subject of the nation, not of a king, owing loyalty not to the king, but the nation. But what was the nation?

The view that asserted that nation and language were one and the same is not of primary importance here, though there are hints of it and more in some of the Revolutionary writing of the period. Sieyès's doctrine was that a nation was a collectivity of people under a common law, represented by a common assembly (Sieyès 1963:58, see also Bastid 1970:574, and Godechot 1968:24). Similarly the *Encyclopédie* (1751–65) defined 'Nation' as 'A considerable quantity of people who live within a certain territory enclosed within certain limits and who owe obedience to the same government' (vol. 22, p. 221).

These definitions were not concerned with language, though they may have been predicated on an unspoken assumption of pre-existent linguistic unity, and certainly that unity is implied by many of the principles and proposals with which Sieyès was associated, for example in the field of education (Bastid 1970:504–12). It is significant that the *cahiers de doléance* of 1789, the lists of grievances and demands for reform prepared by the local assemblies, make little reference to language. A number mention the bilingual status of their localities (e.g. in Alsace and Roussillon) which they wish to retain (Beatrice Hyslop 1934:47–9). Of the rest, which total over 600, only six discuss the desirability of spreading the use of French and encouraging linguistic uniformity. One was from the clergy of Autun where Talleyrand was Bishop. (He is said to have dictated the contents of their *cahier* on his one and only visit to the diocese; Duff Cooper 1958:27.) Hyslop concludes: 'From these isolated references to language, it is obvious that language played very little part in the concept of nationality on the eve of the Revolution' (1934:48). However, as the Grégoire Report and other documents show, only a little later, the relationship between language and nation did become an important issue, and advocacy of the linguistic unification of the polity a common demand. The reasons advanced for such a unification were practical, political, economic and philosophical, and the various strands are not always easily separated. The variety of opinion, and the tenor of the discourse in terms of which the debate was conducted, emerge in letters and memoranda which form the basis of Grégoire's report.

FOR THE UNIVERSALISATION OF FRENCH

Grégoire himself had for several years been concerned with the language issue. De Certeau *et al.* (1975:21) cite a passage from his 1789 essay on the Jewish question in which he said:

> No national language in Europe, nor anywhere else that I know of in the world, is commonly spoken by every person in that nation. France is home to perhaps 8 million subjects of which some can barely mumble a few malformed words or one or two disjointed sentences of our language: the rest know none at all. We know that in Lower Brittany, and beyond the Loire, in many places, the clergy is still obliged to preach in the local patois, for fear, if they spoke French, of not being understood. The governments either do not know or are insufficiently aware how important is the eradication of the patois to the spread of enlightened ideas, to an unclouded knowledge of religion, to the easy execution of the laws, to the national well-being and political tranquility.

The terms in which Grégoire then couched the problem informed a detailed questionnaire which he drew up and circulated in August 1790 and to which he received some fifty or more replies covering most parts of France. A survey of his correspondents has shown that they consisted in the main of professional people (doctors, lawyers, teachers) and clergy. There was also a substantial number of collective replies from branches of the Société des Amis de la Constitution (de Certeau *et al.* 1975:30). Of particular interest are the replies to Question 27 ('What is the respective influence of patois on manners and of the latter on your dialect?'), 29 ('What would be the religious and political importance of destroying this patois entirely?'), and 30 ('By what means could it be done?').

Some are laconic ('L'importance . . . nulle', from an unknown correspondent from Provence scribbled on the margin of Grégoire's circular, see Gazier 1969:79–82); others evasive: 'No one, sir, is in a better position than you to judge the political and religious importance . . .' (Pierre Riou, a cultivator from Brittany, Gazier 1969:283). Most make detailed comments, and one, François Chabot from Aveyron, submitted a 4,000 word dissertation. Most, too, accepted the desirability, indeed the inevitability, of the destruction of the patois, even if they thought it would be a lengthy business.

'It will elevate the soul, reunite hearts, and enlighten spirits' (Gazier 1969:215). 'The French language is better for praying . . . our patois is not worthy of God . . . It favours superstition' (Gazier, pp. 94–5). It will facilitate religious instruction. It will facilitate political instruction and knowledge of the law. It will facilitate communication. And commerce. It will overcome the distrust between countrymen and townsfolk. Above all it will encourage education and literacy. 'The peasant whose ideas are very restricted will be continually cut off from education so long as he does not know the language spoken by educated persons' (Gazier, pp. 170–1).

One word sums up these replies: 'enlightenment'. Access to the French language will give access to 'instruction' (education was both end and means), and through instruction enlightenment. The people will become informed *citizens*, able to participate on equal terms, without inter-mediaries, in the political process. Intellectual, moral and political improvement – all seen as much the same thing – will come from speaking and writing the national language. But critically the language which will bring about these improvements is *French*.

'Instruction' is the key here. As Brunot points out, some of the issues later discussed by Grégoire were brought out in an earlier speech to the National Assembly by Talleyrand (*Archives Parliamentaires*, 10 September 1791) during the presentation of a report on education. In this speech Talleyrand praises *reason* – 'this essential element of man which distinguishes him from everything which he is not'. But man has to be taught to be a reasoning being. Hence the importance of education, of 'instruction', for which Talleyrand regarded mathematics as the supreme model: 'thrusting aside all that serves only to distract the mind, marching directly and speedily toward its goal, leaning on what is perfectly known to arrive surely at what is not, it does not shy from any obstacle. It offers the means if not always to discover the truth of a principle, at least to pursue with certainty its implications to the very end.' Shifting from reason and thought to communication and language, he continued:

A striking feature of the state from which we liberated ourselves is without question the fact that the national language, while every day extending its conquests further beyond France's borders, remained in our midst as if inaccessible to a very large number of her inhabitants, and that it was possible for the principal means of communication to be regarded by many of our regions as an insurmountable barrier. Such an absurdity, it is true, owes its existence to various factors acting haphazardly and without plan; but it was with deliberate intent that the consequences were turned against the people. Primary schools will do away with this bizarre inequality. There the language of the Constitution and of the laws will be taught to everyone; and that host of corrupt dialects, last remnants of the feudal system, will of necessity disappear. The force of circumstances demands it.

Though, says Talleyrand, the French language had undergone many changes, some of which had 'impoverished and degraded it' (hence a need for reform), 'the true riches of a language consist in being able to express everything with force, clarity and economy', and France's greatest writers had achieved that. Ordinary people, too, had the right to such a language. There are benefits to be derived from learning other languages, but the existence of a multitude of tongues is a hindrance to the free communication of minds. Following Leibnitz, he claimed the necessity to 'create or adopt one (language) which will be a sort of central point, a meeting place for every idea, in a word, which might become for thought what algebra is for computation' (p. 473).

Leibnitz's search for a quasi-mathematical, universal, language also influenced Grégoire, as is revealed by this contribution he made to a debate of January 1794 on the use of French for the inscriptions on monuments: 'Leibnitz desired a universal idiom which would be a common bond for human understanding. His hopes begin to be realised. Our language, recognised because of its clarity as being that of reason, will become, through the application of our principles, that of liberty' (cited in Brunot 1967:278). 'Universal idiom' also reveals the influence of Rivarol, to whose essay *De l'universalité de la langue française* Grégoire refers in the first paragraph of his report. Rivarol had argued that French was the supreme vehicle for the expression of reason: 'Sure, sociale, raisonnable, ce n'est plus la langue française, c'est la langue humaine' (Rivarol 1930:271). The morphology of French was closest to that of natural logic, and its 'clarity' offered the best instrument yet devised for the articulation of human reason whose form was universal. Thus, 'universalise' in the title of Grégoire's report implies more than making French common throughout a given territory, or even, as the term was sometimes employed, the vehicle of international diplomacy. It means recognising it as the universal language in Leibnitz's and Rivarol's sense. Moreover, 'French' was the language of the 'Franks', and thus by etymology the language of the free (cf. *franc-maçon*, 'free-mason', *franc-tireur*, 'sniper'). *Franciser* thus was construed as making both French and free at one and the same time (cf. Guiomar 1974:92). Universalising the language was thus a liberal, liberating measure: 'Our language, this lightning conductor of liberty, equality and reason' (Domergue, cited by Brunot 1967:182), and many hoped that it would become the language of Europe, spread by conquest and occupation, with the result that 'all the conquered peoples . . . will become republicans' (in Brunot 1967:186).

The view that the eradication of the patois would be for the benefit and well-being of the people was not shared by all. If one of the features of the patois was widely assumed to be their 'coarseness', which rendered them unsuitable for prayer or elevated thought, others were their 'simplicity' and 'honesty', reflecting an honest and simple country life which learning French might destroy: 'The peasants who know how to speak French are, it

33

is true, less coarse, in general, in their conversation, but they are also more dissolute and depraved. Proximity to the towns spoils them' (in de Certeau *et al.* 1975:223).

A policy of linguistic change also formed part of an overall policy for the social and ideological transformation of French society. The 'Committee of Public Instruction', which began work in October 1791, was concerned not only with education in the narrow sense but also with such matters as the reorganisation of the calendar. Time, more rationally defined and divided, was to begin anew on 5 October 1793, backdated to 22 September 1792, Year I of the Republic. There were changes too in the names of streets and communes – Royaumeix became Libremeix, for example. The choice of personal names was influenced (Godechot 1968:423–6), and there was the Revolutionary ritual, the ceremonies, the Cult of Reason, and the harnessing of the arts and sciences in the Revolutionary cause.

Barère was closely involved with much of this. His biographer says of him, 'he had in his mind a single vision of cultural and artistic indoctrination in which all the creative arts would work as one in inspiring in the breasts of Frenchman a burning and lofty love of the Republic . . . He became in fact if not in title the Minister of Cultural Propaganda' (Gershoy 1962:232–3). This is not anachronistic if we recall that 'propaganda' was a Revolutionary term, though as J. M. Thompson, writing in 1944, commented, such 'mild attempts . . . to mould the minds of Frenchmen would be thought laughable by present-day professors of these arts of government' (Thompson 1944:399). The universalisation of French would assist this ideological transformation, though the French language, too, required revolutionising through a pruning of aristocratic usage, and in the views of some a thorough rationalisation of anomalies of grammar and spelling (see the later letters to Grégoire, in Gazier 1969:314–40, and Higonnet 1980:55–6).

If enlightenment was one major reason for promoting the universalisation of French, a second was the practicalities of administration. Heterogeneity can lead to complexity and is often seen as a hindrance to centralisation. As De Gaulle said, how can you govern a country that has 200 different sorts of cheese?

The theme of administrative inconvenience runs through much of the evidence from official sources assembled by Brunot. Noting later complaints on the part of the prefects about the persistence of the patois, he remarks they do not reflect disdain for the dialects as such but a 'detestation of everything that stood in the way of the development of the country and the orderly running of affairs' (p. 480). A third reason was political.

LINGUISTIC FEDERALISM

Long live the Republic and the National Convention! Long live the Jacobin societies! Long live the defenders of the fatherland! May scoundrels and persecutors of patriots perish! Citizens, you are invited to cultivate study of the French language!
(PRESIDENT OF THE CLUB DE LA RUE THUBANEAU, MARSEILLE, 1793, CITED IN BRUN 1927: 101)

For the Revolutionaries, diversity of language was associated with the old régime, with feudalism. Chabot's memorandum to Grégoire argued:

The multiplicity of idioms could be used in the ninth century and during the overlong reign of feudalism. The former vassals gave up the satisfaction of changing their master for fear of having to change their speech. But today, when we all have the same law for master, today when we are no longer Rougeras, Burgundians etc., when we are all French, we must have only one common language, just as we all share a common heart.   (GAZIER 1969: 71)

Linguistic heterogeneity was associated with a policy of divide and rule. 'Despotism preferred that there should be diversity of language' (Barère).

In the earlier years of the Revolution, during a period which Higonnet (1980) thinks of as anomalous, some encouragement was given to linguistic diversity. For example, anxious that Revolutionary ideas and enactments should be as widely known as possible the Assembly agreed on 14 January 1790 a policy of translating decrees, etc. into the idioms and dialects. Grégoire alludes to this in his report:

By doing this you increase costs, and at the same time you make the government machine more complicated, which slows down its working; furthermore you must take into account the fact that it is virtually impossible to translate into most vernacular dialects, or at best you will achieve only a very imperfect rendering. How can we expect a political vocabulary which is still in the process of being created in our own language to be translated into languages of which some, if the truth were told, abound in sentimental expressions with which to paint the gentle effusions of the heart but are completely devoid of the vocabulary of politics; while others are crude, clumsy speech forms, lacking any specific grammar, because language is always the measure of the genius of a people; words only grow with the progression of ideas and needs. Leibnitz was right. Words are the common currency of the understanding; if therefore we acquire new ideas, we must simultaneously create new words or the balance will be upset. Rather than leave this task of creation to the caprice of ignorance, it would surely be better to give it your own language; besides, country folk, unused to generalising their ideas, will always lack abstract terms; and this inevitable poverty of language, which restricts the spirit, will mutilate your speeches and your decrees, if indeed it can translate them at all.

35

Despite the difficulties (the sheer number of dialects, some lacking an established orthography, the weight of legislation, the problem of finding suitable terms in the patois in which to render the new political discourse) a substantial amount of translation was undertaken by 1792, especially for the southern half of the country (Brunot 1967:25–39, Brun 1927:96 ff., de Certeau *et al.* 1975:287–8). The work continued in a 'Commission for Translation' of which Grégoire himself was a member (Brunot 1967:158). Against the prevailing opinion, other voices argued that some of the dialects and idioms, especially German, were entirely suitable languages for instruction, and indeed that instruction in the mother tongue was the only means available for the rapid spread of republican ideas. According to Brunot 1967:29), such views presented 'a daring project for linguistic federalism . . . a return to before 1539'. This perspective is found in a memorandum which Gazier omitted from his edition of the Grégoire correspondence because he felt the Prussians might use it to uphold their occupation of Alsace (de Certeau *et al.* 1975:280). Both Brunot (1967:80–3) and de Certeau (pp. 280–3) publish it in full. The memorandum concerned the legal system and argued for bilingualism within the judicial process, so that, *inter alia*, no one need have recourse to an intermediary:

How can the people of Alsace prepare themselves for a new order of things which would lead to their being deprived of so sacred and incontestable a right . . . The surest and most legitimate way of spreading French is to demand a knowledge of both languages . . . It is of moment to the Nation that the German language, which is the mother tongue, one of the richest, and I dare say it, one of the most widely used and most noble of Europe, be preserved at its bosom.

Generally such proposals had little support either at the centre or in the provinces. In December 1792, however, a report of the Committee of Public Instruction, which sought to promote French in schools as Talleyrand advocated, at the same time proposed that in German-speaking areas children should learn to read and write in French *and* in German. Where other idioms were spoken, reading and writing would be learnt in French, but other parts of the curriculum would be 'at the same time' in French and the local language (Brunot 1967:136, Higonnet 1980). There was, therefore, a moment when a kind of linguistic federalism seemed possible, and it could have been built into the administrative system by using linguistic criteria to. determine the boundaries of the new departments. In fact where linguistic boundary claims were made (in the Basque/Béarnais area, in parts of the West, and in Lorraine), they were swiftly dismissed (Brunot 1967:75–8), and certainly by 1793–4 there were serious obstacles to any linguistic or indeed other kinds of federalism.

Brunot's history (1967:83–7) contains an account of an anonymous Alsatian pamphlet, published in late 1790, which takes the form of a Platonic dialogue on the use of French and German. In the course of the dialogue, one of the characters, Stark, a blacksmith, exclaims: 'Are we not good French citizens and patriots at heart because we cannot speak French fluently? That would make a cow laugh. There's a big difference between speaking French and having French feelings.' This complaint was echoed in August 1794 by the Société des Amis de la Constitution of Ribeauville, in a memorandum to the Convention: 'Is it sufficient to speak German to be thought a counter-Revolutionary?' According to Barère the answer was definitely 'yes'. In a frequently cited passage from his speech of 8 Pluviôse he stated the case as bluntly as possible: 'Federalism and superstition speak Bas-Breton; emigration and hatred of the Republic speak German. The counter-Revolution speaks Italian, and religious fanaticism speaks Basque. These instruments of harm and error should be suppressed.'

Loyalty to the country meant loyalty to the language, and *vice versa*. To speak French was sign and symbol of patriotism. Grégoire's language is less emotive, but his own position is nonetheless clear:

In our border areas, especially, the fact that there are dialects common to people on both sides of the boundary line encourages the setting up of potentially dangerous relationships with the enemy, while in the main body of the Republic the existence of so many crude dialect forms obstructs the free flow of commerce and weakens social relations. Because of the mutual influence of behaviour on language and language on behaviour, these dialects prevent the formation of a political whole, and make thirty peoples where there should be one. This observation acquires added weight if you consider how many men have cut each other's throats because they were unable to communicate, and how often bloody battles between nations, like the ridiculous quarrels of the scholastics, were really no more than disputes about the meaning of words. We must ensure that children of the same family share a common bond of language. This will obliterate the last traces of that insularity which was the natural result of the old provincial divisions and will strengthen those ties of friendship which should unite all brothers.

Barère's speech of 8 Pluviôse was made as *rapporteur* from the Committee of Public Safety to the Convention. He was famous for his oratory in which he attacked the enemies of Revolution on both the extreme left and the right, inside and outside the country. This particular speech was made after a year of great peril for the Republic with war both beyond and within the frontiers. In 1793 there had been insurrection in Lyons, Marseilles, Toulon, the Vendée. And after that and because of that there was the Terror. Grégoire's report in fact came just a week before the Law of 22 Prairial on suspects and one of the grimmest passages of the Revolution. These are not philosophical and administrative debates conducted in a seminar-like atmosphere of calm and persuasion. The choice of words such as 'feudalism', 'counter-Revolution', and perhaps above all 'federalism' (made a capital crime in December 1792 [Sydenham 1961:137]) to characterise linguistic diversity must have had the effect of conjuring up fear, loathing and hatred.

In the latter part of 1793 concern about counter-Revolution in Alsace led to a period of what Brunot calls 'linguistic terror'. Revolutionary commissars had arrived in the province to find it close to revolt. They ordered the rapid establishment of French schools in each canton of the Bas-Rhin, and forbade the use of German at a ceremony at Strasbourg to honour martyrs of the Revolution. With that, says Brunot (1967:189), 'the era of violence began'. On 25 Germinal, Year II (14 April 1794) the Directorate of the Bas-Rhin ordered that all administrative papers, including those addressed to them, be in French. The Jacobin Clubs were forbidden to use German in their proceedings. The press was ordered to print the German language using a French alphabet. French signs were to replace German ones in public places. And in what Brunot calls a 'virulent' pamphlet on 'The *fransilisation* of the former Alsace', one Rousseville argued that 'anything of any importance should be in French', and urged: 'Why not have a sort of mass conscription of the young men and women citizens of the former Alsace, and billet them for a time in the homes of French people of the interior? Why not decree that any civil or military office of the Republic may be taken only by persons who know French?' (in Brunot 1967:194). It was also proposed that German speakers be deported and replaced by colonies of *sans-culottes*, with 'a parade to the guillotine, to effect their conversion'. Although such extreme proposals were never carried out, 'they remained', says Brunot (1967:195), 'in the memory of the inhabitants and served to nourish hatred of the Republic'.

LINGUISTIC CENTRALISM, CAUSES AND EFFECTS

In Alsace, as elsewhere, the subject of education figured prominently in the discussion of language, and vice versa. Under the Ancien Régime primary education had been almost entirely in the hands of the Church. Under the Revolution it was to become a matter of state.

Through the Revolutionary period there was a stream of reports and decrees concerned with the organisation of schooling and with the curriculum. Barère's speech, and the proposals it brought to the Convention, were the culmination of this debate. Rejecting any suggestion of education in mother tongues, he insisted: 'Let us crush ignorance! Let us send teachers of French to the countryside.' It was, therefore, decreed that teachers (*instituteurs*), named by the popular societies, would be appointed in the principal non-French-speaking areas to:

teach the French language and the Declaration of the Rights of Man every day to all the young citizens of both sexes whom their fathers, mothers and tutors will be under obligation to send to the state schools; every tenth day they will read out loud to the people the laws of the Republic and translate them orally, giving preference to those relating to agriculture and to the citizens' rights.

This policy of linguistic centralisation was also promoted by the decree of July 1794 which forbade the use of the idioms in judicial documents, including private contracts (Brunot 1967: 186), and later by the movement, in which Grégoire took a leading role, to make French the language of the Catholic service.

There was, apparently, widespread support for this measure, but also significant opposition. In a letter to Grégoire, cited in Brunot (1967: 378–9), the Bishop of Rennes made the standard point that a Catholic, by contrast to a Protestant, 'is not a foreigner in any country of the Latin Church'. Moreover, if church services are to be translated into French, what of the Bretons 'whose language is even older than the Greeks, or the Picards, or the Auvergnats, the Gascons and the Basques, the Provençals, do they not have the same right to desire our liturgy in their language or jargon?' Grégoire replied that the patois 'have neither the reach, nor the accuracy, nor the stability of French' (Brunot 1967: 397), and were thus unsuitable for the liturgy. Besides, the use of French will help the spread of the language 'with advantage for both religious and temporal affairs'.

Few of these measures, however, had any serious effect in the short run. The Church succeeded in repudiating the attack on Latin, and as for the proposals concerning primary education, they failed for the most elementary reason: there were no means. In many areas schools simply did not exist. In the Moselle, for example, which Brunot describes as a 'model' department for its relative success in forwarding these matters, by 1804 562 out of the 931 municipalities had no teacher (Brunot 1967: 499, see also 518–22). The poor and uneven development of school provision until the last quarter of the nineteenth century is abundantly documented in Furet and Ozouf's account of the spread of literacy in France (1982). The universalisation of education and the French language was quite beyond the resources of the Republic. The policy, too, was less important to the post-1794 Revolutionaries (Higonnet 1980), and Bonaparte, whose mother tongue was Corsican and who learned French as an adult, apparently saw no advantage in the *francisation* of France, even though he promoted the use of French abroad, in the conquered territories. Brunot suggests that a well-known, if apocryphal, saying of Bonaparte's perhaps summarised his view: 'Let these brave fellows have their Alsatian dialect. They sabre well enough in French.'

Eugen Weber has pointed out that linguistically, as well as in many other ways, France remained a diversified country until well into the nineteenth century, in fact until World War I. Figures he cites for 1863 show that a fifth of the population lived in non-French-speaking communes (Weber 1976:67, 498–501), and the evidence suggests that official figures over-estimated the extent to which the language of France was at the time predominantly French. Nevertheless, the Revolutionary period did have its effects. Through the fervent oral and written political debates in the hundreds of clubs and societies throughout the land, through the participation of hundreds of thousands of Frenchmen in a mass army (Brunot 1967:524, describes the regiment as 'the school of French'), through the popular songs such as the Marseillaise (composed in Alsace, popularised in Provence) – 'French was introduced alongside the various spoken languages in places where previously it had never had a hold' (Brunot 1967:409).

This may be illustrated from Auguste Brun's account of the sociolinguistic environment of the Provençal village of Saint-Michel which in the 1920s had a population of some 500. In a reconstruction of that environment before and after the Revolution Brun (1927:118–19) paints the following picture of social and linguistic change.

On the eve of the Revolution, the population was 900. Until then the only French that most of the inhabitants would have heard was the occasional speech when the Seigneur or the bishop made an irregular visit. Talk in the village would have been local and particularistic. Politics would have been, quite literally, of the parish pump, and in Provençal. Then followed the events of 1789 – the preparation for the States General, the *cahiers de doléance*, elections, leaflets, decrees, *ordonnances*:

No lack of matters to attend to. The council meets several times a week; the survey of the nobility's property; addresses to the assembly; civic oaths . . . nominating functionaries; subscriptions to journals; civic certificates; church inventory. The meetings of the Popular Society – reading, speaking, discussing. Then the war . . . conscription; requisitioning of provisions; harvest census; hoe census . . . The village changes its name – Montmichel . . .   (BRUN 1927: 119)

In short, the Revolution imposed a wholly new dimension of public life, the language of which was French, not Provençal. Even when Provençal was used in political discourse, the key terms of the new political language were often French ones (see, for example, the Provençal translation of the Constitution made in 1790, cited in Brun 1927:108). Above all, a society in which the state had had only a moderate interest in the language spoken by most of its inhabitants became one in which language was seen as a serious object of civil concern. What was previously a matter for philosophers now became a matter of state.

To say this is, of course, to place considerable weight on ideology and policy, and it is well to take note of Gellner's objections (1983) to such an analytical strategy when seeking an understanding of the roots, or causes, of a phenomenon such as nationalism. In the French Revolution, as Furet and Ozouf remind us, 'There was . . . an ideology of the school and a history of the school, and the two were quite distinct. If we fail to make this distinction, we run the risk of trying to deduce the history of education under the Revolution from the Revolution's ideas about the school' (1982:97). For Gellner what matters is not nationalist ideology, for which he reveals only contempt, but 'the objective need for homogeneity which is reflected in nationalism' (1983:46). But whence the particular 'objective need' for linguistic unification?

One possibility is suggested by Patrice Higonnet who takes the view that the linguistic issue offers an illuminating test case through which to 'reveal the operation of ideology in the politics of 1789–99, as well as the scope of the futile egalitarian ambitions of the French bourgeoisie in those years' (1980:69). There was, he argued, no material or political necessity for the eradication of the patois. The policy was the result of deep contradictions in Revolutionary politics, in a way enabling the bourgeois Revolutionaries to proclaim equality while defending property. It thus had an ideological 'function', meaning by that a 'mystifying' effect: 'The persecution of dialects . . . diverted attention from more material social problems, like the redistribution of land' (Higonnet, p. 49).

This simplifies a complex argument, and perhaps does Higonnet a disservice, but I think he misses the crucial point that, failing a federalist régime, entailing a multilingual society, linguistic unification was in important respects an egalitarian measure. As the Revolutionaries themselves argued, it made many areas of the society directly accessible to all citizens. When Higonnet comments that this and like measures meant that 'equality which could not be achieved in any practical sense would be achieved on an ideological and illusory plane' (p. 59 – he equates ideological and illusory), he relegates culture to a peripheral zone. That paradoxically, as he puts it, another kind of linguistic stratification was created through the construction of Republican French is an issue to which we will turn in chapters 9 and 10.

Though he sees Revolutionary linguistic ideology as essentially mystifying, in emphasising its bourgeois, capitalist, roots Higonnet is in accord with Balibar and Laporte (1974), who demonstrate a direct connection between the pressure to make the language uniform and the need to construct an internal national market. For Balibar and Laporte it is 'the development of the mode of production (which) imposes linguistic uniformity' (1974:80). Both Higonnet and Balibar and Laporte, however, neglect entirely the role of language in the formation of the French *nation-state*, in ideological, cultural and indeed practical terms. This is not to accept the Revolutionary premise that a nation must inevitably have a single, common, national language. But the problem of political unity posed by the end of the monarchy had to be solved, and the concept of the nation as unified, homogeneous, socially, culturally and linguistically, provided one way of solving it.

The French solution provided a model which found considerable support elsewhere, for example in the Iberian peninsula (Kohn 1944:152–3, Díaz López 1982, Heiberg 1975, 1980), and the ideology of linguistic unity generally played an important part in the construction of post-absolutist, post-agrarian states. For Gellner a crucial factor in the development of these new formations was communication. Building on ideas first set out in his essay on 'Nationalism' (1964:155) Gellner argues that 'in industrialising societies communication and hence culture assumes a new and un-precedented importance' (1983:74). He thus locates the roots of the homogenising process, and indeed the roots of nationalism generally, in 'the distinctive structural requirements of industrial society' (1983:35). Hence the stress he lays on education (something he shares with Balibar), and on the state's involvement in education. The French evidence strongly supports Gellner on this point, for Revolutionary debates about language and education were firmly entwined.

The drive towards linguistic uniformity was, in this view, a necessary, even rational, complement to the economic and political developments of the period. It was an inevitable adjunct to change. However, if these developments had their supporters, they also had their opponents. Indeed it might be said that the advocacy and implementation of policies which sought to promote these changes created their own opposition. That opposition, however, as we shall see in chapter 4, found an intellectual and ideological basis in a somewhat different view of nation and language.

3

AND THE VIEW FROM ENGLAND

LANGUAGE AND NATIONAL IDENTITY IN BRITAIN

TO TURN from France to the British Isles (England, Wales, Scotland, Northern Ireland, and the Republic of Ireland) is to turn not only to a different social, political and economic context, but also to a different tradition of writing about language and society. Whatever the reasons for this – and one may be the (apparent) differences in the two societies in question – until very recently social historians in Britain have paid little attention to language. There is, for example, nothing comparable to Brun's account of the penetration of French into Provence. Dorian (1981) and Durkacz (1983) on Scotland, O Murchu (1970) and De Freine (1978) on Ireland, and several Williams on Wales have begun to remedy this deficiency, but Peter Burke's call for historians to engage with the social history of language (Burke 1987:1) has been very recent indeed.

So far as English is concerned its history has generally been left to the 'Eng. Lit.' tradition. In that tradition the social history of English is at its best for 'Middle English', from the subordination of the language to Anglo-Norman (the French dialect of the Norman conquest) until the emergence, during the fourteenth and fifteenth centuries of 'Standard English'. The status of the language (or rather of one variety of the language) apparently assured, scholarly attention has focused on the internal development of the standard (Milroy 1984:14) with endless discussion of the changing grammar and accumulating lexicon (see, for instance, Onions 1950, but there are many others) and little attention to the external – social – context of its development. The scope becomes narrower. Histories of English are not usually concerned with the written language as a whole, including the totality of *scripta*, nor even with literature generally, including the highways

43

and byways, but simply with the 'great tradition', the major, exemplary, users of the language.

There are three exceptions. First, the Romantically-inclined folklorists of the nineteenth century sought to record 'dialect', mainly of rural England, and observe its geographical distribution as minutely as possible (see Price 1984: 183–5, and Wakelin 1984 for a survey of more recent work in this field). Secondly, the development since the sixteenth century of pronunciation, especially 'Received Pronunciation' or RP, the 'correct' way of speaking, has been well-documented by historians and more recently by other types of research. Thirdly, perhaps influenced by the attention paid since the 1950s to popular, working-class culture, there has recently been a keen interest in the history of class dialects, especially in Victorian England (the work of social historians such as Asa Briggs (1960) on the 'language of class' deals with a somewhat different issue). The second and third of these lines of investigation will be discussed in chapter 8 along with the contribution of the modern school of sociolinguists which is largely concerned with the varieties of spoken English found among the different strata of present-day Britain.

Particularly striking, by comparison with France, is the almost total lack of attention to any relationship between English language and national identity. This may be attributed to the different ways in which the French and British nation-states have evolved, and the different ways in which that evolution has been conceived. This is not easy to demonstrate. The literature on nationality and nationalism in Britain (or at any rate England) is itself meagre, and sources are few and far between. Detailed studies such as Nairn's (1977) are rare, and even Nairn is forced to concentrate on more recent events, as in his discussion of Enoch Powell.

Apart from brief moments during the Anglo-Norman period when English assumed some significance as a symbol in the conflict between Britain (or rather England) and France, language has not figured conspicuously in the articulation of British or English identity within the British Isles. During the last hundred years or so the prevailing view of the nature of the British nation-state may be characterised as the 'unionist' perspective. In an essay on 'Nationalism' originally published in 1862, Lord Acton argued against the 'ethnologizing' of nationality that occurred during and after the French Revolution. He considered political systems in which nation and state were conflated to be dangerous ones, inimical to freedom. The British system was among the 'most perfect' because it included 'various distinct nationalities without oppressing them' (1909: 298), the sovereign power transcended the nation's ethnic constituents. This *Gesellschaft*-like view of the British nation is echoed in a later essay on

'Nationality and liberty' by Lewis Namier (1952, originally 1948), who concluded that the British concept of nation was a 'territorial' one, by contrast with the German which was 'linguistic and racial' rather than 'political and territorial' (p. 24). In Britain, language could not be the basis for nationality 'or else Scotland and Wales would be split internally' (p. 21). Sir Ernest Barker, too, in his discussion *National character* (1939) emphasises the complex, heterogeneous, but interlocking, nature of British society (p. 130). For Barker, the growth of a national spirit in Britain and France was a result of the extension of state power (the power of the kingdom) and of a common law and a common language employed as a standard in the courts and in chancery. Language was not a fundamental element in the definition of nationality, but a facilitating factor in the formation of the nation-state.

A conventional political history of the English language in Britain would run as follows. Prior to the Roman invasion, the languages of this island were Celtic, conventionally divided into two groups ('q' and 'p') by reference to phonetic differences. The p-group included Brythonic, from which emerged Breton, Cornish and Welsh; the q-group gave rise to the Gaelic languages, Irish and Scottish and Manx (Price 1984:16–17, Thomson 1984:242). Despite subordination to Rome (and the dominance of Latin) the population of the British Isles remained Celtic (or at any rate Romano-British) culturally and linguistically through to the fifth century. For the next 600 years the islands were subject to a succession of invasions, raids, migrations and settlements of which the first and last had the greatest significance for the sociolinguistic history of Britain.

Bede's eighth-century *Ecclesiastical history of the English people* concluded that the 'Germanic' incursion of the fifth and following centuries consisted of three related tribes – Angles, Saxons and Jutes – who eventually settled in different parts of the island. Hence the predominance in their respective areas of the dialects of what came to be called 'Old English'. Whether those dialects in fact came with the invaders or whether dialectal differentiation occurred after settlement (Bloomfield and Newmark 1963:135, Price 1984:171) does not really matter. It is sufficient that by the eighth century speakers of Old English had either assimilated the indigenous Romano-British population or driven it to the margins of the country (for example, beyond Offa's dyke).

The main dialects of Old English were Northumbrian, Mercian, West Saxon and Kentish, each with a centre of power. West Saxon, as the language of King Alfred's Wessex, achieved a wider prominence. It is the predominant dialect of the manuscripts that have survived, and may well have been a literary standard for the island as a whole (cf. Bloomfield and Newmark

1963:138, Pyles 1971:121). Bolton (1975) refers to late West Saxon as the 'premier dialect' (p. 275) and even 'the national preferred form' (p. 290). It was certainly a politically important language, as that of Alfred the Great, and the vehicle for an important literature which includes the *Beowulf* epic. But this status collapsed quite swiftly with the Norman conquest, and for some 3–400 years the dominant language of the islands ceased to be English.

The Normans (originally Norsemen who had settled in Western France) spoke a dialect of the *langue d' Oïl* usually called 'Anglo-Norman' (Price 1984: ch. 17). From the eleventh until the fourteenth century (and in some respects until later) there existed a diglossic situation in England, accompanied by a certain, and much disputed, degree of bilingualism. Anglo-Norman was above all the language of the Court, of the administration, in due course of Parliament, of writing, and predominantly 'for two hundred years after the Norman conquest . . . the language of ordinary intercourse among the upper classes of England' (Baugh 1957:135). English remained the language of the lower orders. Anglo-Norman was the mother tongue of most of the monarchs of England who through perhaps to the fifteenth century had their attention focused as much on France and their French possessions (including Aquitaine) as on England. Certainly until the thirteenth century the French and Anglo-Norman nobility constituted what Baugh (1957:152) calls 'an interlocking aristocracy'. So close were the connections between England and France that they may be viewed as a single social, economic, political, religious and, to a certain extent, linguistic field. That field also included the states of 'Occitanie'. Simon de Montfort, for example, victor of the battle of Lewes, in Sussex, in 1264, was the son of the Simon de Montfort who led the crusade against the Albigensian heresy in the South of France earlier in the century. By the thirteenth century, however, though English was apparently not spoken by King John, knowledge of the language had begun to spread within the Anglo-Norman nobility: 'Among churchmen and men of education it was even to be expected; and . . . among those whose activities brought them into contact with both upper and lower classes the ability to speak both languages was quite general' (Baugh 1957:146).

The decline of French accelerated with the unlinking of the English and French nobilities at about this time, and by the fourteenth century English was widely known and used by all classes. Its spread appears to have been such that in 1332, as Baugh records, a decree was passed urging the upper classes to ensure that their children were taught the language. There is some slight evidence, too, that the status of English *vis-à-vis* Anglo-Norman was a matter of political identity. Cottle cites the author of the *Cursor Mundi* written *c*.1300 in the Northern dialect, saying that his book 'is translated into the English tongue to be read, for the love of the English people, the English people of England, for the common people of England to understand. I have normally read French verses everywhere here . . . what is there for him who knows no French?' (trans. in Cottle 1969:17). Baugh interprets this as a 'patriotic espousal of English' (1957:164).

Despite such pleas, French (or Latin) remained the principal literary language for some time, and was the preferred language of private correspondence until well into the fifteenth century (Baugh 1957:182). And it long remained the language of authority. Petitions to the Commons, for example, are recorded in French until after 1423, and from 1300 until Henry VII the statutes are also in French (previously in Latin). It was only in 1362 that the Statute of Pleading (itself in French) enacted that English should be the language of the courts:

that all pleas which shall be pleaded in [the King's] courts whatsoever, before any of his justices whatsoever, or in his other places, or before any of his other ministers whatsoever, or in the courts or places of any lords whatsoever within the realm, shall be pleaded, shewed, defended, answered, debated, and judged in the English tongue, and that they be entered and enrolled in Latin.

(TRANS. IN BAUGH 1957: 178)

Thus, in ways which will be explored further in chapter 8, English became the language of state – of the Court and of the courts – during the period 1400–1600 when the English crown began to impose its authority on what were later to become the constituent parts of a united kingdom. A comparison with the Ordonnance of Villers-Cotteret is intriguing. Assuming that by this time English is the 'maternal language' of the English king (and assuming the conventional interpretation of the Ordonnance of 1539) both the Ordonnance and the Statute impose their respective monarch's tongue as the language of the courts. Whereas in France a consequence of Villers-Cotteret was to impose what for the mass of people was an alien language, here the effect was to re-establish the *native* tongue, at least so far as most parts of *England* were concerned. Since then there has been a largely unspoken assumption of its pre-eminence, at least on the part of the English, and the case *for* English as the dominant language of the British Isles has rarely had to be made – by the English. The case *against* English, on the other hand, and *for* the other languages of Britain – here French experience is similar – had to be argued, was argued, certainly from the eighteenth century onwards as speakers of what, by then, were the subordinate languages of Wales, Scotland and Ireland were caught up in the fervour of Romanticism.

It is not surprising, therefore, to find an abundant literature, scholarly and polemical, on language and identity in the British Isles *outside* England. Drawing on this literature, the rest of this chapter turns to the relationship between English, as a dominant language and symbol of cultural identity, and the other languages spoken historically in the British Isles to consider the consequences of the dominance of the English language in the formation of the British nation-state.

LINGUISTIC DECLINE IN THE BRITISH PERIPHERY

We have lost the old tongue, and with it the old ways too.
(HERBERT WILLIAMS 'THE OLD TONGUE' IN ABSE 1971: 129)

There are exceptions to which we will come, but in general the 'eradication of the patois' was never pursued as a conscious, whole-hearted policy designed to forward the development of the British state. Nonetheless, the effect of the unification of Britain on the dialects of England, and the languages of Britain, has been devastating. 'English', as Granville Price (1984: 170) puts it, 'is a killer.' The commonest word to be found in writing on the traditional languages of Britain – other that is than English – is 'decline'. (If English is said to be 'in decline' the problem to which reference is made is a quite different one.) It is well-known that Cornish long ago ceased to exist as a spoken language (its last speaker died in 1777). Less well-known, perhaps, is that the last speaker of Manx died in 1974. Yet a century earlier a survey on the Isle of Man estimated that some 12,340 persons, 30% of the island's population, spoke the language. By 1901 there were 4,567 and by the 1950s no more than a few dozen (Price 1984: ch. 6). There are always problems with statistical data collected in censuses and surveys which seek to record ('yes/no') who speaks a particular language, but a picture of a similar, if not so precipitous, retreat is revealed in figures for the other Celtic tongues. Over the last hundred years or so monolingual speakers of Welsh and Scots Gaelic have virtually disappeared. In Scotland there has also been a major decline in the number of bilinguals. Between 1901, when Gaelic speakers in Scotland formed 6% of the total population, and 1981 (1.5%), the number of mono- and bi-linguals fell by more than two-thirds. In Wales the fall was 50%, and in a country where Welsh speakers formed a majority in 1900, they now form only 19% of the total population. In Ireland, various estimates (see De Freine 1977:80) suggest that in 1800 there were two million monolingual Irish speakers in the country and a further one and a half million bilinguals out of a total population of 5 million. In 1901, the figure had been 620,000 of whom 21,000 were monolingual (De Freine 1977:86, Edwards, J. R. 1984a).

The nineteenth century saw a major language shift in Ireland – from predominantly Irish-speaking, to predominantly bilingual, to largely English speaking. This shift continued into the present century, though the interpretation of more recent Irish figures is complicated by the fact that, for reasons to be discussed later, the Irish language became the official language of the Irish state and was for many years compulsorily studied at school. One consequence is that the number who report that they can use the language is considerably greater than the number of those who would normally do so in their everyday lives. By 1926, four years after the creation of the Free State, there were reported to be some half million Irish speakers (Macaodha thinks this may have been an overestimate). In Irish censuses of the 1960s about a quarter of the population of the Republic rated themselves as able to speak the language (O Murchu 1970:30). Macaodha (1972:25), however, estimates that currently some 70,000 only are at all fluent, and in numerous visits to all parts of the Republic during the 1960s and 1970s I personally only once heard Irish spoken in ordinary conversation, outside the scheduled areas known as the Gaeltacht and the Irish programmes of radio and television (in the Government Stationery Office in Dublin). The Gaeltacht itself numbered 72,706 in 1926, 2.5% of the total population, as against 85,703 (3%) in 1956 (Census of Population of Ireland 1966, vol. I, p. 159). Despite its status as an official language and support through the educational system, Irish is less widely used now in ordinary discourse than it was at the founding of the state. 'Decline' is certainly not too strong a word. (See Edwards, J. R. 1984a and 1985:53 ff. for excellent accounts of the anglicisation of Ireland, and Fennell 1981 for the Gaeltacht.)

Although the overall pattern is similar, each of these three countries has a distinct sociolinguistic profile. In Wales, Welsh – just within living memory – was the majority language. In Scotland, Gaelic was already by the turn of the century the language of a small minority which has since become minute. In Ireland, Irish has since 1922 been an official language used widely only in a limited number of domains. Although there are many points in common I will heed Nairn's (1977) warning against treating them as identical, and take each in turn.

SCOTLAND

Even in the Middle Ages, Scotland – or rather the area north of the present border – was not homogeneous linguistically. The southeast spoke

49

Northumbrian, a dialect of English (Aitken 1981, 1984), the far northern islands, and the northwest coast, Norse. Gaelic was spoken throughout the rest of the country, though in certain areas it had not long ousted the non-Celtic language Pictish (Dorian 1981:10–11). Until the eleventh or twelfth centuries Gaelic was also the dominant language, the language of the kings of the Scots and of an important bardic tradition shared with Wales and Ireland (Mackinnon 1977:45, 1984:505–6). From the twelfth century onwards, however, Gaelic began to lose its predominance through the anglicisation of the Court and the influence of the burghs, military and trading towns which were centres of an English-oriented population (Price 1984:51). Price's review of the available evidence shows that by the fourteenth century, with the exception of the southwest, Scotland south of the Clyde–Forth no longer spoke Gaelic but 'Scots' (Scots-English or 'Lallans', see Aitken 1981, 1984, Thomson 1981). Scotland had already become 'two nations not one' (Nairn 1977:167).

From the fourteenth to eighteenth centuries Gaelic withdrew into the north and west. Surveys at the end of the eighteenth century show the language steadily retreating throughout the *northern* half of the country, especially in those areas with commercial links with the Lowlands. This was after the defeat of the Highlanders in 1745, and the beginning of the Highland clearances. By then it was common, according to a report for Perthshire, that 'the language spoken by persons of rank . . . is English; but the language of the lower classes is Gaelic' (in Price 1984:57).

Nancy Dorian, who has long been engaged in a study of East Sutherland Gaelic (ESG), notes that in fact by the sixteenth century Sutherland had become a linguistically stratified society: 'a Gaelic speaking tenantry and an English-speaking aristocracy; a vernacular virtually universal among the general populace but probably not shared by the highest social stratum, whose language in turn is certainly not understood by ordinary folk' (Dorian 1981:15). The sociolinguistic stratification of the countryside, coupled with the anglicisation of the burghs (see Dorian, p. 52, on Dornoch in Sutherland), in Dorian's view ensured a high status for English. Anglicisation followed lines of status, as it did in Wales.

By the end of the nineteenth century, Gaelic was virtually confined to the area beyond the 'Highland Line', but in that area, at the time of the 1891 census, the countryside was still over 75% Gaelic-speaking (Mackinnon 1984:503). Since then (with the usual proviso about the reliability of such data) the 'retreat' or 'decline' of Gaelic can be traced fairly accurately via census returns (see, for example, Mackinnon 1984, Price 1984). Thus, nowadays Gaelic speakers form a majority only in the Highlands and Islands areas of the Western Isles and Skye and Lochalsh. Though 32% of all speakers of Gaelic (migrant workers and devoted students of the language included) actually live in Strathclyde – especially Glasgow – there, of course, they are only a tiny fraction of the local population.

The 1981 census found that 80% of the inhabitants of the Western Isles still spoke Gaelic – almost all now as bilingual Gaelic–English speakers – and the only area within the Islands where there has been a significant decline in recent years is South Uist. The decline of Gaelic elsewhere in the Highlands other than in the islands has led Donald Mackinnon to reflect:

The continued existence of the Gaelic community into the last third of the twentieth century is a problem requiring explanation . . . As the result of clearances of population, lack of economic development and consequential high outward migration, tacit policies inimical to the language in education and public life, it is surprising that there should be anyone at all alive who can speak the Gaelic today.

(1977: 5)

Dorian came to a similar conclusion: 'The survival of the dialect into the late twentieth century is the most extraordinary thing about ESG' (1981:9). (See Evans and Rhys 1968:220 for a similar view of Wales.) In fact, by 1981 only 11.3% of Sutherland's population spoke Gaelic, all as bilinguals, and in 1971, only 70 of the 1,300 Gaelic speakers in the county were aged between 5–25 (Dorian 1981:7). Dorian's comment implies that the situation might have been expected to be worse.

A distinctive feature of Dorian's work is the account she gives of the social history of Sutherland which shows how linguistic change has occurred, and how, occasionally, survival has been possible. What emerges from this account is the close relationship between the socio-economic structure of the region and the distribution of languages. In Sutherland, the countryside and therewith the bulk of the population remained Gaelic-speaking through to the early nineteenth century and the time of the agricultural 'improvements' known more generally as the 'clearances'. The widespread forcible removal of tenant farmers from their holdings obliged many of them to quit the region entirely. Others, however, were encouraged by their landlords to enter the embryo local fishing industry which was being developed in a number of villages along the coast. It was these villages which in Dorian's opinion provided a 'niche' within which Gaelic could be maintained: 'The existence of fishing communities with a strong economic base and a remarkable degree of social separateness from the rest of the population was crucial in fostering Gaelic and maintaining the language long after it had died out otherwise in the villages and had begun to die even in the isolated crofting areas' (Dorian 1981:67).

These relatively endogamous economic communities, whose interaction with the wider society was on a strictly limited economic basis, were able for a time to maintain enclaves of Gaelic speakers whose occupation and language was stigmatised by that society (Dorian sees them as caste-like in structure). Their separation was maintained even in religion, for as Dorian records, in the village of Golspie the Free Presbyterian Church offered two Sunday services: one in English, the other in Gaelic for the 'fisherfolk' (Dorian 1981:64).

A sustainable, if despised, occupation provided the resource for a community which could, up to a point, maintain its language and culture despite what was happening more generally in Scotland. When the fishing economy collapsed and the young men had to leave to become 'golf professionals, gardeners, policemen' (p. 48), then this 'led inexorably to a gradual integration with the rest of the community, linguistically as well as economically' (p. 72).

Several of the themes in Dorian's account of 'language death' on mainland northeast Scotland recur in the literature on the Western Isles where we are fortunate to possess a number of detailed studies enabling us to look closely at the connection between language maintenance and socioeconomic change (see Ennew 1980, Mewett 1982, and Prattis 1981 for Lewis, and Mackinnon 1977 for Harris).

Judith Ennew's account of Lewis rightly criticises the view that the Western Isles are 'communities' for long isolated from the mainstream of politics and economics. Certainly from the seventeenth century, when they were 'colonised' by James I of England (VI of Scotland), their fate has been closely bound up with the 'centre' whether that has been situated in the Lowlands of Scotland, or in London.

Agriculture always provided the basic livelihood, but after the breakdown of the clan system land was generally held on tenure from absentee landlords. The iniquities of the tenurial system throughout the Highlands in the nineteenth century, with its frequent indebtedness and consequent evictions, led to the Crofting Act of 1886 which allowed inheritance of tenure and introduced a number of important reforms (Ennew 1980:17). 'Crofting', the working of small farms with family labour on holdings controlled by the Act, has since become what Mackinnon (1977:161) calls the 'core', and Ennew (1980:59) 'the base-line of all other economic activity'. But it is only a base-line, for another feature of the local economy is what Ennew calls 'occupational pluralism'.

Crofting is mainly a subsistence activity. To obtain cash islanders have to participate in a range of industries which are, and have always been, owned and controlled by outside agencies. Ennew records that in the early nineteenth century, for example, during the Napoleonic wars, the harvesting of kelp was an important source of income. Later there was fishing which gave employment to men (on boats), and women as herring-gutters who followed the fleet as far as Yarmouth (Ennew 1980:29), and the Harris tweed industry, dominated by business interests outside the island, which achieved a maximum production of 7 million yards of cloth in 1966 (Ennew 1980:44). Government and the tertiary sector have also long been major providers of jobs. Besides seeking employment locally or short-term seasonal work outside the Islands, many islanders have left for longer periods, or permanently, as in the 1920s, and in the period after World War II when the population fell by about a fifth. Some of these emigrants were attracted back to the island in the 1970s to the developing oil-related industries (Prattis 1981:24).

Where does language fit into this pattern of economic activity? First, this century has seen the virtual disappearance of *monolingual* Gaelic speakers. The 1971 census found only a few dozen on Harris, for example, in this the principal Gaelic-speaking area. Almost all islanders now speak both Gaelic and English, and very young children are increasingly encouraged in the language. A survey of Harris primary schools, conducted by Mackinnon in 1972–3, found that 59% of the children were reckoned to be fluent in English compared with 11% in a survey in 1957–8 (Mackinnon 1977:88–9). A report that two-thirds of the children in the more recent survey (compared with 83% in the earlier) used only Gaelic in the playground reveals the advance of bilingualism, and perhaps of the predominance of English. Following from this bilingual advance is a sociolinguistic division of labour which may be observed in Mackinnon's analysis of the domains (or 'demesnes' as he insists on calling them) of the two languages. The results are unsurprising. As Ennew shows in outline for Lewis, and Mackinnon in much greater detail for Harris, there is a significant difference in the contexts of domains in which each language is used. A rough approximation is that Gaelic is the language of the countryside and the home; English that of the town and matters outside the home. Thus the principal commercial and administrative centres (Stornoway on Lewis, Tarbert on Harris) are largely the domain of English. Rough distinctions of this kind are inadequate, however, for Gaelic has not, by a long way, been 'reduced to domesticity', to the 'private' world, leaving English dominant in the 'public' domains.

Mackinnon shows that language domains can be mapped on a matrix of power and solidarity:

	Solidarity (+)	Solidarity (−)
Power (+)	Gaelic (i)	English (iii)
Power (−)	Gaelic (ii)	Optional (iv)

(Adapted from Mackinnon 1977:28–9)

(i) e.g. church, post-office
(ii) e.g. home life, shopping, croft work or equivalent
(iii) e.g. school, supervisors at work, public administration
(iv) e.g. encounters with strangers

Crucial here is 'solidarity' which reflects an internal/external, insider/outsider, *ethnic* dimension. English is the domain of what Emmett (1964, 1982a, 1982b) calls, in a Welsh context, 'colonial England' (see below): employment, administration, bureaucracy, the law. A significant contrast is between the use of Gaelic in the local post-office (a site of local relationships) and of English in a bank; of Gaelic in public bars, but of English in hotels ('English reigns supreme wherever there is a carpet on the floor', Mackinnon 1977:54–5).

Within the public sphere there is a difference between the language of politics and that of the Church, though the same people may be involved in both sorts of activity (ministers of religion often standing for public office). English predominates on the local council where, says Ennew, 'educational qualifications and certificates, the marks of success in the English-speaking external world, carry as much weight as natural political ability' (1980:72). Mackinnon shows, however, that on Harris language-switching may occur at meetings. Gaelic is sometimes used by chairmen trying to persuade some councillor to undertake a particular task (1977:56). (This reinforces the point about solidarity.) Gaelic is also used for the prayers which conclude council meetings, and it is perhaps in the Church that the Gaelic-speaking tradition is most strongly maintained outside the family, with Gaelic the predominant language of religion and ritual (cf. Dorian 1981:75 on ESG).

These domains are not exclusively the province of one language rather than the other, as the language-switching example shows. Individuals may also vary in their use of Gaelic or English in the same context – though variation is greater in some domains than in others. Few people, for example, use anything other than English for writing letters. Mackinnon also suggests that there is, currently, some weakening of Gaelic across almost all the domains he investigated, though he detected an increasing inclination among young people to use Gaelic in some situations in which their parents would have used English – for example, when discussing a problem with a local councillor, in a bank, or to a policeman. (He also points out that the two Harris policemen spoke only English, and 'one would become very annoyed when addressed in Gaelic', 1977:154.)

On Lewis and Harris, therefore, there is both continuity and change. Unlike the mainland Highlands where clearances and mass emigration devastated the population socially and linguistically from the nineteenth century onwards, there had been a much slower erosion on the islands. The family farm economy of crofting with its co-operative work groups has remained basic to the islands, and within that, and the moral community of the Church, Gaelic has survived (see Mewett 1982). The need for English among the earlier generations employed off the islands on fishing boats and as herring-gutters was minimal. They would have formed relatively self-contained seasonal migratory working groups. Local employment in the Harris tweed industry, too, would have needed little English, and the relatively homogeneous labour force could sustain the use of Gaelic (Mackinnon 1977:35).

For longer-term migrants to the mainland – for example, those going down to Glasgow – English becomes as essential as it is for those who deal with officialdom. And newer local employment opportunities for women – hotels, catering, offices, banks and shops – is often in contexts where English predominates. Thus women's experience of employment and the opportunity structure is likely to be different from that of men, with consequences for their linguistic attitudes and practices. Mackinnon in fact shows that in terms of tests of 'language loyalty', young women on the island of Harris were least likely to express support for Gaelic (1977:160–2). This, he feels, does not augur well for the future of the language. On the other hand, teenage girls interviewed in another survey he undertook among children away at secondary school on the mainland were among the strongest supporters of Gaelic. He comments: 'The local culture promotes the extrusion of the academically brighter young people and of them the girls in significantly greater numbers than the boys. It is ironic that these young women demonstrate a conspicuous attachment to their home, language and culture and yet are placed in the position of finding a career and a husband elsewhere' (1977:114).

WALES

Briefly, if crudely, the fate of the Welsh language over the last 200 years has closely reflected the fate of the Welsh countryside, and on the negative side that may be summed up as the interrelated experiences of the anglicisation of the gentry, the penetration of capitalism and of the state, emigration, tourism, and the media.

At the present time the bulk of Welsh speakers are to be found in the northern and western parts of the country, in areas which in recent times have voted strongly for Welsh nationalist candidates. These are areas which have been static or declining. Over the last hundred years the population of

Wales as a whole nearly doubled, that of the rural areas hardly changed. In the industrial south between 1881 and 1981 (and mainly in the earlier part of that period) the population of Gwent and Glamorgan rose by 800,000 (80%), that of Gwynedd and Dyfed (north and west) by 60,000 (12%). In many areas there has been an actual decline: the county of Merioneth, for example (nowadays Meirionnydd) counted 30,000 inhabitants in 1801, 52,000 in 1881, but 39,000 in 1961 and 30,450 in 1981.

Although the south does not lack Welsh speakers (18,000 in Swansea, for example, and 15,000 in Cardiff), 56% are concentrated in the rural counties of Gwynedd and Dyfed, throughout most of which they constitute the majority of the population (exceptions are the southern part of Pembroke-shire, and in the north around Conway). If commitment to Welsh is measured by ability to read and write the language and not just speak it, then nearly 60% of 'committed' Welsh language adherents are in these two counties.

Ethnographic studies of Welsh-speaking rural Wales show what has been happening to people and language in the countryside: Alwyn Rees's account of the parish of Llanfihangel, northern Montgomeryshire, in the period before World War II (Rees 1950), four short post-war studies in Cardiganshire, the Lleyn Peninsula, and Merioneth (Davies and Rees 1962), Isabel Emmett's 1964 account of the parish of 'Llan', also in Merioneth, her later studies (1982a, 1982b) of the town of Blaenau Ffestiniog, in the same county and Frankenberg's description of 'Pentre-diwaith' (1957) all contain valuable information.

Essential to any understanding of rural Welsh society in the nineteenth and early twentieth centuries is the fact that it consisted of agricultural communities where upland sheep farming and lowland cattle farming prevailed. Like much of rural Scotland and Ireland this was a family farm economy. The bulk of labour was provided by the farmer and his immediate relatives, with traditionally co-operation between families on work-parties for threshing, sheep-dipping and harvesting (cf. for Ireland, Arensberg 1937, Arensberg and Kimball 1940). Most of the land was traditionally held in tenure from large owners who often as not were themselves absent from the countryside. In Wales, a powerful land-owning Welsh gentry class emerged in the fifteenth century, coming into its own after the union with England in 1536. This gentry formed the basis of the power structure in Wales, and also achieved prominence outside Wales, for example at the court of Elizabeth I of England. In the mid-eighteenth century:

Some thirty to forty parliamentary families worth perhaps £3,000 to £5,000 a year monopolised Commons seats and the patronage that went with them. Beneath them, the local gentry, the £500-a-year men, perhaps twenty-five to fifty families a county, served as JPs and, with their parsons, ran the place through their country clubs of a Quarter Sessions.

(GWYN WILLIAMS 1985: 146, CF. GLANMOR WILLIAMS, 1979: 148)

Whatever other feelings they may have had about Welsh culture – and there continued to be what Gwyn Williams describes as an 'antiquarian' concern with, for example, Welsh poetry – their principal orientation was towards England and English (Glanmor Williams 1979:160 ff.). From the sixteenth century onwards the Welsh gentry was increasingly an anglicised gentry, as indeed was that of Ireland (Beckett 1966:37). Philip Jenkins writing of the Glamorgan gentry in the eighteenth century describes what he calls the process of 'desertion' through which 'the ruling class in a few decades detached themselves from the values and cultures of the local Welsh community. Edward Thomas Wenvre, the Cromwellian lord, could talk freely to his tenants and poorer neighbours in Welsh; his descendant and namesake in the 1750s would have required an interpreter – a fact of enormous significance for social relationships' (Jenkins 1983:194). There was thus a 'barrier of language between governors and governed' (Williams 1985:149).

We catch glimpses of this gentry in more recent ethnography. In the parish of Llanfihangel (pop. *c.* 500), three-quarters of the inhabitants were, until 1946, tenants of the Llwydiarth Estate with holdings of usually less than 100 acres. The Estate itself passed through several hands since the eighteenth century, and in the late nineteenth was held by the William Wynns who hunted and shot over the land and generally played the part of the squire. They were village benefactors, supporting the school and the church, and providing periodic feasts for the entire population to celebrate important events in the William Wynn family (Rees 1951:152). At such feasts the squire's praises would be sung in Welsh, illustrating Gwyn Williams's point about the gentry's interest in Welsh culture (cf. Jenkins 1983:205), but Rees suggests that their attitude towards Welsh was revealed in a remark of the then landlord, Sir Watkin, at a 'great feast' in 1875 when he opened the proceedings by saying: 'You will hear most of the toasts given in *your* native tongue.' Rees comments: 'the only words that he himself seems to have uttered in that tongue were *Iechyd da i chwi* (Good health to you)' (Rees 1951:155).

In Llanfrothen, Merioneth, Emmett reports that in the 1950s there were two estates whose families occupied the position of gentry. Both families were of Welsh descent, but long since anglicised. One was a well-known London publisher whose family spoke only English. The other spoke what

Emmett describes as 'a kind of broken Welsh' (1964:24). The equations landlord = English, tenant = Welsh, signal what was for years the basic structure of the Welsh countryside, until the break-up of many of the estates after World War II, a structure symbolised in the nomenclature of animals: 'Cows have homely Welsh names . . . whereas horses have English names and aristocratic ones at that – Prince, Duke, Captain . . . cows are spoken to in Welsh, but horses are treated as though they did not understand Welsh: all the words of command are addressed to them in English' (Rees 1951:58).

All of the rural studies of the 1940s and 1950s emphasise the *Welshness* of both language and culture of the rural farming communities, as opposed to the *Englishness* of the gentry, and in many cases of the towns. But these were not self-contained, unchanging communities, isolated from that Englishness. Each of the studies records a history of emigration. The population of Llanfihangel, for example, was in 1940 half what it had been in 1841. Many of the young men left agricultural work for mining, quarrying and transport; the women to become maids in wealthier farming areas, or to go into service in the towns. Others emigrated overseas. The town of Tregaron (Cardiganshire) was in the early nineteenth century a centre of the cattle trade, at one end of the drovers' road to England. A later generation followed that route to London, to work in dairying, or left for the South Wales coalfields (Jones 1962:79). It was not just the decline or relative poverty of agriculture which forced the population out. In many areas the inhabitants had long been engaged in other work alongside farming. In Glan-llyn (Merioneth), for example, there had been a thriving local, home-based, stocking knitting industry until well into the nineteenth century in which everyone, male and female, young and old, participated. 30,000 dozen pairs were sold annually in the town of Bala in the 1830s (Owen 1962:206–7). Competition with factory-produced goods from the Midlands destroyed this industry, and here too the population halved in a hundred years (Owen 1962:188). For those who remained the agricultural economy, too, was changing, with increased mechanisation and the decline of co-operative working parties. Many local crafts were no longer practised as rural areas became progressively and permanently integrated in wider regional and national markets.

What have been the linguistic consequences of these changes? A great deal of English is and was spoken, more perhaps than the censuses record. Emmett suggests that many people in the area she studied seem to have listed themselves as speaking 'Welsh only' even when knowing at least some English. For 'if they cannot understand the official language, they cannot be expected to comply with official regulations' (1964:33). But if one thing stands out from the figures cited earlier it is the decline of monolingualism.

In Merioneth in 1901 over half the population spoke Welsh only; by 1951 9% (in Emmett 1964: 132). By the end of World War II the vast majority of people were bilingual.

If the main sources of employment other than in agriculture, or in declining local industries such as slate-quarrying, are located in non-Welsh-speaking areas, then the incentive to learn English simply to get a job is obvious. But additionally, employment which brings prestige and respect is that for which a knowledge of English is essential.

David Jenkins divides the population of Aber-porth (Cardiganshire) into two groups, *buchedd A*, and *buchedd B*. (*Buchedd*, means 'way of life', as for example in *buchedd rinweddol*, 'a virtuous life'). In Aber-porth, adherents of *buchedd A* form a more strongly religious element in the community. They are thrifty people who place a high value on education and upward mobility, own their homes, and do not frequent the pub. Some are professionals, but included among them are 'the roadman or farm labourer who is a Sunday school teacher and deacon, and whose children are given the best education that circumstances allow – often better than they allow' (Jenkins 1962: 17). In the 1950s this meant education in an English language environment.

English, comments Emrys Jones, is the 'language of success' (1962: 102). In Tregaron some 20% of school-leavers in the post-war years went on to a college course of some kind, as against 11% who went into farming. 53% of the girls were recorded as wanting to be *teachers* on leaving school. Noting the importance of this 'English prestige ladder', and the attraction generally of jobs outside Welsh-speaking Wales, Isabel Emmett remarks: 'It is easy for any young person to go to London, Birmingham or abroad now, in the police force or merchant navy, as a nurse, as a civil servant, working in a shop or in an office . . . If . . . the economic incentive to give English first place continues high, the best-paid jobs going to the people who speak English well, then even a Welsh government in Wales . . . could not save the Welsh language' (1964: 137–8). That was written at a time of low unemployment, nationally and internationally, and the effect of the high unemployment of the 1980s on such communities is not yet clear.

A final point about the bilingual situation in Wales concerns the domains in which English and Welsh are spoken (cf. Clayton 1978). Even with the general advance of English, Welsh remains, as it has long been, the language of the home and of agricultural work, of the local shop and the pub. It has also remained the premier language of religion and of *internal* authority. The parallel with the Western Isles will be obvious, though in Wales the local language appears to be of far greater importance for personal writing – let alone 'literature' – than it is on Harris. Until recently, the language of *external* authority, of officialdom and of education has been English.

59

'Officialdom', writes Emmett, 'is seen as an English phenomenon' (1964:74): 'Until the 1939–45 war, Welsh-speaking people were met by English-speaking officials, received letters and forms in English which they often could not understand and could less often reply to in English' (1964:84). In the world of external authority, of 'ruling England', the poor speaker of English was likely as not to be ashamed of his or her poor grasp of the language.

This comes through clearly in another passage from Emmett:

Speaking good English and being accredited with social superiority are closely connected. When a Welsh-speaking person telephones the hospital to ask after a sick relative and cannot understand clearly what is said because the ward sister speaks English, he feels inferior. So does he when he feels ill but cannot explain quite what he feels like to the English doctor; or when he has to ask someone else to fill in a form for him because he is not sure about the big words in English . . . It is humiliating for a man to feel inadequate on many of the important occasions in his life: prize-giving at his daughter's school; answering a summons in court; or calling a doctor. Court cases are heard in English and interpreters only occasionally allowed . . . Ellis Cae Du, who is 29 years of age, pleaded guilty when he meant to plead not guilty to a motoring offence in 1957 and was too embarrassed to explain his error. He preferred to take the consequences of the mistake than to try to explain anything in English, show his inferior education or risk being laughed at.

(EMMETT 1964: 33–4)

There have, of course, been significant changes in this respect over the last two decades. There has, for example, been a considerable increase in professional and other types of employment by the state for which were recruited large numbers of Welsh-speaking men and women (Emmett 1982a:177), as often as not, perhaps, the children of Aber-porth's *buchedd A*. 'Ruling England' was increasingly Welsh-speaking. To understand the reasons for this and its significance we must look more broadly at the politics of language on the Celtic fringe. This will be the subject matter of chapter 5.

CONCLUSION

There is, or was, a conventional view, expressed in the writings of historians such as Elton, Barker and Namier, of the United Kingdom, as a territorially based polity whose constituent units were joined together as a totality through their adherence to common institutions, one of which was Standard English. As the language of authority, of Court and courts, of literature, of education, of commerce and industry it facilitated communication and established enduring bonds. But the *Triumph of English*, to cite the title of

Basil Cottle's well-known book (1969), had important consequences for the languages and cultures of the non-English speaking parts of the Kingdom.

In general terms there were two principal phases in the penetration of English into the Celtic-speaking areas of Britain. The first follows from 'the triumph of English' as the language of authority and status and is associated with the incorporation of local elites (aristocrats and gentry) within an English-dominated culture, an incorporation backed by exhortation and in some instances Act of Parliament (see chapter 5). O Fiaich (1969:103) records that in 1541 the Speaker's address to the Dublin Parliament 'had to be translated into Irish before several members of the Commons could follow it'. But from the mid-sixteenth century onwards in Ireland, Wales and Scotland there emerged two sociolinguistically distinct strata: an English-speaking, land-owning, minority, and a non-English-speaking tenantry or peasantry. The rural and provincial towns, too, were predominantly centres of English language and culture. Until roughly the mid-eighteenth century penetration of English outside the ranks of the gentry and the urban classes generally proceeded at a feeble pace, and even among the gentry, for example in Wales, anglicisation was not as rapid or as uniforms or complete as is sometimes supposed (cf. Jenkins 1983:204). And, apart from the purpose of converting the Catholic population to Protestantism, the pace of penetration was not usually a matter of profound concern to the authorities.

By the time the second phase began in the latter half of the eighteenth century the vast majority of the rural population of Wales, Scotland and Ireland still spoke their native tongues (see Brody 1974:49). The rapidity with which these languages declined in the *nineteenth* century is the most striking feature of the material we have surveyed. Here the real 'killer' was not so much English but the combined forces of industrialisation, urbanisation, agricultural change, education and eventually the rise of centralised institutions of state concerned with economic and social management and welfare. Even in the nineteenth century, however, the pace of penetration was neither uniform nor inexorable. Where local economies were poorly integrated with the wider society (as perhaps in the Aran Islands) or integrated in such a way as to provide a relatively autonomous ecological niche, then language and culture could survive, as happened, for example, in the Sutherland fishing villages.

Many, of course, bitterly regretted this decline, and, as we shall see in chapter 5, fought an ideological battle for Irish, Welsh and Scottish subjectivity which on the more favourable terrain of Wales could be partially won in the fusing of religion, literacy and the Welsh tongue. For others the decline was welcome. The language shift in nineteenth-century

Ireland was so massive – 'unparalleled' (Greene 1972:9), 'unprecedented rout' (De Freine 1978:72) – that Greene calls it 'linguistic suicide'. De Freine believes it was of a chiliastic or millenarian nature: '(It is) only by seeing it as a millenial or utopian movement that the mass flight from the Irish language becomes explicable' (1977:83). It is all too easy to blame the decline of Irish in the nineteenth century on the education system (as did Douglas Hyde, for example), or the Catholic Church, or Daniel O'Connell (see chapter 5). Leaving aside the economic and other forces (famine and emigration) which devastated the population, and hence the language and culture of the Irish countryside, it is not at all clear that the Irish themselves *wanted* to save the language. Writing of the 'tally sticks', for example, the petty, humiliating penalty imposed on children speaking Irish similar to the devices reported widely for Wales, Scotland and Brittany, Greene (1972:10–11) argues that these were used at the insistence of the parents. 'The people in general', writes De Freine, 'accepted the ethnocentric Ascendancy viewpoint that Irish was a backward language and that even to speak it was a hindrance to progress' (1977:84). De Freine's point shows both that the decline of the language must be set in the wider context of social and economic change, and that the struggle for the language was part of a larger struggle.

In the present day, even in an area ('Inis Beag') remote from the centres of change, and which has received strong institutional and financial support from the Gaeltacht authorities, John Messenger records:

English is spoken as much as Irish in the presence of children in some households so as to prepare them for eventual emigration, in spite of the protestations of some priests and neighbours who insist that the alien tongue not be spoken on moral and nativistic grounds. The language revival movement [see chapter 5] receives much criticism because it results in emigrants being placed at a disadvantage; a frequently heard utterance in Inis Beag, even among those who hesitate to use English before their offspring, is, 'What good will Irish do a person?'

(MESSENGER 1969: 129)

4

A VIEW FROM THE PERIPHERY:
'OCCITANIE'

*The princes speak French, and soon everybody will follow their example;
and then behold, perfect bliss; the golden age, when all the world will speak
one tongue, one universal language is dawning again! There will be one
flock, and one shepherd! National cultures, where are you?*

(J. G. HERDER, CITED IN BARNARD 1969: 209)

> *La lenguo d'O, pamens fièro coume toujour.*
> *Lengo d'amour, se i'a d'arlèri*
> *E de bastard, ah! pèr sant Ceri*
> *Auras dóu terradou li mascle à toun cousta;*
> *E tant que lou Mistrau ferouge*
> *Braimara dins li roco, – aurouge,*
> *T'apararen à boulet rouge*
> *Car es tu la patrio e tu la liberta*

(MISTRAL 'CALENDAU, CANT. IV, VV. 20, 21)

THIS chapter is principally concerned with the view of language and nation epitomised by Mistral and his poetry.

Fishman (1973:10), and others (e.g. Smith 1983), represent modern nationalism as a striving to reverse what Tönnies, Durkheim and Weber saw as an historic trend in European societies from *Gemeinschaft* to *Gesellschaft*. The tendency of nationalist movements to seek out 'original' national languages is, according to Fishman (1973:70), a reflection of 'a more general yearning for community'. Anderson, too, refers to the 'beauty of *Gemeinschaft*' represented by appeals to 'nature' of the kind made, for example, in the poem *Último adiós* of the martyred Filipino nationalist, Rizal, which he cites (Anderson 1983:130–1).

Those who see nationalism embodying a desire for a return to the society of former days take the opposite position to that of Gellner (1983), who sees nationalism's genesis in the structural needs of a modernising society. In fact, as suggested in chapter 2, nation as *Gemeinschaft* is only *one* view of the nature of the entity. Anderson rightly says that 'the nation is always conceived as a deep, horizontal comradeship' (1983:16), but 'comradeship' may be conceived in different ways, for example as co-citizenship, as in the *Gesellschaft* or Enlightenment model of nation. Comradeship of the *Gemeinschaft*-like type is distinctive of a second great intellectual, philosophical, political and social, trend or movement of the eighteenth and nineteenth centuries – Romanticism – a movement often said to be in creative opposition or tension with Enlightenment.

The eighteenth-century German philosopher J. G. Herder (1744–1803) was closely associated with the origins of this movement, and shaped Romantic ideas about language, nation and history (Kohn 1944:430 ff., and Blackall 1978, Edwards, J. R. 1985:23–4, Furst 1969, Schenk 1966). His concept of culture, what one generation transmits to another largely, though not exclusively, through language, was essentially relativist, a position which was, as it were, prepared for Romanticism by the age of discovery outside Europe (Anderson 1983:68ff.). As such Herder's ideas had an important influence on the development of modern anthropology (Clark 1955:188, Dumont 1979, Lovejoy 1941:277), and there is a line of descent from his predecessor Hamann, through Herder himself, to von Humboldt, the American anthropologist Boas and thence to the linguistic relativists Sapir and Whorf (see especially Haugen 1977). It is, however, Herder's political heritage which concerns us here.

F. M. Barnard (1965, 1969) has provided an excellent synthesis of the Herderian conception of language from the *Treatise on the origin of language* and other writings (see also Kohn 1944:432 ff.). Central to this was the idea of a direct relationship between language and reason ('Each nation speaks in the manner it thinks and thinks in the manner it speaks', in Barnard 1965:56), and between language and consciousness, both individual and collective: 'Those sharing a particular historical tradition grounded in language Herder identifies with a *Volk* or nationality, and it is in this essentially spiritual quality that he sees the most natural and organic basis for political association' (Barnard 1965:57). The *Volk* had a natural foundation:

The natural state of man is society. He is born and brought up in it . . . words which are associated in his mind with the most tender feelings are father, mother, son, brother, sister, lover, friend; all these entail natural ties which exist in the most primitive societies . . . It is nature which educates families: the most natural state is, therefore, one nation, an extended family with one national character . . . A nation is as natural a plant as any family, only with more branches.

(HERDER IN BARNARD 1969: 317, 324)

Language is the crucial element, 'the most determinative characteristic' (Barnard 1965: 141) of a nation, a form of organisation which has for Herder an 'organic' nature which he opposes to the 'mechanical' type of bureaucratic society (Durkheim's usage of organic/mechanical is nearly the reverse of Herder's).

Herderian ideas were important for the development of German literature of the eighteenth and nineteenth centuries (in particular Goethe and the *Sturm und Drang* School), and were elaborated by Fichte, Schlegel and Arndt (Chambers 1946, Edwards, J. R. 1985:25 ff., Kohn 1967). A passage from Fichte's *Lectures to the German nation* (1807–8) in which, especially in Lectures 4 and 5, he 'placed language in the foreground of nationalism' (Engelbrecht 1968:114) illustrates this. For Fichte, language is not something accidental or unimportant. Language is the most fundamental expression of the soul of a people; it reveals its entire character.' Unlike Herder, however, who had a concern for cultures world-wide, Fichte was more interested in *German* nationalism, its specificity, its essential unity, and ultimately its historic destiny. Another passage from Fichte from the *Patriotic dialogues* (1806–7) contains the following comment by one of the participants: 'The separation of Prussians from the rest of the Germans is purely artificial . . . The separation of the Germans from the other European nations is based on nature. Through a common language and through German national characteristics which unite Germans, they are separated from the others' (in Engelbrecht 1968:97).

The relativistic and deterministic relationship between language, thought, culture and society posited in this Romantic, *Gemeinschaft*-like view of nation entails a major theoretical problem for anthropological linguistics, but its significance as political ideology is unquestionable. This chapter examines its influence on the perception of the situation of subordinate language groups in France in the nineteenth and twentieth centuries through the case of 'Occitanie'. The discussion is continued in chapter 5 where the focus shifts from France to Britain.

OCCITANIE/PROVENCE

In a celebrated essay, the historian Gwyn Williams asks 'When was Wales?' (Williams 1982, 1985). A similar question is as appropriate for 'Occitanie' as it is for the principality. Consider.

A short while ago an historian wrote: 'There never was an Occitanie' . . . The reason for non-existence: 'There never was any unity between the Alps and the Pyrennees.' *Political* unity is what is meant. The reader should be aware that in our view such a conception of history is entirely outmoded. It is also conceptually absurd. Does the existence of a human group of any kind depend on its being united by a state?

(ARMENGAUD'S INTRODUCTION TO ARMENGAUD AND LAFONT 1979:XI)

What Armengaud, Lafont and others mean by 'Occitanie' is an area of France constituted by the 'countries of the Oc' which in their view share a common culture and language. This area, they agree, was never a single nation-state, nor was it by Sieyès's definition a nation. In fact Armengaud (p. xiii) specifically dissociates himself from that definition, but insists that Occitanie is (was, will be) what Lafont (1968) has called an *ethnie.*

The linguistic argument for this is as follows. Within what is now France there were two major groups of dialects: the *langue d' Oïl* and the *langue d' Oc*, the boundary between which is sometimes seen as a major social and cultural divide with origins in prehistoric times. Both groups of dialects are thought of as branches of the Gallo-Roman division of the Western Latin languages which evolved after the break-up of the Roman Empire (others include Ibero-Roman). However, a leading Occitanian linguist argues that the *langue d' Oïl* and the *langue d' Oc* differ considerably in linguistic terms and the latter has more in common with Catalan than with 'French', and has proposed the inclusion of the *langue d' Oc* with Catalan in a separate 'Occito-Roman' language group (Bec in Armengaud and Lafont 1979, p. 116).

Called in the Middle Ages *la lengua romana*, or sometimes *limousin* or *proensal*, Bec records that the term *langue d' Oc* itself first appears in Dante's *De Vulgari Eloquentia* (as *lingua d'oco*). From the fourteenth century *patria linguae occitanae* referred to the southern fiefdoms of the Kings of France, and such usage encouraged the early nineteenth-century writer Fabre d'Olivet to resurrect the term *occitan* for the title of a collection of poetry (*Poésies Occitaniques*) which he published in 1804.

Whether or not 'Occitanie' was originally only a geographical expression, it has since connoted a great deal more. This connotation may be observed in contemporary Occitanian historiography from which the following picture is derived. Out of the chaos of the barbarian invasions, the fall of Rome, and the eras of the Merovingians and Carolingians, there emerged in the southern part of France (an area which may have been more thoroughly romanised than the north) a region of small feudal polities maintaining strong links with other societies of the Mediterranean, including Catalan-speaking northwest Spain. In the twelfth century, four powerful states competed for the terrain and people of a region which Martel (in Armengaud and Lafont 1979:255) describes as a 'nebula, still lacking a centre of gravity'. To the west, the duchies of Aquitaine and their successors, the Plantagenets – an English influence; in the centre, Toulouse with influence across the Rhône; to the south, Catalonia which at that time also held sway over the Comte de Provence in the west. To the north, France, or rather the Kingdom based on the Ile de France which having consolidated its authority locally was building on an excellent economic base, and good relations with the Church, to extend its political influence.

Gradual French encroachment on the south was followed by the crusade against the Albigensian heresy, an event which figures prominently in contemporary Occitanian historiography. The crusade ended with the accord of Meaux in 1229 in which the nobles of 'Occitania' were integrated within the feudal hierarchy of the 'French' king. The 'autochthonous' dynasties (Martel in Armengaud and Lafont 1979: 335) were replaced by the King of France and an externally imposed administration.

Occitanian historians search the Middle Ages for signs of an 'Occitanian' consciousness, as opposed to a mere resistance offered by local potentates and their followers. They find it in Raimond VI, of Toulouse, who called those who fought with him 'homines nostre idiome', 'men of our tongue' (in Armengaud and Lafont 1979: 325, 402), in the war songs of the period, in particular in the *Cançon de la crusada*, and in the 'occitanian' values (*valor, pretz, mesura, paratge*) which they extol (Armengaud and Lafont 1979:323).

A similar process of incorporation occurred elsewhere in France at this time or later. For example, in the Middle Ages the Brittany peninsula (settled in the fifth to sixth centuries by Celtic immigrants from Britain who maintained an enclave against Frankish incursions) was a relatively autonomous 'Duchy'. Its independence was contested by England and France, and with the Pact of Union of 1532 it became a province of the French crown.

In the south, the 'annexation', as it is called, of 1228 was followed by a long, slow process of political and administrative integration with the north which only became effective in 1481. The integrative process involved language to the extent that after the Ordonnance of Villers-Cotterets the Occitanian dialects lost status as French became the *official* language, the language of power, and increasingly the principal vehicle for literary expression.

In his study of the language of Provence, an important part of Occitanie situated in the lower valley of the Rhône which includes the towns of Aix, Avignon and Marseilles, Auguste Brun records that by 1650, although a Provençal literature still existed, French had become the primary language of writing of all kinds. Many people of all classes still, however, spoke Provençal, though French was available (and often necessary) as a second language, employed according to the situation. Thus: 'The use of French or

Provençal was not a matter of class, but of circumstance: French was nobler and more suitable for public discourse, for ceremonies and meetings, Provençal was more suitable for ordinary, everyday needs' (Brun 1927:12). Provençal was used in church, for example, for the homilies, but serious religious discussion of dogma warranted French (Brun, p. 13).

In the early eighteenth century, while Provençal remained the language of the lower orders and the countryside, French increasingly became the ordinary everyday speech of the upper classes. Brun provides some interesting evidence for the stratification of language, and of language switching, from an examination of popular eighteenth century drama. Surveying the plays produced locally, whose characters consisted of a range of social stereotypes, he says:

The seigneur, the bourgeois, the gentleman do not customarily speak patois, though they condescend to do so with their inferiors. These – peasants, servants, artisans, fishermen, sailors – understand French, force themselves to use it when speaking to their masters, but are at ease only in Provençal. In between, the middle classes, and those who have been abroad, affect French, and are made fun of for speaking it badly: theirs is poor French, *franciot*. Functionaries, judges, etc., speak French impeccably. (p. 29)

This is probably an accurate reflection of the urban scene where there also begins to emerge, as at Marseilles, a distinct French *regional* dialect and accent, though it is not until the next century, when French becomes much more common among the urban working class, that that dialect emerges as a major phenomenon.

Linguistic stratification of the eighteenth century was a consequence, Brun argues, of other changes taking place in the south. These include the increasing pre-eminence of French as a literary vehicle – it now dominates the scene – the growth of a popular (French language) theatre and press, the dominance of French in technical, scientific, administrative, and commercial jargon, and the expansion of education (for the upper classes) and its orientation towards contemporary French language and literature (now of 'classic' stature). In a time of prosperity, the large towns such as Marseilles also became major centres of commerce and industry. The demand for labour brought in migrant workers from the countryside and other provinces, making of Marseilles a sort of social and linguistic melting pot. The expansion of markets meant that the local commercial classes were now in contact with customers and suppliers from all parts of the Kingdom (Brun 1927:83) and needed French for their everyday business.

By the time of the Revolution, however, the habitual use of French had not spread below the bourgeoisie or outside the larger towns. This began only after, and in part because of, the Revolution. Thus, Brun (1927:117) estimates that 10% of the male population of Provence probably served in the Grande Armée during the Napoleonic wars. He also places particular emphasis on the emergence, during the post-Revolutionary era, of a state which increasingly made its presence felt in all corners of life where: 'The individual came up against the barrier of the *guichet*, symbol of the State . . . and a bureaucracy which did not understand Breton, or Basque or Provençal' (Brun 1927:141).

Brun's description of the changes taking place in Provence is probably a reasonable guide to what was happening in other parts of Occitanie, and indeed much of the rest of France, though the area of the lower Rhône was more 'advanced' economically, and certainly better endowed, than many other regions. In Brittany, for example, by the eve of the Revolution, the aristocracy and bourgeoisie of the principal towns were still bilingual in speech, but read and wrote only in French. Outside the towns French was rarely understood, except along the coasts where the sea provided the main means of movement and communication. The interior of the country was poor and scarcely penetrable (Dauzat 1946:107–8).

The spread of literacy in the eighteenth and nineteenth centuries and the spread of French probably followed similar paths. This is not to equate literacy and French, simply to point out that the social, economic and political processes at work in the two instances were much the same. Consequently, the following overview of the history of literacy could equally apply to the French language:

By the 17th century, the élites of the old Kingdom of France could read, write and count, while the peasantry was still massively illiterate. Most of the spectacular progress made in the 18th century occurred among the middle ranks of the old society: merchants, shopkeepers, artisans, tenant farmers and rich peasants. Wage-labourers, especially in the countryside, formed a kind of residual though substantial stock, undented by progress in the surrounding milieu. It was only in the 19th century that they too became caught up in the general movement towards literacy, the timing of the process keeping pace with its gradual 'trickling down' through society . . . the market economy, backed by and relying upon the machinery of the centralised state, expanded the role of writing as a necessary condition of modernisation.   (FURET AND OZOUF 1982: 303–4)

Although the patois and idioms in fact remained important well into the nineteenth century and beyond, even early in the century it seemed to some that *francisation* and the centralisation with which it was associated had gone too far, too fast, destroying their cultures and languages. It was at this time, that Fabre d'Olivet sought to promote the poetry of an earlier age in the language he called 'Occitan'. D'Olivet, like others, was influenced by the so-called 'Ossian' epic, a spurious poem, published in Britain in the 1760s, purporting to be a translation of ancient Gaelic verses, which excited widespread interest on the Continent, including Herder's. Thus the early years of the nineteenth century saw a 'renaissance', as it was called, for Occitan, or strictly speaking Provençal, literature which Brun believes was a direct response to the political and linguistic centralisation fostered by the Revolution. In this renaissance a prominent part was played by the poet, Frédéric Mistral (1830–1914).

MISTRAL AND THE FÉLIBRIGE

Mistral was born in the village of Maillane, not far from Arles. His father was a *ménager*, a yeoman farmer living on and working his own homestead or *mas* with hired help. Mistral described the social background:

Around Arles, the *ménagers* are a class apart, a sort of aristocracy coming between peasants and bourgeoisie and who, like all others, are proud of their caste. For if the peasant, who lives in villages, works his little bit of land with his hands, with spade or hoe, the *ménager* works his large holding upright, singing his songs, hands to the plough. (MISTRAL 1906: 4)

This rural community where there still existed an almost feudal relationship between the labourer and the *ménager* (known locally as *maître*, but Mistral refers to his father as *seigneur*, 1906:27–8), provided much of the material for Mistral's poetry. English writers on Mistral, carried away by their subject, reproduce his thought and style in their own. Tudor Edwards's account of Mistral's childhood, which follows Mistral's own description very closely, provides a typical example of the way in which Mistral becomes the Romantic personified: 'The life at the *mas* was a life in close contact with the soil and with elementals, still dominated by the ancient cycle of times and seasons, traditions and beliefs, where even the simplest meals had an almost monastic ritual . . . It was [his mother] who first kindled in him the love of local history and legend, firing his imagination as she sat turning her spinning wheel in the corner of that great fireplace' (Edwards 1964:7).

Already interested in the Provençal language, which he spoke at home, Mistral was sent to school at Avignon where one of his teachers was Joseph Roumanille who himself wrote poetry in Provençal. A myth-like story attaches to Roumanille, telling how at first he wrote in French, but noticing one day his mother's tears because she could not understand his words, he henceforth vowed never to write anything his mother could not comprehend. Mistral says of him: 'Until [meeting Roumanille] I had read, in fits and starts, a bit of Provençal. What annoyed me was seeing modern writers in general . . . use our language derisively. Roumanille expressed the deepest feelings of the heart in the popular speech of contemporary Provence, with dignity and in simple and fresh form' (1906:116).

The two began to contribute to a journal of Provençal poetry (*Boui-Abais*) published in Marseilles between 1841 and 1846. In 1854 they and five of their followers founded what they called the Félibrige, a Provençal word of uncertain meaning and derivation, discovered by Mistral in an ancient hymn. In 1876 the Félibrige became a society with branches in various parts of Provence and further afield, including Paris, and Mistral its first president or *Capoulie*. Their aim: 'to preserve the language of the land of Oc' (cited in Downer 1901:19).

From the outset the Félibrige attacked 'the false idea that popular speech was suitable only for low subjects or for ribaldry' (Mistral 1906:118). The great Provençal literary tradition of the troubadours of the twelfth and thirteenth centuries had since the 'annexation' been submerged, and the language been 'reduced to domesticity' (Mistral 1906:223). They sought, therefore, to relegitimate Provençal as a literary vehicle.

One problem, according to the Félibrige, was that social and political pressures had caused the break-up of what was previously a uniform language into a large number of local dialects. The 'corrupted, bastardised form of the francisised patois of the streets' (Mistral 1906:120), could not provide a suitable linguistic model for their poetry. That had to be found elsewhere, in the countryside. They chose the dialect of Maillane. But though it provided a good basis, that language too required renewal. The spelling needed to be regularised and words reflecting French influence needed replacing with 'older and more genuine forms' (Downer 1901:44). Where the vocabulary they needed was unavailable in the patois or the medieval poems they drew on Latin and exploited the use of suffixes to create new forms. Thus *eigagno* – dew – from *aigo* – water – and *agno* – a diminutive.

This selection of one local dialect as a model for standardisation of a widespread and varied language led inevitably to conflict with other groups (in Marseilles, for example, and in Gascony) who wished to continue to use their own local variants. It also ran counter to the wishes of those seeking a standard, which would somehow encompass all of the dialects of the *langue d'Oc*. This is an example of the particularism for which the Félibrige was criticised by later Occitanians. In another way, however, the Félibrige were far from particularistic, seeing themselves as part of a great movement which included all the 'Latin' languages and 'races': Italian, Catalan, Rumanian, as well as the *langue d'Oc*. (See Mistral's poem 'Cant a la raço latino', translated in Lyle 1953: 34.) In similar fashion later Breton nationalists saw themselves as part of a wider Celtic 'race' and movement.

The Félibrige therefore aligned themselves with the revival of Catalan literature and political aspirations in Spain, and discovered an ancient symbol of Latin unity in the 'Floral Games', which took place annually from 1859. In that year Mistral was visited by the Catalan poet Calvet, and a link was established with the Catalan political leader Victor Balaguer. In 1867, the Catalans presented the Félibrige with a gilded chalice (the *Coupo Santo*). Mistral replied to the presentation with a poem (*La Coupo*) which became virtually a Provençal national anthem (Edwards 1964: 103). These Latin links were furthered by the celebration in 1874 of the fifth centenary of the death of Petrarch, and by the participation of Rumanian poets in the Félibrige's prize competitions. (Mistral wrote approvingly of attempts to revive a national language in Rumania, again by seeking its pure form in the rural areas and in the mountains.)

Mistral's interest in a 'Latin Federation' led to accusations of separatist or 'federalist' aspirations. In the 1790s, Federalism, with which, as we have seen, Barère and Grégoire charged the users of the idioms, often seems little more than a political *tendency* or current of opinion. Its vagueness was such that one of the Girondins declared that as a term applied to an opponent 'federalism' meant simply 'marked for execution' (Sydenham 1961: 193). Sydenham himself distinguishes federalism 'in its literal sense' from a general hostility towards the policies of Robespierre and the radical Revolutionaries of Paris which he believes characterised the so-called federalism of the Girondins. At the most, the Girondins wanted only 'departmentalism' (Soboul 1977: 43-4), a relative degree of autonomy for the new departments. Federalism in the literal sense refers to support for a federal republic for the France of the 1790s, perhaps along the lines of Switzerland or the United States (Sydenham 1961: 195). Soboul also shows how varied were the aims of the insurrectionists of 1793 – there was no common platform, and the support given by different classes of the population to the risings varied from region to region and place to place. Only in Brittany was there any sign of a distinct separatist viewpoint, in that case linked to the counter-Revolution, though Brunot (1967: 177-8) reports that there were very few counter-Revolutionary tracts in the idioms.

The Occitanian historian, Claude Delpla, admits that federalism was a vague and variegated phenomenon, distinguishing three kinds: an 'aristocratic' (as in Brittany), 'bourgeois', and 'popular' (in Armengaud and Lafont 1979:701-11). But he argues that federalist ideas were strongly supported throughout the Midi (i.e. Occitanie), and that various areas (e.g.

Marseilles, Bordeaux, Toulon, and Lyons) for a period in 1793 virtually seceded from the Republic. He also records that in June 1793 a meeting in Nîmes of representatives from throughout the south proposed what he calls *La République Fédérative du Midi* 'creating from the 24 departments of the Midi a federated republic from Lyons to Bordeaux' (cited in Armengaud and Lafont 1979:708). This idea came to nothing, but a federalist orientation or perspective remained part of the political discourse of the south throughout the nineteenth century.

Mistral certainly espoused a kind of federalism for France and for Spain: 'Our French republicans dream of the advantages of the American and Swiss constitution, but nearly all ignore or reject the only means of attaining them, which is federation' (cited in Edwards 1964:117). But he never advocated a separate, autonomous Provençal, or Occitanian, state. His 'separatism', says Aldington (1956:137), 'was a moral, spiritual and practical repudiation of the standard of Paris'. He certainly opposed that centralisation which characterised the French state in the nineteenth century, and what he saw as the evil effects of modernity: '(Agricultural machinery) is Progress, the terrible, fatal harrow against which nothing can be done or said: the bitter fruit of science' (1906:164). The ideas of the Félibrige were on a ritual, rather than practical or political plane – the *Coupo Santo*, the Floral Games, the significance of the number seven, their poetry, much of which celebrated the legendary and mythical past of Provence, interwoven with contemporary folklore.

First and foremost was the language in which 'that which one thinks comes easily to the lips' (Mistral 1906:227). Mistral celebrated the language in a speech at the annual Saint Estello banquet (another ritual) in 1877:

A language is like the shaft of a mine for at the bottom of it there have been deposited all the fears, all the feelings, all the thoughts, of ten, twenty, thirty, a hundred generations. It is a pile, an ancient hoard, whither every passer-by has brought his gold or silver or leather coin. It is a great monument whither every family has carried its stone, where every city has built its column, where a whole race has worked, body and soul, for hundreds and thousands of years. A language, in a word, is the revelation of actual life, the manifestation of human thought, the all-holy instrument of civilizations, and the speaking testament of dead and living societies.

(GIRDLESTONE'S TRANSLATION, CITED IN EDWARDS 1964:141)

In 1892, however, there was a serious split within the Félibrige (Nguyen 1977:249) when Amouretti and Charles Maurras issued a manifesto declaring that freedom for the language would come only from political autonomy: 'We are autonomists. We are federalists. We want a sovereign assembly at Bordeaux, Toulouse, Montpellier, and one at Marseilles and

Aix. And these assemblies will run our administration, our courts, our schools, our universities, our public works' (cited in Delpla in Armengaud and Lafont 1979:761). Besides this felibrigean federalism of the Maurrasian kind (which became increasingly royalist and antisemitic, for Maurras was, of course, one of the precursors of French fascism) there was also a federalism of the left, what Delpla (p. 762) calls the 'red Félibrige', associated with Louis-Xavier de Ricard who favoured a socialist Occitanian republic federated with France. It is often suggested that it is Ricard, rather than Mistral, still less Maurras, who is at the origin of much contemporary Occitanian political thought.

Though there was a renaissance of Provençal or Occitanian as a literary, especially a poetic language, crowned by Mistral's Nobel Prize of 1904, the language failed to become, as did Catalan, the language of literature generally. And though the 1863 survey cited in chapter 2 showed that in many parts of the South over three quarters of the population were still monolingual patois speakers, there was a further decline in oral usage. For the authorities, however, continued use of the language was considered as intolerable as when Grégoire wrote his report (Armengaud 1977). Education was once again looked to as the instrument of change, and reforms in education in the latter part of the century pressed hard on the patois, with a policy which Robert Lafont has described as 'ethnocide'. Breton nationalists similarly characterise use in nineteenth century schools of the *symbole*, the clog hung by teachers round the necks of children who persisted in speaking Breton as a vicious psychological weapon for destroying a belief in the value of local languages and cultures, making children ashamed of their tongue (Reece 1977:31–3, Timm 1980:30).

After 1914, the popular language entered a period of what Teulat calls 'catastrophic setbacks':

The [First World War] itself caused this setback: many were killed and for those who survived amidst the camaraderie of the trenches the national language gained a new significance. Another setback was caused by World War II, above all through the influx of refugees from the North, another fraternity with whom the common language could only be French. The third setback dates from the 1960s, the new industrialisation, the installation of another wave of French speakers [the former colonials, the *pieds noirs* from North Africa], and above all the audiovisual media which use only French. At the same time . . . the school and the university continue their work of destruction. (TEULAT 1979:883)

In the early 1920s there were some 9 million people for whom Occitan was the usual language. By 1971 Lafont (1974) estimates only 2 million full-time users (plus another 7 million speaking it occasionally). Though the situation may have changed less than these figures suggest, they indicate the evidence

74

which persuades contemporary Occitanians of the perilous situation of their language and culture. In this period of decline (cause and consequence) there occurred another attempt to revive the concept of Occitanie.

MODERN OCCITANISM

Robert Lafont, described as the 'founder and theoretician of modern Occitanism' (Armengaud and Lafont 1979:896), wrote in 1974: 'The Occitanian claim – linguistic, cultural, socioeconomic, and political – is today so widespread that no one in France can fail to know of it' (1974:7). What form does this claim take, and what is being done about it? One answer is the massive corpus of *writing* – permanently published and ephemeral, scholarly (for example historical and linguistic), political, polemical, and literary, and sometimes all of these at once. In what ways is the Occitanian 'movement' more than this?

Three things distinguish this modern revival from that of the Félibrige: its attitude to the language, the political framework within which it locates the past and present history of Occitanie; and the intellectual and political connection it makes not with some supposed 'Latin race', but with the political claims of other regions of France, and of regionalists elsewhere in Europe. Thus contemporary Occitanists often characterise the Félibrige as particularistic (because of their elevation of the Provençal dialect), élitist (because of their attempt to recreate a 'high' culture), and politically unsophisticated (because they had no real understanding of the power structure of French society and were unable to formulate any serious political programme).

The accusation of particularism refers to the Félibrige's conscious choice as a standard of one dialect of Oc which was not even representative of Provençal as a whole, but only that part of it known as 'Rhodanie' (the lower valley of the Rhône, Mistral's homeland). The Félibrige's difficult relationship with the poets Jasmin (who wrote in Gascon) and Gelu (Marseilles) stemmed from this insistence on *their* standard, the claims of which were contested in a series of rival grammars. Their chosen orthography was also thought to suffer from the influence of French conventions and was therefore not always appropriate to the dialects of Oc. Even if it were made more appropriate for Provençal, it could not easily be employed elsewhere.

The intellectual, and political, problem was to reconcile an 'imagined community' of Oc, as Anderson might call it, with an existent diversity. A partial solution was proposed by the grammarian Louis Alibert in 1935, who devised an orthography capable of representing the diverse dialects (Teulat

1979:884–5, Lafont 1974:204), This system was adopted by the Institut des Etudes Occitanes in 1946, but current opinion favours a kind of grammatical and orthographic democracy:

> The new theoreticians recognise all forms of the spoken language (except French words introduced through diglossia) as authentic Occitan. The spoken language of an area is the Occitan of that area. That language has the right to be written down, and careful thought about the traditional orthography allows all forms of speech to be provided with a written form. The dialects can be used in all kinds of writing. A treatise on mathematics written in Provençal is as legitimate as one written in langue d'Oc.
>
> (TEULAT 1979:887)

Much of the early phase of the modern Occitanian revival was concerned with such issues and societies and associations, like the Escola Occitana (1919), Collegi d'Occitania (1927), Societat d'Estudios Occitans (1931) and the Institut d'Etudes Occitanes (1946, but originally founded by a group of Résistants, clandestinely, in 1943), whether in or out of sympathy with the principles of the Félibrige, essentially confined themselves to language, literature, and education.

The status of Occitan in the school system has long exercised the movement. One of the criticisms of the Félibrige (Giordan 1975, Lafont 1974:216) was of their failure to evolve an educational policy to counter the centralising influence of French. It was not until the 1920s that there was founded a Comité d'Action en faveur de la langue d'oc à l'école. Pressure from that and similar groups in the South and in other regions of France, for example Brittany, led eventually to the Loi Deixonne of 1951 (No. 51–46 of 1951, text in Lafont *et al.* 1982:144–5). This measure provided for the teaching in primary and secondary schools of a number of designated regional languages (including Occitan, though not immediately). Both teaching and learning were optional (depending on the wishes of both teachers and taught) and limited to one hour per week maximum, with additional time available, if desired, for local history and culture (Marcellesi 1975).

Although the Loi Deixonne was an important innovation for France, its limited provisions meant limited success for the languages. Only in the higher reaches of secondary education was this success marked, and then only after further initiatives in the 1960s (Lafont 1974:233). Then the numbers taking Occitan as part of the *baccalauréat* exam rose from 342 in 1961–2, to 977 in 1965–6, to 5,422 in 1973–3 (Giordan 1975:100), and over 10,000 in 1980–1 (Lafont *et al.* 1982:156). In the Académie de Rennes (Brittany), 946 candidates (in 13 *lycées*) presented themselves for a *baccalauréat* examination in Breton in 1973 (Reece 1977:219–20), over 3000 in 1980–1, 90% from private schools.

A view from the periphery: 'Occitanie'

Writing in 1979, and in the face of the apparent slow progress of the movement, the linguist Teulat argued that Occitan, like Catalan and Basque in post-Franco Spain, should be recognised as a national language for the region in which it is spoken, involving the compulsory use of Occitan in public administration, a panoccitan newspaper, and radio service supported from public funds. He also advocates an official policy of implanting 'teams of two or three Occitano-phone activists in each village, charged with speaking the language in all social situations, especially those involving commercial exchanges' (1979:897). Shades of Barère!

Lafont sees the Occitanian struggle on the educational front as illustrative of the political values which increasingly dominated the Occitanian movement in the 1960s and 1970s. After 1968, he claims, Occitanian teachers (there is a Fédération de l'Enseignant Occitan) moved beyond demands for more time and resources for teaching Occitan towards a radical perspective on the role of education in centralisation and in the creation of a 'colonial mentality': 'One can well say that if the Oc Renaissance has been marked by many setbacks since the nineteenth century, it has recently raised the educational struggle to a level of real effectiveness. It is in that struggle that Occitanie has begun to be built' (1974:238).

What of Occitanie and Occitanism outside the fields of literature and education? Relatedly, there has been the upsurge in Occitanian historiography – best represented, perhaps, in the mammoth *Histoire d'Occitanie* of 1979. The main thrusts of this history include a questioning of the accepted 'myth of France' and French unification, the identification of a distinct Occitanian-wide culture and society, and the location of an 'Occitanian resistance' in the opposition to the Albigensian crusade of the thirteenth century, the federalist movement of 1793, and the 'Revolt of the Midi' in 1907 (the widespread disturbances among the Southern winegrowers, see Armengaud and Lafont 1979:780 and Lafont 1974:92). Occitanian writers are not alone in this. Breton nationalists too have found themselves as much through a rewriting of the history of the hexagon and a recovery of the past, as they have through a revival of the language (see Deniel 1976, McDonald 1986, Nicolas 1982, Reece 1977, Serant 1971). And beyond revisionist history, the rejection of France One and Indivisible?

Leaving aside the literary and educational societies there exists a complex network of organisations of varying duration, many of them what the French call *groupuscules*, little groups of a sectarian nature, and mainly of the left. For many years after World War II, the principal body grouping together Occitanists was the Institut d'Etudes Occitanes (IEO). In 1961–2 members of that organisation became involved with the long and bitter miners' strike at Decazeville. Differences within the IEO on the issue of political involvement led in 1962 to the Comité Occitan d'Etudes et d'Action

(COEA) which had Robert Lafont, a former President of the IEO, as secretary general. In 1969 this body was succeeded by Lutte Occitane, of which Lafont writes: 'The preparation of the new organisation was the work of Occitanian action committees composed of all strands of the revolutionary left: Maoists, Trotskyists, anarchists, peasants' unions and some workers' unions' (1974: 308). Such a coalition was manifestly destined not to last, and in 1974 Lutte Occitane gave way to the VVAP ('Volem viure al pais') largely under the influence of Lafont (Touraine *et al.* 1981:48). Other groupings of the 1960s and 1970s included the Parti Nationaliste Occitan (which supported De Gaulle for his opposition to NATO and firm stand on Europe), the journal *Viure* and its adherents, a Parti Socialiste Occitan, a Movimento Autonomista Occitanico, a Fédération Anarchiste Communiste d'Occitanie (opposed to the French imperialism of the Paris-based Organisation Révolutionnaire Anarchiste), Jeune Languedoc (later Poble d'Oc) and a number of subregional groupings (for example FORS in Béarne). In the late seventies a Green tendency was also apparent.

I cannot here disentangle the ideological and other disputes which distinguish such groups and the different ways in which they construct 'Occitanie'. Nor can I tackle the relationship between the *groupuscules*, the popular causes which they supported throughout the region (such as the protest concerning the military base at Larzac), and the national political parties (Socialist, Communist and others), who have accommodated a regionalist dimension. What is significant is the sheer proliferation of groupings, the apparent fragmentation of the movement.

In a survey which looks more closely at some of these issues, Alain Touraine and his colleagues summarise the end of the 1970s as follows:

The Occitanian struggle, fragmented as it is, is always trying to bring itself together to form an Occitanian movement. Even if this effort fails it has important consequences. It forms part of the defence of society against the State, of the weak against the strong. If it cannot overturn domination, it can call it into question and weaken it. Too fragile to launch a major attack, it is strong enough to influence public opinion. It cannot start a revolution or a war of national liberation, but it is an important factor in the social conflict which occurs. (1981:303)

THE LIMITATION OF DOMAINS: DEPENDENT PERIPHERIES AND INTERNAL COLONIES

Let me conclude this chapter with some discussion of the 'diglossic process' in this region of France.

The material shows the necessity for studying diglossia dynamically. The domains of a language are the result of the interplay between complex social and political forces, and in that interplay the domain that a language occupies, or is sometimes forced into, may be the site of intense ideological and political struggle.

There had long been diglossia in the south. French was spoken in some areas of social life and by some classes, Provençal in and by others. But after the Revolution the diglossia was of a different order. 'Certainly', says Brun, 'the peasants kept their Provençal among themselves, and within the home, but the linguistic tradition is breached by the daily necessities of public life' (1927:120). This was a significant diminution of the domains remaining to Provençal after it had been driven from the law, the Court, the administration, and literature in the preceding centuries. Thus, as Mistral put it, Provençal was 'reduced to domesticity'.

Did this mean, then that Provençal was destined to disappear? In 1800 there was still a long way to go. Writing of Saint-Michel in the 1920s (the old name had long since been recovered) Brun (1927:164–7) notes that everyone now understood French and spoke it when necessary. Monolingual speakers of Provençal had virtually disappeared. However, the older generation, those over 50, still spoke it amongst themselves, and the younger men used it when working or chatting in the cafés or playing *boule*. Younger women, on the other hand, usually preferred to speak French amongst themselves. Within families, males of the grandparental generation usually spoke to their wives and their sons in Provençal, but to their grandchildren, especially their granddaughters, in French. Fathers spoke to their adult sons in Provençal, to their daughters in French. In the streets of the village shop-owners would often switch from Provençal with a male customer to French with a female. This and other evidence led Brun to suggest that in the 1920s Provençal was no longer the *maternal* language; that it was *men* who maintained the traditional speech. He believed this had serious implications for the future.

Quite remarkably, however, a study by Maurand (1981) conducted some fifty years later in a small farming village similar to Saint-Michel, though in a different part of Occitanie, paints a picture very similar to Brun's (see also the Provençal village studied by Schlieben-Lange 1977). The grandparental generation (the teenagers of the 1920s) still speak to each other largely in Provençal, which is also the language of the men at work (and speaking to livestock). French is still the preferred language of women, and of the younger generation. Maurand's survey recorded not one instance of young girls using Occitan to each other. All villagers, however, used French with the village notables – the curate and the teacher – though both were Occitan speakers from nearby villages. French was used with the postman and exclusively in all kinds of office: *mairie*, bank, post-office, *caisse d'assurance*, etc.). This material indicates that over the last fifty years the diglossia has stabilised, taking the form illustrated by Figure 4.1, derived from one of Maurand's diagrams.

A temporary balance of forces, so to speak, has been reached. But Maurand also notes that among younger people there is a detectable change of attitude towards Occitan, and an increasing desire for a revaluation of the language. There is, he says, 'a search for a new diglossic balance, which has only just begun' (Maurand 1981:115).

Throughout contemporary Occitanian writing, especially that influenced by Lafont, diglossia is seen as a function of relations between a dominant

Figure 4.1 Sociolinguistic functions of Occitan and French (from Maurand 1981, p. 113)

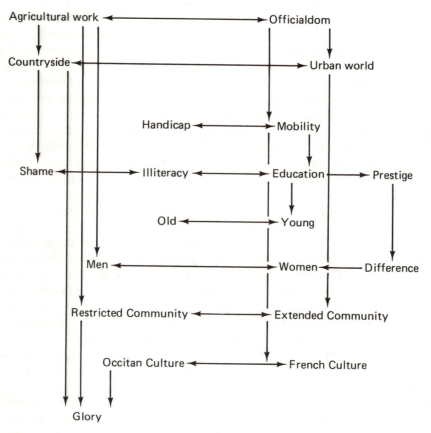

centre ('France') and a subordinate periphery ('Occitanie') which has made of the latter an 'internal colony' (see Lafont 1967: chs. 2, 3; 1974:279 ff., and Lafont *et al.* 1982:69 for a similar perspective on Brittany).

This perspective represents a major difference between the Occitanian movement of the present day and the Provençal movement of the nineteenth century. For although the earlier federalist tendency had grown out of opposition to Paris, and in the nineteenth century Mistral had set the Provençal renaissance against centralisation, it cannot be said that Mistral had any sustained theoretical view of the causes of centralisation. The contemporary use of 'centre–periphery' theory, or the 'theory of under-development', provides a seemingly powerful vision enabling activists to incorporate issues of language and culture with those of politics and economics. It provides the basis for a political economy of diglossia. In order to understand what this view of language says it is first necessary to set out the main propositions of the 'underdevelopment' perspective. In the theory of underdevelopment great weight is attached to the operation of the economic order, or rather to the inner logic of the capitalist mode of production. In this order there are 'core' or 'central' places which in predatory fashion seek to incorporate and exploit resources, labour, markets in other areas which then become socially, economically, politically and geographically their 'dependent periphery'. 'Underdevelopment' is not a state of being 'undeveloped' (i.e. with high levels of poverty, malnutrition, illiteracy), but a *process*. Peripheral regions are *made* peripheral. The centre acts on them in such a way that they *become* underdeveloped, and hence dependent, for the economic benefit of capitalism at the 'advanced' centre.

This economic and political model has, since the late 1950s, been extensively applied to relationships between countries of the First and Third Worlds in both the colonial and post-colonial periods. It was popularised, initially, through writing mainly on Latin America (especially, in the English-speaking world through the work of Gunder Frank and Immanuel Wallerstein), though it has an anterior history to be found in the writings of Lenin on imperialism and in the work of the Italian Marxist, Antonio Gramsci. It is to Gramsci that we owe what may now be seen as a variant of the underdevelopment thesis. In his essay on 'The southern question' (in Gramsci 1957), written in 1926–7, he took up and elaborated the proposition that southern Italy and the islands, which he characterised as areas of 'extreme social disintegration' (p. 42), had historically been 'reduced . . . to the state of exploited colonies' (p. 28). That is, the economic and social processes which a later generation envisaged as characteristic of the relationship between (First World) colonisers and (Third World) colonised, Gramsci saw as fundamental to the relationship between the regions in a European country like Italy, a theme taken up widely in the 1970s (see Seers *et al.* 1979). The 'internal colonialism' variant of the theory) of underdevelopment was explored in 1975 in an important book on the regions of Britain by Michael Hechter. Applying the standard economic arguments of underdevelopment (as outlined above), Hechter sought to explain how and why nationalism and ethnicity flourished in peripheral regions. An important element of this, he argued, was the way in which the economy assigned a subordinate role in the division of labour to inhabitants in (and from) those regions. This creates a 'cultural division of labour' (Hechter 1975:38 ff.) which might be reinforced by law, more often, perhaps, through practice: 'through policies providing differential access to institutions conferring status in the society at large, such as the educational, military, or ecclesiastical systems' (Hechter 1975:39–40).

This cultural division of labour, through which divergence from, rather than convergence with, the centre is maintained, provides the material for ethnicity and nationalism. And it is the existence, in Wales, Scotland and Ireland, of a sustained cultural divergence from England which Hechter seeks to document through much of his book.

Hechter's work has been much criticised for lumping together disparate regions and periods of history, for misreading economics, for economic reductionism, for confusing unofficial practices with official, state, policies, and for misuse and misunderstanding of the term 'colonialism' (see *inter alia* Nairn 1977:201 ff., and Edwards, J. R. 1985:73–4, Grillo 1980: 14 ff., Jenkins 1983:214–15, Williams 1982:196–7). His model has great difficulty in accommodating the changes in peripheral cultures (for example the decline of regional languages) as Hechter himself recognises. For the British evidence, which Hechter reviews and which is considered here in chapters 3 and 5, does, as he admits: 'weigh against the internal colonial model, which predicts the maintenance of indigenous cultural identity in the periphery despite heightened exposure to the core culture' (1975:207).

The sociolinguistic evidence for France, as much as for Britain, does not simply 'weigh against' Hechter's view of internal colonialism, but seems completely at variance with it. The process of nation-state formation in France appears to have required not divergence, but convergence. It is precisely against such convergence that the Félibrige and the later Occitanian movement inveighed. This does not mean that the evidence supports a simple diffusion model of core–periphery relations (in which culture inexorably seeps from one area to the other) which Hechter rightly rejects. As I have argued elsewhere (Grillo 1980:10) the dependency/ internal colonial model 'says everything, and nothing'. We are dealing with very complex social processes which cannot effectively be reduced to any one factor, and which cannot be expected to have uniform consequences across a vast range of social and cultural practices or across a wide range of diverse regions. Interestingly, in France, as to some extent in Britain, the sociolinguistic evidence is taken to *confirm* a colonial model of relations between centre and periphery because, it is argued, incorporation has historically entailed the *destruction* of languages and cultures, not their maintenance. Again the evidence does not all point in the same direction, and here, surely, Hechter is right to note, for example, the divergence from England of religious practice in Wales, Scotland and Ireland.

In seeking to understand these complex processes it is important not to confuse rhetoric and reason. Nairn (1977) has criticised many writers on nationalism who, he says, take nationalism's own ideological constructions (for example of 'nation') as the bases for objective analysis. In this instance he was referring to the widespread acceptance of the Romantic definition, but his point could equally well be applied to the view of subnations as internal colonies. As he says of the latter view: 'It may be effective ideology, but it rests on rather poor history' (1977:201–2).

5

THE POLITICS OF LANGUAGE IN WALES, IRELAND AND SCOTLAND

Also be it enacted by auctoritie aforesaid that all Justices Commissioners Shireves Coroners Eschetours Stewardes and their Lieuten'ntes, and all other Officers and Ministers of the Lawe, shall pclayme and kepe the Sessions Courtes . . . and all other Courtes, in the Englisshe Tongue, and all others of Officers Juries and Enquetes and all other affidavithes verdictes and wagers of Lawe to be geven and don in the Englisshe Tongue. And also that fromhensforth no psonne or psonnes that use the Welsshe speche or langage shall have or enjoy any maner office or fees within the realme of Englond Wales or other the Kinges dominions, upon peyn of forfaiting the same office or fees onles he or they use and exercise the speche or langage or Englishe.
(THE ACT OF UNION OF ENGLAND AND WALES, 1536, 27 HENRY VIII, CH. 26, CLAUSE XVII)

There was no English Grégoire. But to say that England never had a policy of 'eradicating the patois' would not be entirely correct. In fourteenth century Ireland, concern over the assimilation into Gaelic culture of the Anglo-Norman nobility led to an order in 1360 that 'anyone of English race shall forfeit English liberty, if after the next feast of St. John the Baptist he shall speak Irish with other Englishmen' (cited in Hyde 1967:609), and in 1366, by the Statutes of Kilkenny, Englishmen using Irish were threatened with forfeiture of their lands. These were the defensive measures of a small, isolated, threatened minority in eastern Ireland (cf. Edwards 1968:29). As Hyde says, they cannot have been very effective as for the next two centuries English influence in Ireland was very low, scarcely extending beyond Dublin and the coast (cf. Beckett 1966). More significant was Tudor

84

legislation (cited in Hyde 1967:610) which established the use of English in town courts, and an Act of Henry VIII, which stated: 'every person or persons, the King's true subjects, inhabiting this land of Ireland, of what estate condition or degree he or they be, or shall be, to the uttermost of their power, cunning and knowledge, shall use and speak commonly the English tongue and language' (cited in O Murchu 1970:40).

In general such legislation was exhortatory, but along with the contemporary Act of Union of England and Wales it made the King's maternal tongue the language of the administration, the courts, and the records. By these measures, but not these alone, English became the established language in the Celtic periphery. They were not, however, hostile to the Celtic langues *per se*. In this they differed from later Scottish legislation such as the Statutes of Iona (1609), which suppressed the Bards, and two Acts of 1616, designed to strengthen the position of the King (James VI of Scotland) and the power of the Lowlands against the clan chiefs. The first (*Act anent the upbringing of the bairns of Chiftanes in the Ilis*, 26 July 1616) ordained that the children of the highland chiefs and clan leaders should be educated in English:

Forsamekle as the Lordis of Secrete Counsall vundirstanding that the cheif and principall causs quhilk hes procuirit and procuiris the continewance of barbaritie impietie and inciuilitie within the Yllis of this Kingdome, hes proceidit from the small cair that the chiftanes and principall clannit [men] of the Yllis hes haid of the education and vpbringing of thair children in vertew and learning . . . ordanes and commandis the haill chiftanes and principall clanit men of the Yllis that they may and euery ane of thame send their bairnis being past nine yeiris of age to the scoolis in the inland to be trayned vp in vertew learning and the Inglish tunge.

(CITED IN APPENDIX TO NICOLSON 1866:170)

The second, for the Settling of Parochial Schools, argued similarly:

That the vulgar Inglish toung be vniversallie plantit and the Irishe language which is one of the cheif and principall causis of the continewance of barbaritie and incivilitie amongis the inhabitantis of the Ilis and Heylandis may be abolisheit and removeit. (IBID., p. 171)

To go by the content of official acts of government, however, there was no general, concerted policy of state to attack the Celtic languages, and indeed in certain circumstances their use was encouraged (see below). But the extent and nature of hostility to a language cannot be judged solely by Acts of Parliament. Though often ineffectual in accomplishing what they proposed (as was the Parochial Schools Act) they often had unintended consequences of a profound nature. Thus, for example, the Act of Union accelerated the anglicisation of the Welsh gentry, even if it did not initiate it

(Williams 1979). Legislation also reflected and helped to create a climate of opinion. That the kind of comment found in the Acts of 1616 was not confined to the statute books is confirmed by a letter (cited in Dorian 1981:18) to the 13th Earl of Sutherland in which he is advised to 'use your diligence to take away the reliques of the Irishe barbaritie . . . to wit the Irishe langage'. The well-known remarks of Dr. Samuel Johnson in *Journey to the Western Islands of Scotland* (1775) show that similar thoughts prevailed 160 years later: 'Of the Earse language, as I understand nothing, I cannot say more than I have been told. It is the rude speech of a barbarous people, who had few thoughts to express, and were content, as they conceived grossly, to be grossly understood' (1971 edition, p. 114). Alexander Nicolson's *Report on the state of education in the Hebrides* of 1866 reveals that the very language of the 1616 Acts was still widespread a century after that. Consider what must have lain behind this reflection on the plight of the natives:

[They] find themselves, in fact, in the predicament of dumb persons; and their sensitiveness to ridicule often exposes them to the pain of being reckoned barbarous by persons perhaps inferior to themselves in all the elements that constitute real civility, but endowed with the precious faculty of speaking some more or less intelligible form of the English language. (NICOLSON 1866:126)

What irked Johnson was the absence of a literary tradition. In this respect, 'Earse' compared unfavourably with Welsh and Irish which he thought 'cultivated tongues' (p. 115). For Jonathan Swift, however, Irish was equally damned for the contribution it made to the wretched condition of the country:

I have been lately looking over the advertisements in some of your Dublin newspapers . . . In one of the advertisements . . . I encountered near a hundred words together which I defy any creature in human shape, except an Irishman of the savage kind, to pronounce . . . I am deceived, if anything hath more contributed to prevent the Irish being tamed, than this encouragement of their language, which might easily be abolished and become a dead one in half an age, with little expense, and less trouble.

('ON BARBAROUS DENOMINATIONS IN IRELAND' IN DAVIS 1939, VOL. IV, p. 280)

And:

It is indeed in the Power of the Lawgivers to found a School in every Parish of the Kingdom, for teaching the meaner and poorer Sort of Children to speak and read the English Tongue, and to provide a reasonable Maintenance for the Teachers. This would in Time abolish that Part of Barbarity and Ignorance, for which our Natives are so despised by all Foreigners; this would bring them to think and act according to the Rules of Reason, by which a Spirit of Industry, and Thrift, and Honesty, would be introduced among them.

('CAUSES OF THE WRETCHED CONDITION OF IRELAND'IN DAVIS
1948:202)

A nineteenth century source shows the continuity of the tradition: 'The common Irish are naturally shrewd, but very ignorant and deficient in mental culture from the barbarous tongue in which they converse which operates as an effectual bar to any literary attainment' (Pamphlet of 1822, cited in O hAilin 1969:92). The idea that the language was a cause of, or at the very least contributed to, economic, political and social backwardness emerged also in the Kay-Shuttleworth *Reports of the Commissioners on the state of education in Wales* of 1847 – the 'infamous Blue Books' – which documented at great length the inadequacies, as they were portrayed, of the Welsh village schools.

The Welsh language is a vast drawback to Wales, and a manifold barrier to the moral progress and commercial prosperity of the people. It is not easy to overestimate its evil effects . . . It dissevers the people from intercourse which would greatly advance their civilization, and bars the access of improving knowledge to their minds. As a proof of this, there is no Welsh literature worthy of the name.

(J. C. SYMON'S REPORT ON BRECKNOCK, CARDIGAN, RADNOR AND
MONMOUTH, IN PT. II, p. 66)

'My district exhibits the phenomenon of a peculiar language isolating the mass from the upper portion of society', wrote R. W. Lingen, Commissioner for Carmarthen, Glamorgan and Pembrokeshire:

His language keeps him [the Welsh workman] under the hatches, being one in which he can neither acquire nor communicate the necessary information. It is a language of old-fashioned agriculture, of theology, and of simple rustic life, while all the world about him is English. (Report Pt. I, p. 3)

The Welsh language thus maintained in its own ground, and the peculiar moral atmosphere which, under the shadow of it, surrounds the population, appear to be so far correlative conditions, that all attempts to employ the former as the vehicle of other conceptions than those which accord with the latter seem doomed to failure.

(IBID. p. 7)

As C. J. Hampton commented in his evidence:

Their [the Welsh people's] intelligence is not very high certainly, and this is owing, in my opinion, to the circumstance of the adult population not having had the advantage of education in the English language. The prevalence of the Welsh

87

language is, I think, a great obstacle to the moral and intellectual improvement of the people. (REPORT, PT. I, p. 482)

Hampton's remarks are not typical of all evidence submitted, nonetheless the general tenor of the Commissioners' summary reports and recommendations clearly tends towards such views. And as the Commissioner for North Wales averred: 'Nor are [the] imperfect results of civilisation confined to the intellectual state of the inhabitants: they are seen also in the social and moral condition of the poorer classes in every county of North Wales' (Pt. III, p. 63).

It was perverse of Johnson to castigate Gaelic for lacking literature. For it was the establishment of the English language which made it the authoritative vehicle for the written word. After the Statutes of Iona Gaelic lost any status it had as a language of 'high' culture to become 'the repository of a "little tradition" of vernacular poetry and song' (Mackinnon, 1984:506). Similarly, as De Freine (1978:53) points out, in the twelfth century Irish had a 'unique position' among the vernaculars of Europe. Some of the first translations of medieval Latin medical treatises were into Irish. But even if a Welsh, or Irish or Gaelic Shakespeare were to have emerged, the (virtually non-existent) independent Celtic language press would have made it extremely difficult for him or her to get into print.

The legislation also made English the authorised language of names. 'When English was first used in an official bureaucratic context in predominantly Gaelic-speaking areas the [very different forms of names in English and Gaelic] caused difficulties. English-speaking bureaucrats could not spell Gaelic names. Gaelic-speakers might not know the English equivalents of their names, equivalents which did not sound or look like the names by which they had been known to others and to themselves throughout their lives' (Ennew 1980:77). Gwyn Williams records that an instrumental figure in Wales was the sixteenth century 'hanging judge' Bishop Rowland Lee who 'wearied of the long strings of *ap*', and had them deleted. 'In the process many of the Welsh got surnames much as Jews got them at Ellis Island. They were saddled with incomprehensible English distortions of Welsh names, nicknames, insults' (Williams 1985:118). So Enoch ap Hywel, Enoch Powell, and, in Ireland, Sean O'Cinneide, John Kennedy (cf. Dowling, 1935:103). Dispensing with the *ap* was standard among the gentry by the late seventeenth century (Morgan 1983:52), though Jenkins (1983:16) cites one Glamorgan family who did not take up this practice until 1830. The landscape, too, and the names of places became anglicised. Brian Friel's play *Translations*, centring on the activities of the military survey in 1833 which produced the first ordnance map of Ireland, portrays this process of redesignating the countryside: 'Lis na Muc', 'Swinefort', 'Cnoc na Ri', 'Kings Head' (Friel 1981:62).

The climate of opinion in the seventeenth, eighteenth and nineteenth centuries was thus hostile to the languages and cultures of inhabitants of the Celtic fringe, seeing them as 'barbarous', dangerous, and in the case of Ireland and the Highlands, priest-ridden, though in complementary fashion they were also figures of fun. Lest it be thought that such views represent an older, now discarded opinion, consider a remark by Lord Raglan in a magazine article in 1958, cited by Isabel Emmett (1964:133), which reveals a persistent, unofficial, casual hostility to the Celtic tongues through to our own time:

The Welsh language is . . . used for at least three undesirable purposes, to conceal the results of scholarship, to try to lower the standards of official competence and, worst of all, to create enmity where none existed.

LANGUAGE AND THE NATIONAL IDEAL

In anglicising ourselves wholesale, we have thrown away with a light heart the best claim we have upon the world's recognition of us as a separate nationality.
(DOUGLAS HYDE 1899, CITED IN NOWLAN 1972:43)

Though English became dominant administratively, legally, socially and economically, so that eventually many people became apologetic for speaking it 'badly', or ashamed of not speaking it at all, the Celtic languages did not always go gently into the good night. For Emmett (1982a:167), 'life in Welsh-speaking North Wales could be made sense of only in terms of a struggle which in many important manifestations is cultural'. For Mackinnon (1977:170), 'there is a sense in which Harris is a battleground of language issues'. In Wales, Scotland and Ireland, language constitutes a terrain on which, during the last 400 years, there have been fought a number of engagements and larger encounters. Thus, for Wales alone: the decision to make and print a Bible in Welsh; Griffith Jones's fight to use Welsh in the circulating schools; the opposition to the 1847 Blue Books; the disputes over the 1870 Education Act; the establishment of the Welsh Board of Education in 1907; Saunders Lewis's 1962 broadcast on *The fate of the language* (in Jones and Thomas 1973); the setting up of the Welsh Language Society which followed his appeal; and the campaign of civil disobedience which came later; the Welsh Language Act of 1967; the argument over the Welsh Channel 4, and so on, and so on. Some issues might seem trivial – for example whether rate demands should be in Welsh (see Saunders Lewis in Jones and Thomas 1973:133). But each represents a symbolic and practical attempt to defend or extend the domains of the language, to reverse what has appeared to be an inexorable trend.

In Wales, Scotland and Ireland, at different times and in different ways, language has also been an important element in the defining of national identity and aspirations. Its significance has been least in Scotland, for the most obvious reasons. Although in the late nineteenth and early twentieth centuries the predecessors of the Scottish Nationalist Party (SNP) found in Gaelic language and culture an inspiring symbol of national unity, and there was, for a time, a kind of Highland nationalism based on the crofters movement of the 1880s, the fact that the vast majority of Scots were outside the Highlands, and indeed had spoken a dialect of English for centuries, made it unlikely that Gaelic would become any more than a symbol. Consequently, says Nairn, 'few Scots easily understand or sympathise with the anguishing dilemmas of the language-problem [in Wales]' (1977:197). An exception might be Hugh MacDiarmid, poet, nationalist, and communist, though in his essay on Scotland in Owen Dudley Edwards's collection on *Celtic nationalism*, he has more to say about 'Scots' or 'Lallans' than about Gaelic, finding in the language of Burns a genuine, Scottish, working class voice on which to base a modern literary revival (MacDiairmid, 1968:347–8).

This does not mean that the SNP neglects the plight of the Gaelic minority in the Highlands – for example in its education policy – simply that in Wales and Ireland the connection between language and identity has had much greater salience. To understand this requires a digression.

The Welsh gentry, although increasingly anglicised during the seventeenth and eighteenth centuries, never entirely lost touch with Welsh bardic culture which continued 'to serve its ancient and immemorial function of praising the patron's status as a gentleman' (Williams, 1979:163). There was, too, an important, if dying, tradition of gentlemanly historical scholarship which had flourished, for example in Glamorgan (cf. Jenkins, 1983:234 ff.). In the eighteenth century, however, such interest took a new form, and Jenkins notes the irony of the fact that 'just as the Glamorgan gentry were rejecting the historical and architectural heritage of their county, so others were discovering it' (1983:272).

Previously we observed the significance for the development of linguistic nationalism of the Romantic movement in philosophy and literature. The 'discovery' of the ancient Gaelic Ossianic poetry was an important source of inspiration for that movement on the Continent, and in the British Isles. From the mid-eighteenth century onwards there emerged a succession of mainly aristocratic or middle-class societies promoting the cause of Celtic culture. Many of them were based on the émigré societies of London (the London Welsh, Scottish and Irish), others existed in Edinburgh and Dublin, though not, it seems, Cardiff (Glanmor Williams 1979:138–9, Gwyn Williams 1985:163 ff., Durkacz 1983:190).

In Ireland, where the gentry also maintained an interest in language and culture, Romanticism found expression in the Royal Irish Academy (founded 1785) which had strong aristocratic ties within the Ascendancy (Greene 1972:13). Their interests were largely antiquarian, and of course they were of the Protestant faith, as indeed were many of the early supporters of Gaelic (MacDonagh 1983:105 ff). During the nineteenth century, however, a number of other clubs and societies emerged, such as an Ossianic Society (1853), and a Society for the Preservation of the Irish Language (1877), with a more varied membership socially, and intellectually a more serious concern with the contemporary language and the speech of everyday life (Greene 1972:14–16). The latter Society, for example, lobbied the government on the part of Irish in education, and secured some important concessions. From a split in the Society in 1879 there emerged the Gaelic union, one of whose members was Douglas Hyde (1860–1949), a co-founder in 1893 of the Gaelic League.

Like the Gaelic Athletic Assocation, the League sought to combat at the cultural and linguistic level the anglicisation of the country. In line with the Romantic tradition (Hyde, for instance, was influenced by Mazzini) it emphasised the connection between national identity and Irish language and culture, which it accused earlier nationalists, such as Daniel O'Connell, of neglecting (see Hyde 1967:626). In this the League echoed one of O'Connell's chief opponents, Thomas Davis, who under the influence of German Romantic thought, especially that of Fichte (MacDonagh 1983:110) had urged: 'To lose our native tongue, and learn that of an alien, is the worst badge of conquest – it is the chain on the soul' (in Edwards 1968:111).

The League developed a system of full-time travelling organisers (*Timiri*) who set up branches throughout the country, teaching language, dance, music and history and arranging cultural and folkloric activities (Macaodha 1972:22). By 1904 it claimed 50,000 members in 600 branches which, if true, meant it was reaching and influencing a substantial part of the adult population. Its importance was threefold. First, it rejuvenated interest in Irish nationalism, and brought into the movement many people who later played a part in Sinn Fein and the Easter Rising. Secondly, it gave the movement a new dimension, *Gaelic* nationalism, through its project of an 'Ireland not only free, but Gaelic as well', which, suggests Beckett, 'helped to prepare the way for partition' (1966:417). Thirdly, the Gaelic League ensured that Irish would be installed as the official language of the Free State in 1922. Hence the educational policies which forbade the use of English in infant classes, and made Irish the principal vehicle of instruction in primary schools. Hence, too, the policy of designating and hopefully preserving the Gaelic-speaking areas, the Gaeltacht, and subsidising the inhabitants.

In *The Gaelic vision in Scottish culture* Malcolm Chapman uses the term 'symbolic appropriation' to refer to 'the way in which Gaelic culture, language and life has become the focus of statements and associations not intrinsic to an autonomous Gaelic life, but required by an external discourse of the English language' (1978:131). Nairn (1977:167) employs a similar turn of phrase in referring to the way in which English-speaking Lowlanders 'plundered the Gaelic raw material of nationality for their own use'. Romanticism has always involved a symbolic – and ideological – appropriation. The Gaelic League is a case in point, making as it did of the remnants of Irish-speaking rural society (cf. De Freine 1978:51) a symbol for a nationalism which was largely (but certainly not exclusively) based in a more urban, middle class, constituency.

Wales, too, has had its fair share of Romantic revivalism and mythologising, as Prys Morgan's instructive account (1983) of the invention of Welsh 'tradition' in the eighteenth and nineteenth centuries has recently shown. The Romanticism which makes the 'ancient' Welsh such a crucial element in national identity can be discovered in many places. It is obvious in the nationalist essay by Gwynfor Evans and Ioan Rhys (1968:221), who remark that 'A language is . . . far more than a means of expression: it is a way of thinking and feeling, even a way of life.' It can be found in Bud Khleif's *Language, ethnicity and education in Wales*, one of whose informants declared: 'One's language gives one a primordial or mystical feeling, a celebration of heritage . . . The Danes have a mystical notion of language: Language is not lost; it goes to sleep in the minds of each generation' (in Khleif 1980:40). Khleif's own comments ('folk language true to itself', 'fundamental richness of meaning', 'unique ways of seeing the world', p. 41), suggest how thoroughly he himself has absorbed this discourse. It is present, too, in the work of Isabel Emmett ('the language carries the tradition and the people carry the language', 1964:131). Nowhere was the Romantic vision more clearly displayed than in the late Wynford Vaughan Thomas's contribution to the 1985 television programme *The dragon has two tongues*. The second tongue was represented by the Gramscian Marxist, Gwyn Williams, whose lecture 'When was Wales?' (1982) challenged the Romantic vision of Welsh identity as antique and eternal.

This Romanticism finds expression in the key cultural institutions such as the Welsh National Anthem (1856), and the Eisteddfod as it was constituted from 1858 onwards (Williams 1979:27). This is not to deny the vitality of such institutions. Anyone attending Cardiff Arms Park would testify to that of the former, and any observer of rural Wales to that of the latter. Rees, Jenkins, Owen, Emmett and others show the enduring popularity not just of the national but of the *local eisteddfodau* where contestants for awards in music and poetry try their paces before moving on to county, regional and national competitions.

LANGUAGE, NATIONALISM AND POLITICS IN WALES

There is no denying the recent popularity of the Welsh nationalist cause, either, at least in Welsh Wales. In the 1983 general election, when Plaid Cymru's overall support was lower than it had been for some years, it obtained 31% of the vote in the five principal Welsh-speaking constituencies, winning two of them. (It gained a third in 1987.) But half its vote is concentrated in those 5, out of 38 in all. Crucial to the Party's promotion of that nationalist cause has been the issue of language.

There is not the space here to follow every twist of the relationship between language and nationalism in Welsh politics (see *inter alia* Hywel Davies 1983, Khleif 1980, Madgwick *et al.* 1973, Morgan 1981, Glyn Williams 1978, Glanmor Williams 1979, and Gwyn Williams 1985). Instead I concentrate on the contribution to Welsh nationalist thinking of one of its key figures: Saunders Lewis, President of the Welsh Nationalist Party from 1925–39, and a major influence on its policy.

The Welsh Nationalist Party (originally *Plaid Genedlaethol Cymru*, latterly *Plaid Cymru*) was founded in 1925 bringing together various small groups and networks of individuals passionately concerned for the fate of Wales in a Britain, and a Europe, in post war crisis. Inspired by the example of Ireland, and shocked by the decline in the numbers of Welsh speakers revealed in the 1921 Census, they believed that the future of Wales lay in some form of independence or 'home rule'.

They were, mostly, middle class intellectuals. Of 30 committee members between 1925–45, 16 were teachers and lecturers, 2 journalists, 3 ministers of religion, 2 doctors, 2 lawyers, and 1 each from banking, insurance, business, local government and agricultural research (Hywel Davies, 1983:194). In fourteen Parliamentary constituencies fought by the Party up to 1945 much its best performance came in three contests in university seats

(Hywel Davies 1983: Appendix). As late as 1959, 12 of its 20 candidates in the General Election of that year were graduates of the University of Wales (Morgan 1981:381). In the inner circle was the Liverpudlian Welshman Saunders Lewis who with Ambrose Bebb was largely responsible for shaping Party policy on language and nationalism. Both Bebb and Lewis were themselves influenced by right-wing, French Catholic thought (see Hywel Davies 1983:36 ff.), Lewis by Barrès, Bebb by Maurras, the disciple of the Félibrige and of Mistral (see chapter 4). In their writing the Romantic tradition of nationalism is readily apparent. 'The nation', said Bebb in 1926, 'is holy, and sacred . . . ordained by God himself' (cited in Hywel Davies 1983:98). For Lewis it was a 'community of communities' (Hywel Davies 1983:102): 'Family and tribe existed prior to the state, and voluntary organisations existed prior to the authority of the sovereign government . . . A nation's civilisation is rich and complex simply because it is a community of communities' (Lewis in *Canlyn Arthur*, 1938, cited in Jones 1973:34). Nationalism, for Lewis, provided: 'defence of the individual soul against the oppression of the centralist state, and against economic materialism that denies or ignores the spirit and nature of man' (in 1935, cited in Hywel Davies 1983:102).

Central to this conception of nation was cultural identity and language, the two in many respects seen as identical:

Language is the fruit of society, is essential to civilisation, and is the treasury of all the experiences and memories of the nation. It keeps the visions and desires and dreams of the nation, its knowledge of its beginnings, of its youth, its sufferings, its problems, and its victories – all that constitutes the history of a nation.

(IN 1923, CITED IN HYWEL DAVIES 1983:74)

Welsh language and culture had, according to Lewis, flourished in the century before the Act of Union, and he constantly turned to the 'civilisation' of that era as a model for the society which the Nationalist Party would rebuild (Jones 1973:49, 51).

There are many parallels between Lewis and Mistral. Both were poets (though Lewis was never, to my knowledge, a candidate for a Nobel Prize) who opposed the centralising tendencies of a distant colonising state and located the roots of identity in language, extolling the literature and culture of another epoch. The person of Maurras (whose fascism Lewis later rejected) offers a direct, historical link between the two. Nonetheless, there is a major difference between them. Whereas Mistral rejected direct engagement in politics, Lewis was a political activist. In 1936, the 400th anniversary of the Act of Union, Lewis and two other party members undertook a considered act of law-breaking, burning down the RAF

'Bombing School' on the Lleyn Peninsula. Tried at Caernarvon by a jury which failed to reach a verdict, they were retried at the Old Bailey and Lewis was sentenced to nine months imprisonment. At Caernarvon he defended his action thus:

It is the plain historical fact that, from the fifth century on, Lleyn has been Welsh of the Welsh, and that so long as Lleyn remained unanglicised, Welsh life and culture were secure. If once the forces of anglicization are securely established behind as well as in front of the mountains of Snowdonia, the day when Welsh language and culture will be crushed between the iron jaws of these pincers cannot be delayed.

('CAERNARFON COURT SPEECH OCTOBER 1936', IN JONES AND THOMAS
1973:117–18)

At the Old Bailey trial the accused refused to testify in English. That, and their argument with the judge over their use of Welsh in the Caernarvon trial, stimulated the 'National Language Petition' of 1938 which collected 250,000 signatures and led, eventually, to the Welsh Courts Act of 1942 (Hywel Davies 1983:162, 242 ff., Morgan 1981:270).

Although Lewis considered language central to the nationalist cause, others believed that a Welsh practising party faced considerable difficulties in a country where the large (and growing) majority of the population knew no Welsh (Hywel Davies 1983:180 ff.) This debate was resolved largely in favour of those who wished to broaden the Party's appeal to non-Welsh speakers, especially in the heavily populated industrial south. Leadership of the Party passed, in the war years, from Lewis who in Kenneth Morgan's phrase represented 'cultural commitment' to Gwynfor Evans and his 'populist nonconformism' (Morgan 1981:397). The language issue, though not disappearing from the political agenda, went dormant until Lewis's broadcast talk of 1962 on 'The fate of the language'.

Lewis argued that the continuing decline of Welsh speakers which he predicted the 1961 census would reveal meant that shortly 'the measure called the Act of Union of England and Wales in 1536 will at last have succeeded' (Lewis 1962 in Jones and Thomas 1973:127). Appealing to those 'who consider that Wales without the Welsh language will not be Wales' he urged that the Welsh language be saved by making it impossible for government, local and national, to govern without using Welsh. This struck a chord and led to the formation of the 'Welsh Language Society'. Then, 'Beginning with a blockade of traffic in Aberystwyth in February 1963, in protest at the refusal of the Post Office there to use Welsh-language notices and official forms, a series of more militant demonstrations were held in government offices, central and local, throughout Wales. Local taxation officers, borough treasurers, libraries and universities found the peaceful tenor of their lives disrupted . . . by groups of angry, noisy, and determined

95

Welsh-speaking students, demanding equal status for their native language and prepared to use all methods short of overt violence to force their point home' (Morgan 1981:383).

The campaign remained distinct from Plaid Cymru, and it is difficult to estimate its effect on the latter's fortunes. Nonetheless, at the height of the campaign the Party achieved a major breakthrough with the victory of its leader, Gwynfor Evans, at the Carmarthen byelection in July 1966. There followed the Welsh Language Act 1967 which replaced and reinforced the Welsh Courts Act of 1942 and which by putting Welsh and English on an equal legal footing in an administrative context in effect abolished the language clause in the Act of Union. This was accompanied by other measures (for example in broadcasting) which in a way astonishing to many observers transformed the language scene. Thus, says Gwyn Williams: 'In response to a militant campaign whose hunger is by definition insatiable, the British state, ruling a largely indifferent or hostile Welsh population, has, in a manner which has few parallels outside the Soviet Union, countenanced and indeed subsidised cultural Welsh nationalism. Wales is now officially, visibly and audibly a bilingual country' (Williams 1985:292–3).

SITES OF LINGUISTIC STRUGGLE: RELIGION AND EDUCATION

This account of the modern struggle for the legal status of the Welsh language may be set in longer-term perspective through an examination of the links between language, religion and education in rural Wales since the eighteenth century. Ethnography of rural Wales and the Western Isles reveals the centrality of religion in social life, with the churches, one for every 134 inhabitants in Glan-llyn, Merionethshire, in 1951 according to Owen (1962:185), sustaining the 'moral order' (Mackinnon 1977:31). They are, or were, not only a focus for ritual, but also for leisure and learning. 'Llanfihangel', says Rees, 'had many a monoglot English schoolteacher during [the nineteenth century], but the children received a free education in Welsh at the Sunday Schools and the Children's Meetings' (1950:130). In the twentieth century, nonconformist religion was the principal domain of public life in which Welsh and Gaelic held indisputable sway, and it is important to see how this became possible.

Victor Durkacz's survey of Scottish material (1983) reveals evidence of seventeenth century policies extremely hostile to Gaelic, which gave expression to attitudes of the kind found in the 1616 Acts (cf. Dorian 1981). They were not, however, policies of state, or at any rate of *governmental* institutions, but of the church (cf. Price 1984:53) – though the connection between Church and State in this period is such that only fine distinctions can be drawn. At any rate, it was the established churches which seem to have been the principal institutions actually concerned with language at large and of ordinary people, rather than the language of courts and administration and the gentry which was government's concern.

Durkacz shows there were in fact two opposed tendencies within the Protestant Lowland churches, one hostile to Gaelic, the other, generally, supportive of it (cf. Dorian 1981:20 ff.). The hostile element connected Highlander rebelliousness with their language and their Catholicism. It is they who come closest to a discourse of 'eradicating the patois', though the term current in the late seventeenth century was 'extirpation', as in the title of a pamphlet by a member of the supportive camp, James Kirkwood, in *c*. 1690: 'An answer to the Objection against Printing the Bible in Irish [i.e. Gaelic], as being Prejudicial to the Design of Extirpating the Irish Language out of the Highlands of Scotland' (cited in Durkacz 1983:21). 'Extirpation' also occurs in Kirkwood's correspondence (in Durkacz 1983:28, 29). The supportive element stressed the importance of the vernacular for the purpose of conversion – how can you persuade them of the errors of Catholicism if you cannot talk to them? Later, in the eighteenth century, support was justified by theological principle: 'the evangelical belief in the right of every man to read the scriptures in his mother tongue' (Durkacz 1983:35, cf. Dorian 1981:22). The significance that evangelists attached to the vernacular is shown in the 1825 Annual Report of the Edinburgh Gaelic School Society: 'The fundamental principle of the Gaelic Schools Society is, that it is essential for every man to read the Word of God in his own tongue: – in that language in which he thinks and which alone he can thoroughly understand' (in Durkacz 1983:123).

Similarly in Ireland, despite the strictures of Henry VIII, and a demand in 1540 that the clergy employ English (DeFreine 1978:55), the Reformation had been promoted through the Irish language. The first book to be printed in Irish was the Protestant Catechism in 1571 – the font provided by Elizabeth I (O Cuiv 1969:25), who also encouraged the use of Welsh in Wales (Durkacz 1983:34). This Irish policy was continued by James I, again with the hope of enabling the Protestant clergy to hasten the conversion of the native population (O Murchu 1970:41). Later, however, according to Hyde (1967:618), there was an 'unwritten compact' between Church and government 'that they should have no dealings and make no terms with the national Irish language' – a policy posing severe practical problems and one likely to thwart the aim of conversion.

In Ireland and Scotland the debate over translating the Bible was the focus of this conflict on policy which was not resolved for Scotland until the publication of the Gaelic New Testament in 1767 (i.e. after the Jacobite threat had diminished, Durkacz 1983:63). The Irish translation had appeared the previous century. In Wales, however, the issue had been settled much earlier, the first translation appearing in 1588. This event 'ensured the continuity of the literary tradition in Wales' (Glanmor Williams, 1979:133). Indeed, Gwynfor Evans and Ioan Rhys (1968:233) argue that: 'The Welsh Bible . . . probably saved the self-respect of the Welsh language and ensured that, when a new Wales emerged, unpredictably, in the eighteenth century, it would be a Welsh-speaking Wales and a literate Wales'.

The resolution of the questions of biblical translation and religious language had one important consequence in that the Welsh Bible provided an early and outstanding model for the Welsh literary register. It was also important for education, which was largely under the auspices of the religious authorities. The answer to the question 'what is to be the language of religious practice?' was likely to provide the answer to 'what is to be the language of education?'

In each of Wales, Scotland and Ireland there developed in the eighteenth century systems of informal, sometimes clandestine, education promoted by religious groups and individuals outside of, or in conflict with, the established churches. One important example is that of the 'circulating schools' organised in Wales by Griffith Jones (1683–1761) (Williams 1979, Durkacz 1983).

Education had formed part of the 'charitable economy' (Williams 1979:202) of Tudor and Stuart Britain. In Wales this particular charitable activity was practised by the Welsh Trust (1674–81) and later the Society for the Propagation of Christian Knowledge (SPCK) also active in Scotland. Griffith Jones, 'an ill-educated, hypochondriacal Welsh parson' (Glanmor Williams, 1979:203), greatly extended this work often against strong opposition (Williams 1979:209), and insisted that the schools should use Welsh. His purpose was, modestly enough, to ensure that his pupils became 'Christians and heirs of eternal life' (in Williams 1979:204), and for that purpose the Welsh language was essential. His influence was enormous. By 1761 some 3,000 schools had enrolled over 150,000 children who had learned to read the Bible, and read it in Welsh. The schools were also open to adults who formed up to two-thirds of the classes in some places (Williams 1979:207). It is possible therefore that Jones's teachers reached *nearly half the population of the country*. Although the schools declined with Jones's death, their tradition was maintained in the Welsh Sunday Schools, the continued importance of which in the mid-twentieth century is reported in several of the ethnographies of rural Wales.

Literacy, a certain kind of religion (from which developed Welsh non-conformism), and the Welsh language were thus closely connected. Given the anglicised, Anglican, tradition of the gentry, and given that most of Jones's pupils were presumably children of tenant farmers, then a further connection with ethnic identity and economic division was also made. As Jenkins (1983:194) notes: 'the culture abandoned by the gentry was promoted by lower class groups, among whom it acquired plebeian and radical overtones. Culture, language and religion, all conspired to separate landlord and tenant'. Education must be added to this list. For while the education of the tenantry was provided, if at all, by the Welsh-oriented charitable economy, the gentry was, as again Jenkins notes, by the eighteenth century largely in the hands of tutors 'who took great care to eliminate the unfashionable Welsh language among their pupils' (1983:223).

These connections provide some of the reasons (not the only ones) for the survival of Welsh-speaking communities into the twentieth century. They help us understand the hostility towards the critical comments of the 1847 commission on the Welsh nonconformist schools, and the pressure in the latter part of the nineteenth century for the inclusion of Welsh as a subject and medium of instruction within state education. A movement similar to Jones's circulating schools existed in Scotland, though, according to Durkacz, on nothing like the same scale, nor with the same success. Nevertheless the Paisley Society for Gaelic Missions and the Edinburgh Gaelic School Society did important work in this field, albeit at a much later date. Although members of such societies were essentially missionaries, who seemed to see their task in the Highlands as similar to that undertaken by others in Africa or India, a connection was forged here, too, between language, religion and literacy, especially from the 1840s onwards with the growth of the Free Churches (Durkacz 1983:116). But it was a case of too little and too late for all but the remotest of the Gaelic-speaking areas. In the Highlands material factors such as clearances and famines made the religious and cultural task impossible.

In eighteenth century Ireland, the work of educating the peasantry was undertaken clandestinely by 'Hedge Schools' of the kind in which Brian Friel sets *Translations*. Distantly related to the earlier Bardic Schools, the origin of their name can be readily understood from a letter to Rome of 1669, cited by Dowling (1935:18), concerning one Father Gelosse who 'taught a small school in a wretched hovel beside a deep ditch, and there educated a few children furtively'. In the eighteenth century, continues Dowling:

Because the law forbade the schoolmaster to teach, he was compelled to give instruction secretly; because the householder was penalised for harbouring the schoolmaster, he had perforce to teach, and that only when the weather permitted, in some remote spot, the sunny side of a hedge or bank which effectively hid him and his pupils from the eye of a chance passer by.   (DOWLING 1935:45)

Despite the legal and practical difficulties in gathering and retaining a class of pupils (there were severe penalties for Irish teachers until 1792) they flourished, and Dowling estimates that by 1824 the Hedge Schools made up the great majority of the 9,352 'pay schools' then in existence in Ireland. The curriculum ranged from arithmetic to instruction in the classics, but the great claim of these schools is that in the eighteenth century at least the medium of instruction was largely Irish (Dowling 1935:21), and that the schoolmasters maintained a tradition of literacy in Irish by copying and preserving Irish language texts in manuscript form, compiling dictionaries and grammars, and by writing (mainly poetry) in the language. Durkacz (1983:75–80) is sceptical of these claims. As often, it is difficult to separate reality from subsequent mythology, but the Hedge Schools certainly offered a Catholic, Irish education as an alternative to the established, Protestant system (Durkacz 1983:76).

By the early nineteenth century, however, the English language began to predominate. Thus Dowling cites one teacher, in a town school, advertising for pupils in the Limerick Gazette of 1815 who: 'Begs leave to inform the Public, that he teaches to Spell, Read, and Write the English language correctly . . . and that his English Grammar is so clear as to be immediately understood' (Dowling 1935:135). Indeed, when it became possible for Catholics to become teachers the preferred language of instruction in schools became English, as it was at the Catholic College of Maynooth, founded in 1795. Commenting on this O Murchu says: 'In effect, the dominance of English in the domain of *religious practice* was ensured. This must have been the greatest single blow to the Irish language since the seventeenth century . . . because of its prestige and permeating influence, the Catholic Church became a major force of de-ethnicization and anglicization' (1970:28).

As De Freine (1977, 1978) and Greene (1972) have argued, it is easier to blame the decline of Irish in the nineteenth century on the education system (as did Douglas Hyde, for example), or the Catholic Church, or Daniel O'Connell, than accept that for many people English represented the only 'rational' choice in their economic and social circumstances. Certainly Irish was excluded from the National Schools from the 1830s onwards, as indeed were the vernaculars in Wales and Scotland. It is often said they were 'banned', but as Emmett (1964:83) points out there was no governmental proscription. It was rather a matter of official and unofficial pedagogic policy, supported on the one hand by members of the Inspectorate of

Education such as Matthew Arnold, and on the other by the tally stick, the clog, and the 'Welsh-not'.

The reforming Education Acts of 1870 and 1872 made no provision for the teaching of/in anything other than English. For Scotland, Durkacz argues that by the 1870s there was a considerable accumulated experience of using Gaelic, gained through the work of the Gaelic School Societies, and suggests that the educational benefits of employing the language, mainly for the rapid development of literacy skills, were widely known. That this experience was ignored is, he says, 'a serious indictment of those controlling highland educational policy at that time' (1983:164). After 1870, however, and to a certain extent prior to that in Wales, a variety of organisations and societies sought to put pressure on the authorities to provide space in the curriculum for the local languages and by 1875, for example, both Gaelic and Welsh were permitted by the Education Codes governing elementary schools to be used as vehicles for the testing of young children (Durkacz 1983:178–9, Price 1984:104).

In Ireland pressure from the Society for the Preservation of the Irish Language, which enrolled forty MPs in a lobby of government, led to the concession in 1879 that Irish would be permitted as an 'additional subject', to be taught outside normal school hours (Greene 1972:16–17). Some fifty schools had availed themselves of this opportunity by 1893, the year of the founding of the Gaelic League (O Fiaich 1972:64). In Wales, the campaign of the Society for Utilising the Welsh Language, led by Dan Isaac Davies, at HMI, resulted in the 1880s in the recognition of Welsh as a 'grant-earning subject' suitable for study in intermediate schools (Durkacz 1983:166–7, 180–1, 206, Evans 1974:26–7, Khleif 1980:113, Price 1984:104). In Scotland, too, in 1885 Gaelic became a permitted subject (Durkacz 1983:179).

Subsequent experience in each of the countries was, briefly, as follows.

The educational policy of the Gaelic League was avowedly bilingual:

A rational education, such as any self-governing country in Europe would give [the Irish people], would teach them to read and write the language that they spoke, and that their fathers had read and spoken for fifteen hundred years before them. The exigencies of life in the United Kingdom would then make it necessary to teach them a second language – English.

(HYDE 1967:632–3, ORIGINALLY 1899)

Although Irish was permitted within the curriculum as an optional subject from 1900, few schools took it up, and bilingual education made little progress until the creation of the Free State in 1922 (see Edwards, J. R. 1985:56 ff., MacDonagh 1983:116 ff.). In the long run, however, although the Gaelic League's policies successfully carried the nationalist movement, they could not carry the people. The rehabilitation of the language largely failed. Every school child receives what Edwards calls 'a thin wash of competence' in Irish (Edwards, J. R. 1984a:485), until 1973 necessary for matriculation, but in daily life the only space that exists for Irish (other than as a vehicle for official documents also available in English) is 'ceremonial and trivial' (1984a:488). The Gaeltacht are apparently in unstoppable decline (O Tuama 1972:100, Fennell 1981).

In Scotland, too, there was little progress until the Highland Association secured an amendment to the Education (Scotland) Act, 1918, which required 'adequate provision for teaching Gaelic in Gaelic-speaking areas' (Section 6, 1(a), cited by Durkacz 1983:179). This so-called 'Gaelic clause' had little immediate effect, and it was not until 1955 that the Inverness county education authority, which had jurisdiction over the Western Isles, introduced a Gaelic Education Scheme (Mackinnon 1977:60 ff.). Within this Scheme Gaelic was employed in teaching in the early years of primary education. In secondary schools there was teaching of, but not in, the language, except when the Gaelic lesson included project work on local history and geography. Mackinnon's survey of Harris's primary schools in the early seventies found that all eight schools taught Gaelic, but only one taught the first and second years mainly in Gaelic. Six schools provided religious instruction in Gaelic, two taught some other subjects in the language (1977:86–7). Within secondary education Gaelic was, in the 1970s, taught separately from other subjects in the curriculum. Although present in ways in which it had not been previously, it was confined to 'a domain which firmly associated Gaelic with local life, local solidarity and folk-life studies which may be moribund in the present age' (Mackinnon 1977:101). Nevertheless, secondary school children interviewed by Mackinnon remained, by and large, firm supporters of the language.

The position of Welsh in the schools of Wales is, and has long been, much stronger. A crucial development was the establishment in 1907 of the Welsh Department of the Board of Education (Evans 1974, and Durkacz 1983:182, Price 1984:104) when, as the Board itself reported: 'In the Code for 1907, as also in the Regulations for secondary schools and training colleges in Wales . . . the teaching of Welsh was fully and definitely recognised' (in Evans 1974:323). Thereafter, the position of Welsh appears to have been similar to that of Gaelic in Scotland in the Inverness Scheme. The language was quite widely used in the state elementary sector in Welsh-speaking areas. Jones (1962: 100–1), for example, shows that in the Tregaron Council School in the 1940s no English was used in infant classes (Standard 1) but by Standard IV it took up five hours a week compared with two hours for Welsh. In secondary schools English was generally employed for all subjects except the teaching of the Welsh language, and perhaps religious instruction (Price 1984:105). In 1939, however, the first private, fee-paying 'Welsh-medium' school (*Ysgolion Cymraeg*) was opened at Aberystwyth (Khleif 1980:116ff., Davies 1983). The 1944 Education Act provided greater room for manoeuvre than some of its predecessors, and a number of state-financed Welsh-medium primary schools were established. Welsh language schools received support in the 1967 Gittins Report, and sixty-two were open by 1974–5 (Khleif 1980:200). By 1980 there were eleven Welsh medium secondary schools as well, with some 8,000 pupils (Price, 1984:105). In these schools Welsh is used for most subjects except the physical sciences and mathematics, but Khleif emphasises that they are essentially *bilingual*, giving equal weight to proficiency in English and Welsh. In addition some 25% of the English-medium schools, which are of course in the vast majority, offer a Welsh programme within the general curriculum, providing teaching through Welsh for some subjects other than the language (see Khleif 1980:124, 127).

Welsh-medium schools are concerned as much with ethnicity and identity as they are with pedagogic matters in a limited sense. Khleif cites the aims of the Rhydfelen Comprehensive School in Glamorgan which include not only 'To ensure that every pupil is stretched mentally as far as his ability would allow' (clause 3), but also 'To transmit to every pupil pride in being a Welshman and determination to safeguard the Welsh nationhood' (clause 7). This purpose is served by an emphasis on local Welsh matters, the Welsh heritage, and the relationship with England. There is, therefore, a partially bicultural as well as bilingual curriculum, though the detailed secondary syllabuses surveyed by Khleif (1980:244–55) do not suggest that practice diverges greatly in the 'O' and 'A' level courses from what happens elsewhere. 'Tudors and Stuarts' are taught with a Welsh emphasis.

In the post war period, says Morgan (1981:359), 'more than any other feature of Welsh life, education became the battleground for those locked in conflict over the survival of the Welsh language', and clearly there have been victories, in education as much as in administration (cf. Rawkins 1987). 'Wales is now officially, visibly and audibly a bilingual country' (Gwyn Williams 1985:293). Various writers, Emmett (1978, 1982a, 1982b) among them, have detected a revaluation of Welshness among young people. It is no longer 'square', she says, to be Welsh (Emmett 1982b:213). One result is that the opposition dominant, ruling, English/subordinate, ruled, Welsh does not always now apply. A Welsh-speaking headmaster is a headmaster, a Welsh-speaking bureaucrat is a bureaucrat, and perhaps like bureaucrats everywhere. And the Welsh language of the office is not always the same as that of the Church or the home. There are divisions here of a different kind which the (relative) success of the Welsh language movement must make it all the harder to bear. Nevertheless, the advance of Welsh teaching has not gone unopposed. Madgwick *et al.* (1973:118–21) describe the problems caused in Cardiganshire in the early 1970s when the local authority sought to implement the recommendations of the Gittins Report. The proposal to make Welsh *compulsory* for 4–7 year olds led to the formation of a protest committee – the Cardiganshire Education Campaign – which argued that any extension should be optional, and took their case to the Ombudsman. They did not win, but the campaign managed to curtail other measures which the authority had proposed.

Strong local opposition to a bilingual initiative is also recorded by Caitrin Roberts (1986) in a study of a plan by Gwynedd County Council for a Welsh secondary school in Bangor. The local educational authority, responsible for an area in which, according to the 1981 census, over one quarter of the population were Welsh speakers, had in 1976 responded to local pressure by proposing a new, separate establishment to provide education in Welsh for those who wished it. After some delay the (Labour) Secretary of State for Wales referred the proposal back on the grounds that a viable institution required at least 500 pupils and the catchment area of the proposed school was too small to ensure such numbers. The ensuing public reaction from bodies such as the Welsh Language Society and the National Union of Welsh Teachers was such that the Secretary of State was persuaded to allow the council to seek to enlarge the catchment area. This resulted in a new proposal which it was argued would ensure that some 580 places would be filled.

Opposition to both the first and second proposals was centred mainly in the City of Bangor and included representatives of the City council, the local Labour Party, Parent-Teacher associations, and a body named 'Parents for Optional Welsh' or 'POW'. They argued that splitting the existing secondary school to create one English and one Welsh school as the plan entailed would be undesirable. Perhaps influenced by this the Secretary of State delayed a decision until pressed in the House of Commons by the Plaid Cymru MP for the neighbouring constituency. Eventually agreement was given and the school opened in September 1978 with, as Roberts says 'ironically', 380 pupils.

Roberts's account of this episode brings out the conflicting interests behind the two camps and the uneasy alliances that were concluded. One of the key objections to the scheme was that it was likely to be socially and culturally divisive. She comments:

The desirability of separate schools is something which gives rise to much heated debate not merely in the Welsh context, but currently in relation to proposals for separate schools for Muslim children in Britain. Like separate bilingual schools, separate Muslim schools are charged with contravening the spirit of comprehensivisation and introducing a segregation which militates against intercultural understanding and the development of mutual tolerance in children.

(p. 12)

This is an important point to which we will return in Chapter 6.

In the 1970s and early 1980s, says Gwyn Williams:

there has been a growing resentment, impatience and anger which has taken the form of an increasing dislike of the Welsh language itself which at times and in places has become a kind of hatred. An English-speaking working class, neglected and treated with shoddiness, its necessities, not only social but cultural, scorned, not least by some leaders of the Welsh language movement, sees a British state subsidizing the Welsh language production of what is to them a middle-class minority.

(1985:293)

'English-speaking Welsh people are increasingly being denied membership of Wales', he adds (p. 294). The rejection by a majority of 4 to 1 of the referendum proposal on Welsh devolution shows, he suggests, that most Welsh people are now 'choosing a British identity which seems to require the elimination of a Welsh one' (p. 303). This goes too far, perhaps. Nevertheless, whereas the boundaries between the domains occupied by one language rather than another can be shifted marginally, or the encroachment of a dominant language on a subordinate one can be halted, perhaps temporarily, it is difficult to obstruct the social and economic forces which give rise to that encroachment, as the fate of Irish shows. Despite the re-establishing of Welsh in certain crucial domains, the retreat of the language has continued, as the census figures show. Between 1961 (a year before Saunders Lewis's broadcast) and 1981 the number of Welsh speakers fell by 148,000 – 22% Perhaps the only viable 'solution' for the proponents of Welsh is that advocated by supporters of *Adfer* who call for a retreat to a monolingual Welsh stronghold in the remaining Welsh 'heartland'. Summarising the 1960s and 1970s, Kenneth Morgan suggests that in retrospect the nationalist revival and attendant language movement was 'largely ephemeral' (1981:407). Yet in 1974, say, it seemed that the 'unionist' view of Britain as a mosaic state of sub-nations successfully, and peacefully, integrated within a larger framework of 'Great Britain' (not a view universally shared outside England) had not long survived the period in which Namier wrote (1948). Nairn's 1977 book seemed at the time aptly entitled *The break-up of Britain*. The British nation-state, like the French, had been pieced together from the twelfth or thirteenth centuries onwards by conquest, annexation and union, and now, in the late twentieth, things were falling apart with strong nationalist and separatist surges in Scotland, Wales and, in several different ways, Northern Ireland. Although support for nationalist parties at the General Elections of 1979 and 1983 declined (to recover slightly in 1987) nationalist feeling has not disappeared and in certain areas (geographical and social) remains very strong. The *potential* for a further nationalist revival in both Wales and Scotland is still apparent, and of course in Northern Ireland the strength of anti-unionism (small 'u') expressed by those who often describe themselves as 'Unionist' (capital 'U') has grown considerably. What this means is that in the late 1980s the issue of a pluri-ethnic, multicultural Britain is still very much on the agenda.

However, the focus of the debate, especially for England, has shifted from the 'internal colonies' of the Celtic periphery to other kinds of internal colony. These are the subject matter of chapter 6.

6

IMMIGRANTS AND LANGUAGE: THE 'MOTHER TONGUE'

*The English language is a central unifying factor in being 'British',
and is the key to participation on equal terms as a full member of
the society*

(SWANN REPORT 1985:385)

INTRODUCTION

THIS chapter and the next are concerned with people known as immigrant or migrant workers, and discuss certain social linguistic issues raised by their presence in the societies where they live.

With this focus the two chapters might seem to be dealing with material quite distinct from that considered previously. The continuity may, however, be observed in Ernest Gellner's remark that 'genuine cultural pluralism ceases to be viable under current conditions' (1983:55). He argues that by comparison with the past when 'culturally plural societies often worked well', in modern industrial nation-states, national cultures become the 'natural repositories of political legitimacy'. And of course, within that national culture the national language plays a crucial role.

Historically, the most significant source of cultural diversity in nation-states has been *regional*. Over the last century, however, and increasingly since the Second World War, large-scale movement of populations across national boundaries – international migration – has created within many nation-states additional diversities of both long and short-term kinds.

In the literature on European immigration over the past twenty years two closely related social linguistic issues have been widely discussed, both with a direct bearing on Gellner's observation concerning cultural pluralism. The first is usually called the 'mother tongue debate'. This concerns the status of what is, or is thought to be, the mother tongue, or home language of immigrants. It addresses the problem whether, and if so in what form, and how, that language should be preserved, or promoted or fostered. It is obviously related to the debate concerning the status of regional minority languages though the political connection between them is not always made clear. Both debates encompass much broader issues of culture or way of life as a whole (cf. Cicourel, 1982). They thus confront one of the most difficult political questions facing Western European nations: to what extent do we wish to foster a multicultural society? This question is being confronted in many countries of Europe, not least our own, and there is literature from Britain, France, Germany, Switzerland, Belgium, Holland, Scandinavia and the USSR to demonstrate this. And those familiar with the United States or Canada or Australia or Israel can testify that this is a global debate of paramount importance: what to do about so-called minority cultures.

The second issue concerns not the status of immigrants' mother tongues, but the status of their knowledge of, and competence in, the dominant language of the society in which they have settled. The two issues are connected in complex ways – the one affecting the other, the position taken on one affecting the position taken on the other. This complex interweaving can be seen in discussion of the status of the language spoken by a group of immigrants whose mother tongue is in fact English, or perhaps a variety of English sometimes called 'Creole': migrants from the West Indies settled in Britain. Underlying this issue too is the question what kind of society do we wish to foster? What are the implications for *action* and what are the consequences of *inaction* in this area?

Although the two issues are connected, both are vast in scope, and cannot be discussed simultaneously. This chapter will therefore concentrate on the first while the second will be reserved for Chapter 7.

SOME FACTS AND FIGURES

First, and briefly, some facts about contemporary migration in Western Europe, and some preliminary conclusions which bear on the themes of this chapter and the next. Those wishing to know more should consult the standard literature (e.g. Castles and Kosack 1973, Castles *et al.* 1984).

(1)   Labour migration has a lengthy history in modern times and a full account would need to consider what happened in the 19th century. In the post-war era alone, however, tens of millions of men, women and children have left their homes, sometimes permanently, sometimes temporarily, to find work in the core countries of

Western Europe. 'Core' because these countries are at the centre of economic development, and labour migrants come, usually, from areas which are peripheral to, and very often dependent on them. No one knows precisely how many there have been or are now. The numbers are themselves an explosive political issue. In many parts of Europe the question 'How many?' as like not would receive the reply 'Too many'. What constitutes a migrant or foreigner is not a hard and fast matter. It involves a complex mixture of social and political and legal definitions which are constantly changing. An informed guess of some 15 million people currently falling into the migrant category means that they form approximately 5%–10% of the population of the receiving societies concerned.

(2) The classic regions of emigration were areas such as Ireland or southern Italy, and before World War II labour migration in Europe principally involved the movement of peripheral European populations. In France in 1936, for example, of over 2 million foreigners, 700,000 were Italian, 500,000 Polish, 250,000 Spanish. After World War II, until their countries developed their own centres of attraction, Italian and Spanish workers still emigrated in large numbers. But new sending areas also came on stream: Yugoslavia, for example, and Greece, and Portugal. During the 1970s something like 10% of the native population of Portugal lived and worked in France. Most important of all, however, were the new or relatively new streams of migration from *outside* Europe, often from colonial and ex-colonial territories: the West Indies, the Asian subcontinent, North Africa, the Middle East. That is from cultural traditions very different from those of the receiving societies. In 1982, for example, there were over 1.5 million Algerians, Moroccans, Tunisians and Turks in France, and in 1981 in Britain 1.1 million people who had been born in the 'New Commonwealth'.

(3) Global features are misleading. One outstanding feature of labour migration is its concentration: in certain places and jobs, with generally concentration greatest in the urban and industrial centres. But within the conurbations immigrants are not usually distributed evenly through the population. For example, in the city of Lyons and its surrounding communes approximately 12% of the population are by French census definitions classed as foreigners, but within the urban area the proportion varies from 6% in the middle class suburbs to the west to about 18% in the working class suburbs to the east (Grillo 1985). Recent French elections make it clear that there is currently a direct relationship between the size of the

immigrant population in a commune and the vote received by the right wing *Front National*.

(4) One example of concentration is by sector of employment. In France, for example, it was said in the 1970s that one in three motor vehicles was produced by a migrant worker. Within sectors employing large numbers of immigrants, there may be further concentration within certain firms or departments within those firms, and within certain staff grades. One large factory in Lyons in the mid-1970s employed 2,500 North Africans out of a total labour force of 21,000, 91% in the lowest industrial category. Of 6,000 white collar and technical staff, only fifteen were from North Africa.

(5) Labour migration is generally at first a phenomenon of *men* who have gone as bachelors or young marrieds leaving wives and children back home. It is usually only secondly, and at a later stage, a phenomenon of families or of independent women, and whether it becomes that is to some extent a function of policy in the receiving society. Be that as it may, it is now the case that in each of the core countries there is a substantial immigrant family population which increased exceedingly rapidly during the 1970s. And there are now many children of immigrants who have been born and brought up in the societies to which their parents migrated.

(6) Finally, parallel to the population movement generated by labour migration is that which stems from other causes, such as seeking political refuge. Often these two causes are compounded, and certainly from a linguistic point of view the situation of the labour migrant and the refugee is often similar. For example, when children of Polish origin living in Slough go on Saturday mornings to a Polish language class, it may not be of any account that their parents, or maybe even grandparents, came to Britain not as labour migrants but as the remnants of Anders' army.

In sum, a salient feature of contemporary European migration is the growth in the number of families of migrant origin – and hence of course children – and their concentration in certain residential and occupational sectors. Where and how does language fit into this picture?

IMMIGRANTS AND LANGUAGE: THE ETHNIC SCHOOL TRADITION

There are millions of immigrants from China Pakistan that speak all different languages and I think if they come to this country they should try to speak the

language. Alot of the people stay in the own community and speak the own language
I think this should not be aloud. I think they should be chucked out.
(FOURTH YEAR ENGLISH SECONDARY SCHOOL PUPIL, CITED IN SWANN
REPORT 1985:253)

In the 1960s and 1970s, a period when the immigrant child population
expanded very rapidly, there was an increasingly noticeable diversity in the
linguistic profiles of the areas in which migrants settled. This was
documented systematically in England in pioneering studies by the Inner
London Education Authority, and by the Linguistic Minorities Project
(LMP) set up at the Institute of Education, University of London, in the
late 1970s. In a series of surveys the LMP established that, for example, in
the city of Bradford, in 1981, some 18% of all school-children were
bilingual, half of them being speakers of Punjabi, and that in the Borough of
Haringey, London, bilinguals made up 31% of all children enrolled in the
authority's schools (see Linguistic Minorities Project 1985 for the details).
Secondly, in Britain, France and other European countries there was an
increasing interest in, and concern for, immigrant cultures. A major part of
that interest focused on the immigrants' own languages, their mother
tongues, and on an informal and unofficial educational sector concerned
with their support which had experienced a substantial growth during this
same period.

This sector does not have a universally agreed name: it is referred to *inter
alia* as 'complementary' or 'supplementary' schooling, 'mother tongue
classes', or 'community mother tongue provision'. To call it the 'community
school' sector suggests more strongly than is sometimes the case that such
schooling is provided by and for ordinary members of minority communities themselves. In fact a number of parties have sought to promote this
kind of schooling and/or mother tongue teaching generally. These supporters have included, besides the families concerned, the governments of
the countries from which they originate – and in some cases to which they
migrate – the religious institutions (especially of the Catholic, Islamic,
Hindu and Sikh faiths), some (but by no means all) teachers and others
professionally concerned with education, various political groups and
tendencies (within both minority and majority cultures), and last but not
least, the European Economic Community, the EEC. Needless to say, the
precise interests of each of these groups are not always the same.

For convenience I will follow American and Australian (Norst, 1982)
usage and call this the (unofficial) 'ethnic schools' sector, emphasising one of
the defining characteristics of its schools and classes, that they are intended
to cater for a clientele which shares, or is believed to share, a common ethnic
heritage and identity. They are an example of ethnically specific provision

and demands for them, wherever such demands come from, have to be understood as such.

Ethnically specific educational provision, generally though not always external and additional to that provided by the official (state or private) school system, has long been a part of the urban scene in the United States (see Fishman and Nahirny 1966 for an overview). Warner and Srole's classic account of ethnicity in 'Yankee City' in the 1930s records extensive evidence for what they call the 'folk type of ethnic school' among Jews, Greeks, Armenians, Russians and Poles providing tuition in what must be considered the equivalent of the 'three Rs' in such schooling – language, history and religion. These 'afternoon schools', as Greek immigrants called them, permitted a division of educational labour: the public (state) school turned the 'ethnic child' towards American society while the ethnic school oriented her or him towards 'the ancestral system of the community' (Warner and Srole 1945:244).

Such schools certainly existed before the 1930s. Saloutos's history of Greek immigrants in the United States refers to a 'missionary zeal' for the study of the Greek language among the early arrivals. That study was usually promoted by the church committees which ran the Orthodox parishes. He provides a description of one 'afternoon school' prior to World War I: 'The classes were held in dark and dreary rooms; the instructors were dull and uninspired; the children were unhappy over having to attend a Greek school after a full day of classes; cooperation between teachers and parents was lacking' (Saloutos 1964:74). Despite this, demands for such schooling in no way diminished, as Warner and Srole show for the 1930s, and the schools continued to exist, and indeed to flourish after World War II, especially when the Greek community was reinforced by a further wave of immigrants. Moskos (1980) records that in 1978 there were some 400 such schools run by the Orthodox Archdiocesan government and other classes provided independently by private tutors. There were also some eighteen full-time Greek day schools within the parochial schools system. (For Greek language and culture classes in Britain see Constantinides 1977:284–6.)

The unofficial ethnic school sector has a long, but poorly documented history in Britain too. An early example was a school in the Italian colony of Clerkenwell, founded by Giuseppe Mazzini in the 1840s during his years of exile in London, for the benefit of the 4,000 (male) adult migrants who lived in the city at that time (Palmer 1972:74). The Society for the Advancement of Italian Workers had a similar aim. Also founded by Mazzini, it became in 1864 the Circolo Mazzini–Garibaldi which still exists, mainly as a fund-raising body. Palmer points out that Mazzini's school was the historical precursor of a number of Italian ethnic schools established in London in the

1920s and 1930s with the support of Mussolini. They in turn were the predecessors of the *Doposcuole* organised after World War II, initially by the Italian Catholic Mission, subsequently by the Italian government to provide tuition in the Italian language (Palmer 1972:118).

Jewish education provides another example (Fishman and Levy 1964, and discussion in Jeffcoate 1984). A Jewish Religious Education Board was established as early as 1860, and ran schools for Jewish immigrant children, mainly in the East End of London in the latter years of the nineteenth century. It was followed by the Talmud Torah Trust (1905) and the Union of Hebrew and Religious Classes (1907). Between the two World Wars activities were coordinated by a Central Committee for Jewish Education, which in 1945 was succeeded by a Board for the London area, and a Council for the Provinces.

In 1962 the London Board supervised seventy-eight part-time schools plus other classes with a total of 12,000 pupils. There was in addition a number of full-time Jewish (voluntary-aided and private) schools. Organisation of Jewish education was similarly extensive in the major provincial cities such as Manchester, and in smaller centres there were classes often run by the local rabbi. In all some 800 instructors were available providing tuition, for some three hours a week, in Hebrew language (translation, grammar etc.), the history and geography of the diaspora, and religious knowledge. Fishman and Levy (1964:69) estimated that some three-quarters of all Jewish children at some time in their lives received at least some exposure to Jewish education.

In France, ethnic schools were more difficult to organise owing to a law of 1889 which forbade the opening of foreign schools on French soil. One pre-World War II example was among the large Polish community in the mining areas of the Nord and Pas-de-Calais where a network of Polish priests was in existence from 1911 onwards. These priests taught the catechism in Polish, thus encouraging the use of the language among the children of immigrants, and providing a focus for Polish ethnic identity (INED 1954:199). In 1921 a number of private Polish schools were opened by the mining companies, circumventing the 1889 legislation by the device of appointing a French head teacher with Polish assistants. The latter were permitted to teach language, history and geography, using Polish as a medium of instruction, for half the school time. The other half was devoted to French. These schools closed when the mines were nationalised in 1945, though Polish classes continued, albeit outside school hours.

In the 1960s and 1970s, in both Britain and France the ethnic school sector experienced a rapid expansion, and began to involve migrants other than those from Southern and Eastern Europe. For Britain, Verity Saifullah

Khan (1983) distinguishes three main types of provision in this sector corresponding roughly to three groups of immigrant nationalities. (1) Where schools with qualified teachers are run by parents, often members of an ethnic association with close ties with a church (e.g. Polish Saturday Schools and those of other East European refugee groups). (2) Where the government of the country of origin, operating through the embassy or consulates, provides a professional staff using textbooks generally employed in the school system of the country of origin (e.g. Italian schools). (3) Where classes are organised on a local basis with voluntary, untrained teachers (e.g. among many South Asian groups). A further distinction might be made in Britain between those schools which secure financial or material support from the Local Education Authorities (LEAs), and those that do not.

In France, for migrants from the Catholic countries of Southern Europe the lead in the educational field was taken originally by the Catholic Missions and more recently by governments operating through consulates (usually in close contact with the Missions). The work of the Catholic Missions, both in Britain and France, though of long standing, was undoubtedly fortified by the Second Vatican Council, and the attention paid since then to the importance of cultural specificity – the need to respect and foster the cultural patrimony of each national group (for the application of this doctrine to migrants see Ancel 1973). For North African migrants, the provision of mother tongue teaching is largely, though not exclusively, in the hands of government-backed organisations such as the Amicale des Algériens en Europe which also have close ties with the consulates of the North African governments.

Because of its dispersed and localised nature it is very difficult to estimate the extent of the activity in this sector. A Linguistic Minorities Project survey of Coventry, Bradford and Haringey local authorities found in 1981 and 1982 432 classes in languages ranging (geographically) from Chinese to Irish about one third of which received some support from the authorities. But it is hard to know for sure what a 'class' means. In Lyons in the mid-1970s, besides some provision for Spanish and Italian migrants and rather more for Portuguese (155 courses in France as a whole in 1972), it was the Amicale des Algériens en Europe which was the most active organisation. Beginning from a base of some two dozen classes in France in 1966, by 1974 it was claiming to provide 800 classes nationally. In Lyons itself in 1976 it employed fourteen part-time teachers – usually North African graduate or undergraduate students – who held classes outside school hours either in school buildings or in local social centres. The regional branch of the Amicale also held an annual *fête scolaire* where prizes were presented to children who had performed well.

How are these classes seen by those who promote them and those who participate in them? It must be made clear that they are only partly educational in intent. An assessment of the impact of Jewish education in Britain by Esh concluded that as a substantial number of children did not attend classes, or attended only sporadically, 'about half of the growing Jewish generation will be unable to take any active part in Jewish life' (discussion in Gould and Esh 1964:87). Such schools, therefore, are seen as providing an essential preparation for community life which in this, as in many other cases, is crucially centred on religion. As in the Polish 'Saturday Schools' what is at stake is ethnic identity.

These schools, which originated with General Anders' exile Polish Army, have been important in Britain since World War II (Patterson 1977:228). Keith Sword (1982) describes one such school in a small industrial town in the south of England. Locally the school, which was founded in *c.* 1950, is run by a committee of priests, teachers and parents, and is affiliated to a national Polish Education Society which functions rather like a Ministry of Education in exile. The local school has a pre-school group, 6 elementary, 4 advanced and one 'A' level class, with 12 teachers in all. Classes are held on Saturday mornings in LEA premises. Parents contributed (in 1978) a fee of £14 p.a. and raised funds through dances and so on.

The curriculum covers language, history, geography and religious instruction, and clearly much more is at stake than the provision of tuition in the language: 'at each stage of the lesson the children received a renewed sense of their ethnic distinctiveness' (Sword 1982:140). Currently the language of instruction is Polish, which remains the language of the home for many children. There are fears, however, that eventually the Polish spoken in Britain might end as an 'indeterminate argot' of the kind said to be prevalent among Poles in the USA, and that the medium of instruction used in the Saturday school will have to be English. Polish will then be provided as a foreign language.

The close connection between language and national or religious identity (sometimes, as in the case of Greek Orthodoxy, religion *and* national identity) means that ethnic schools are hardly ever concerned solely with the maintenance of the 'mother tongue', if that means the language spoken by children and parents within the household.

As Fishman and Nahirny (1966:93) argue for the USA, the ethnic schools are 'a product of the encounter between ethnic immigrants and urban, industrial American mass culture', and represent, among other things, a 'means to ethnicity'. They can, and in some cases do, survive without actually engaging in mother tongue teaching. Not uncommonly the language of or for instruction is quite different from that actually spoken by children in the home. In France, the Amicale language classes usually teach a form of modern, literary Arabic which is not at all the same as the dialects spoken by most immigrants – a number of whom in fact speak Kabyle, a totally different language. In Sweden, Morris Fred reports, the parents of 'Syriani' immigrant children, who mostly speak Kurdish, insist that their offspring be taught Syrian, which is a church language: 'the choice reflects the group's emphasis on their religion and more particularly on the Syrian-Orthodox Church as the most crucial factor in their cultural identity' (Fred, 1983:89). In a survey of the complex linguistic scene among South Asians in Britain, further details of which are provided in the Linguistic Minorities Project 1985, Reid in fact argues we should abandon

(the) use of the term 'mother tongue' when referring to the languages being learned by large numbers of minority children in voluntary classes . . . There are good reasons, both educational and social, for encouraging the study of the languages of minority communities . . . but these do not all depend on the languages chosen being identical with the languages of the home.   (1984:420)

BILINGUAL AND MULTICULTURAL EDUCATION AND THE MOTHER TONGUE DEBATE

An 'unofficial ethnic school sector' therefore is currently flourishing, so far as it can, given the inevitable lack of financial and organisational resources. But what has been happening in the *official*, state-run, school system?

The desirability of a different – in a sense ethnically specific – kind of schooling for some pupils was officially recognised by the 1944 Education Act. This designated a 'voluntary-aided' sector of schools outside, but overseen by, the state system, run by a variety of religious bodies – principally the Church of England, and by Catholics, Jews and Methodists. It was not until the mid-1970s, however, that ethnically specific provision within the mainstream system for post-World War II immigrants became a serious issue in British education (Saifullah Khan 1977).

The first 'official' discussion of the view that our system might accommodate provision for mother tongue teaching and thus, perhaps, move towards some form of bilingual education is usually said to have been in the Bullock Report (1975) which was mainly concerned with the teaching of reading and writing of the English language – though the matter was in the air prior to that (Edwards 1984a:60, and see Townsend 1971:60, Townsend and Brittan 1972:31).

The Bullock Report has one chapter (ch. 20) on 'Children from families of overseas origin', dealing mostly with their difficulties with English, which was then the principal cause of official pedagogical concern (see chapter 7).

One paragraph, however, raised a new and somewhat different matter: 'The importance of bilingualism, both in education and for society in general, has been increasingly recognised in Europe and in the USA. We believe that its implications for Britain should receive equally serious study.' Bilingualism, they argued, should be seen as an asset, 'as something to be nurtured, and one of the agencies which should nurture it is the school . . . the school should adopt a positive attitude to the pupils' bilingualism and wherever possible should help maintain and deepen their knowledge of their mother-tongues . . . bilingual pupils should be encouraged to maintain their mother-tongues throughout their schooling' (Bullock Report 1975: para. 20.17, pp. 293–4).

Institutional discussion of multilingual education had focused almost exclusively on the regional languages (see chapters 3 and 5). The struggle for the teaching of/in the regional languages had only an indirect effect on demands for immigrant mother-tongue teaching. Indeed the connection between the two is rarely made (though see Cohen 1984 and certain passages in chapter 7 of the Swann Report of 1985). Nonetheless, that struggle did form an important part of the background against which new demands were made.

So far as immigrants and their children were concerned, there were four reasons why in their case the issues of bilingual – and in a more complex way multicultural – education became an important public matter in the mid-1970s.

One of these was the development of policy at a European level for such children. In 1970, the Council of Europe passed a resolution which proposed that the education of the children of migrant workers should seek to maintain their linguistic and cultural ties with their countries of origin. This was followed up by a 1977 Convention, Article 15 of which called specifically for courses in the mother tongues in order, *inter alia*, to facilitate reintegration in the sending societies (Rey-Von Allmen 1983:17).

Slightly earlier, in 1974, the European Community had circulated a draft directive to much the same effect. Saifullah Khan (1977, 1980), and Martin-Jones (1984) trace the reception of this draft directive in Britain, noting the objections lodged to it by the educational authorities. Martin-Jones (1984:430) records that local administrators and teaching unions were 'guardedly negative'. There was a similar response in France when information about the directive was circulated there (Grillo 1985). A revised version, much watered down, was finally adopted by the EEC in 1977, for implementation in 1981. The crucial Article 3 states:

Member States shall in accordance with their national circumstances and legal systems, and in cooperation with States of origin, take appropriate measures to promote, in coordination with normal education, teaching of the mother tongue and culture of the country of origin for the children [who are dependants of any worker who is a national of another Member State].

(ARTICLE 3 OF COUNCIL DIRECTIVE OF 25 JULY 1977 ON THE EDUCATION OF THE CHILDREN OF MIGRANT WORKERS, COUNCIL OF THE EUROPEAN COMMUNITIES 1983:25)

The EEC's initiative aimed to forward one of the basic principles on which it was founded: that there should be every possibility for the 'free circulation of labour' between member states. It also responded to the demands of some labour sending countries, such as Algeria, that they should be able, eventually, to regroup their dispersed population – that it should not be lost to them. Neither of these two considerations had particular relevance to the situation of the bulk of British immigrants. Nevertheless, EEC membership forced British attention on the problem.

Secondly, members of the teaching profession were themselves beginning to think along new lines. Teachers, particularly in the large comprehensive schools in the London area, had found themselves working in an extremely difficult educational context. Apart from the problems created by reorganisation and the long-term erosion of resources which began in the early 1970s, many schools faced large and growing intakes of immigrant children. Teachers were dealing, day by day, with multiracial and multicultural classrooms in schools in which there was often considerable ethnic tension, and were looking, sometimes desperately, for solutions to their difficulties and those of the children they taught. What have been called at different times and in different places 'multiracial', 'multi-ethnic', or 'multicultural' curricula were thought to provide one.[1]

A third influence, again indirect, was the USA, seen to be facing a situation similar to ours if on a much larger scale (cf. Cazden and Dickinson 1981, Cohen 1980, 1984, Kelly 1981, Paulston 1981). There the Bilingual Education Act 1968, and perhaps more important the judgement in the case of Lau v. Nichols in the California courts in 1974, had pushed the education system towards bilingual provision for children whose mother tongue was not English. Although US practice is very varied, and programmes are often confused as to aim (Cohen 1980), bilingual education was by the late 1970s very much a part of the American scene. Of slightly earlier date was the push towards 'Black Studies' – of and for Afro-Americans – which also had supporters among West Indians in Britain.

---

[1] One possible solution was believed to reside in my own discipline – social anthropology. In the early 1970s a number of teachers looked to anthropologists to provide them with guidance on material suitable for use in multiracial and multicultural contexts. Anthropologists, however, generally interpreted this interest on the part of teachers as a desire to have anthropology taught as a subject within the secondary curriculum, and the profession was firmly against that.

Finally, parents, particularly of Asian children, already making extensive private provision for mother tongue teaching within the ethnic school sector, began to demand that that burden be taken on by the state system.

For these and other reasons, then, the latter half of the 1970s was characterised by a major debate in Britain and other countries of Western Europe on multilingual and multicultural education. In Britain it is best described not as a single debate, but a cluster of related discussions with as their focus the issue of social and cultural pluralism and its particular relevance for the educational system. These discussions occurred at many different levels and in many different arenas with protagonists representing a wide variety of interests and perspectives. Thus, although most parties found themselves talking about teaching the mother tongue, it was not always the case that they were actually talking about the same phenomenon. It was not talk alone, either, for a great deal of activity was also taking place – researching, lobbying, implementing test projects, experimenting with curricula (see Edwards 1984a, Martin-Jones 1984).

I do not propose to discuss everything that was at stake, but will concentrate on two issues. One is fairly specific – the question of mother tongue teaching in the educational curriculum. The other, which some-times, though not always, incorporates some considerations of bilingual education, is the much broader question of the multiracial and multicultural school.

MOTHER TONGUE TEACHING IN THE EDUCATIONAL CURRICULUM

What kinds of policies have evolved over the last decade concerning the place of mother tongue teaching in schools?

In France, as in Britain, the debate about the education of migrants' children was initially concerned with the needs of those children whose command of the dominant language was weak. From 1974–5 onwards (again like Britain) the issue of mother tongue teaching and the wider problem of the multicultural or 'intercultural' curriculum came to the fore in policy discussions. In the mid-1970s, French policy towards immigrants was oriented towards the dual goals of integration, for those who wished to stay in France on a long-term basis, and the maintenance of ties with the 'home' country and culture for those who wished in the end to return (Dijoud 1976, Hessel 1976 and Grillo 1985). This second perspective was also shared by the governments of some of the sending countries (especially Algeria) who looked forward to an eventual 'reintegration' of their migrant populations.

The provision of mother tongue teaching was thought to have a part to play in this policy, and thus the French government at least was more receptive to the EEC initiative in 1974 than Britain's, though locally the French teaching profession was as negative in its attitude as was its British counterpart.

From 1974 onwards, a series of circulars from the highly centralised French Education Ministry set in place a limited structure of mother tongue provision (Charlot 1981, Delrieu 1983, Rey-Von Allmen 1983), and a number of bilateral agreements were signed with the principal sending countries (Portugal, Italy, Tunisia, Spain, Morocco, Turkey, Yugoslavia, and finally in 1981, Algeria). Two types of course were to be made available in primary schools: 'integrated' courses offering tuition for three hours per week within normal school time, in periods traditionally set aside for additional activities; 'parallel' courses, allowing the use of official facilities for language classes outside school hours. The teaching staff in both cases were to be provided and paid for by the governments of the sending countries.

Figures cited by Delrieu (1983) for the 1979–80 school year suggest that some 20% of the primary age group of migrant children participate in these classes (*c*. 82,000 out of a total of 400,000). The figures refer to integrated and parallel courses combined, however, and those attending the integrated courses (i.e. during school time) constitute only 8.5% of the total. Regarding national distribution, some 60% of the pupils came from the three principal Southern European groups of immigrants (Italian, Portuguese and Spanish) and 30% from the North African groups. Proportionately North Africans are under-represented in the classes, and in addition a much smaller proportion of all North African children are catered for: whereas some 40% of Italian, Portuguese and Spanish children appear to attend the various courses, only some 15% of those from North Africa do so.[2]

A number of difficulties have been encountered with these courses. The facilities provided within the schools are often poor, there is little coordination between the courses and the main school curriculum, and there is no follow-up in the secondary school, other than where the languages are available as part of the secondary curriculum (this may be the case for Italian or Spanish, but not for Portuguese or Arabic). Nevertheless, despite these difficulties, it is clear that, as Delrieu notes, '[mother tongue] teaching is very much a part of the daily life of the French school' (1983:29).

[2] Campani (1983:36) cites Italian embassy figures of 14,197 Italian children attending courses in language and culture in France as a whole in 1979–80. It is not clear whether these include both those on integrated and those on parallel courses. There were 27,000 primary age Italian children in France in 1977–8 (Charlot 1981:101).

French policy has, therefore, moved towards a limited programme of special provision at primary level, mainly to facilitate reintegration. What kind of provision has been made available in Britain, and with what goals? The short answer is very little indeed. Writing in 1984, Tosi remarks: 'Mother tongue teaching is presently being discussed in Britain in terms of *whether* and *how* it should be incorporated in the timetable rather than for what duration and with what subjects it should be integrated into a bilingual curriculum' (1984:137). In fact the emphasis has been on the 'whether' rather than the 'how'.

The position in Britain in 1984–5 is well summarised in the Swann Report (1985) which gave rise to a very lively debate in educational and social scientific circles over the following year.

The Swann inquiry was initiated in 1979, originally under the chairmanship of Mr Rampton, to 'review in relation to schools the educational needs and attainments of children from ethnic minority groups' (Rampton Report 1981:1). Some of its conclusions regarding multicultural education and the position of West Indian children will be discussed in chapter 7. Here I consider only its views on mother tongue teaching, an issue on which the inquiry received more evidence than on any other topic (Swann Report 1985:397).

In the sections which deal with this issue the Report is concerned essentially with those children whose mother tongue, or home language, is *not* a variety of English, and appears to have in mind a 'model' population, so to speak, of South Asian origin. It distinguishes three possible forms of mother tongue provision: (a) within the context of a bilingual education programme, using the language as a medium of instruction; (b) mother tongue maintenance – by which is meant 'the development of a pupil's fluency in his or her mother tongue as an integral part of a *primary* school's curriculum in order to extend their existing language skills', and (c) mother tongue teaching – in which the language is made available as a subject in the secondary school curriculum (Swann, 1985:399).

Although pronouncing itself 'for' mother tongues, the Report records that it is unable to support (a) or (b). Mother tongue maintenance, it suggests, is an important matter, but one for the communities themselves, and it proposes enhanced support, from local education authorities, for community-based provision (what I have called the ethnic schools). They are, however, in favour of (c) and wish to see 'community languages built into the curriculum' (p. 409), and not just for members of minority communities.

The reasons they give (pp. 406–7) for rejecting bilingual programmes or mother tongue maintenance are that they lead to separatism which 'serves to establish and confirm social divisions between groups of pupils'; that they would not affect the hostile perspective of the majority; that they do nothing for equality of opportunity, the key to which is 'good comand of English'; that the research on bilingual education, which suggests that the learning of the mother tongue prior to, or at least alongside, a second (dominant) language might be positively beneficial, is unconvincing; that such claims are, anyway, invalid if the 'mother tongue' is not actually the language spoken in the child's home; that where a mother tongue is important for the families concerned it is likely to 'survive and flourish regardless of the provision made for its teaching and/or usage within mainstream schools' (p. 408).

The majority of LEAs, and indeed educationists, probably breathed a sigh of relief at these recommendations. How they might be reconciled with the EEC Directive is another matter, but as a senior LEA education officer pointed out, at a conference I attended in 1982, the key word in Article 3, from a legalistic point of view, is 'promote' (cf. Jeffcoate 1984:88), and it could certainly be argued that the proposals do that.

On the more positive side, however, and in line with its generally 'liberal integrationist' stance (see below), the inquiry saw linguistic diversity as a resource and an opportunity and advocated a change in attitudes towards language. They argue (following Bullock) that schools should cultivate awareness of linguistic diversity and of the 'appropriateness' rather than the 'correctness' of language use (p. 419). This involves greater understanding of the nature of language (p. 422), and the Report, in effect, endorses the incorporation of a sociolinguistic approach in teaching of and about language, and in teacher training (see especially Annex H of Swann's chapter 7).

Turning specifically to the comments on bilingual education and bilingualism, it should first be noted that bilingual programmes may have very different goals. A common enough contrast is one made by Paulston (1981:474) between those which are essentially 'transitional' in intent, such as the programmes envisaged by the US 1968 Act, and those which are maintenance-oriented (cf. Edwards, J. R. 1985:126; Skutnabb-Kangas 1981, 1984 and Tosi 1984 describe a more varied range of models). The former seek to use the mother tongue as a vehicle through which to enhance access to the dominant language, the latter seek to sustain equal skills in both languages.

Concerning programmes of the first kind, the pedagogic arguments for 'transitional' bilingualism, at the very least, are much stronger than the Swann Report allows. The evidence *for* bilingual education is too readily swept aside. Admittedly that evidence is not all positive (e.g. Macnamara 1966 on Irish experience), but comparison is very difficult since the same practice may have a quite different meaning in another context. On the other hand, experiments in this country have already demonstrated the value of bilingual practice in education (see Tosi 1984), while it has also been argued that monolingual education, i.e. in the dominant language, without support for the mother tongue may 'produce (a risk of) deficit of a major character' (Skutnabb-Kangas 1984:41).[3] Thus the case for substantial programmes of the kind outlined by John Rex in an Annex to the Swann Report (p. 299) is in fact quite formidable.

Full-scale programmes of the type Rex advocates for immigrants in Britain or France would, however, pose immense problems of organisation and resources. How many teachers of Italian, Greek, Gujarati, Arabic, Chinese etc. would be required, and where would they come from? Who is to provide their training? What teaching materials would they use? What is to happen in areas in which only small numbers of each language minority are present? If, on the other hand, 'there are many areas of the country, and a number of obvious schools, where a large number of children could benefit from [mother tongue] provision' (Saifullah Khan 1980:77), and resources were directed towards those schools, what would be the effect on their intakes and the catchment areas in which they were located? Would there not be a movement towards them on the part of immigrants, and perhaps a movement away from them on the part of 'white' parents? Social and political objections by such parents, which have led to protest marches in some London boroughs against the introduction of an element of multicultural education in local schools, form part of the reality by reference to which proposals for bilingual programmes have to be evaluated.

These are real problems which proponents of such programmes (among which I would include myself) have to face. They do not disappear with Swann's proposals which simply remove them from one area of institutional responsibility (mainstream schools) to another, the communities and presumably their governments, the LEAs and Whitehall. If, as one suspects, the latter will not move speedily, if at all, then the burden of providing mother tongue teaching will rest, as it does now, on the communities themselves. Given that resources are unequally distributed among them, and sending society governments will be variously unwilling or unable to make up the deficit, it is clear that community mother tongue provision, the only kind of bilingual education Swann envisages for the public sector, will be patchy, and above all marginalised.

---

[3] Formulations such as 'semilingualism' or 'double-semilingualism', of the kind employed by Skutnabb-Kangas e.g. in 1978, and others have been severely criticised by several linguists (e.g. Martin-Jones and Romaine 1985). I cannot discuss the issues here, but they are touched upon in later chapters when I look at the concepts of 'competence' and 'deficit'.

WHAT KIND OF A SOCIETY?

[Transitional bilingual education] is a more sophisticated assimilationist policy and does not involve, nor aim for, a truly multicultural, multilingual society where diversity is fostered; where multilingualism is not perceived as a problem but a benefit and resource for the whole society.   (SAIFULLAH KHAN 1980:76)

To the extent that programmes designed to develop competence in minority languages can be justified by reference to equality of opportunity rather than cultural maintenance, they too perhaps should fall into the unexceptionable category.   (JEFFCOATE 1984:94)

We have been considering mother tongue teaching from the point of view of 'transitional' programmes. Can they be justified on other grounds, and what of those cases where the language taught is not that of the home?

Maintenance-oriented programmes may also support a variety of goals. Thus, the EEC interest in promoting mother tongue teaching derives primarily from the Community's economic aim of encouraging the free movement of labour. The so-called 'Bavarian model' (Abadan-Unat 1975, Skutnabb-Kangas 1981, 1984) seems to have this purpose in mind. Such a model, as Skutnabb-Kangas shows, is clearly associated with a 'guest-worker' immigration policy in which immigrants are, by definition, only temporarily in the labour-receiving country. Then:

it is imperative . . . to keep the children unintegrated, prepared to be sent home whenever their parents' labour is not needed any more. This is done by preventing a real integration in German classes and in German society. It is also done by making as much use as possible of syllabuses and teaching materials drawn from the country of origin.   (SKUTNABB-KANGAS 1981:109)

This Skutnabb-Kangas characterises as a system of 'negative separation'. In neither Britain nor France have maintenance programmes usually involved such objectives, though in France government policy in the 1970s certainly envisaged 'keeping open the option' of the eventual return of migrants' children. Generally, in both countries supporters of mother tongue maintenance programmes have sought objectives either of a 'pluralist' kind, or at any rate which are justified by reference to pluralist arguments. But to what extent should provision for the mother tongue be the responsibility of the mainstream school system? In fact, should the school be concerned at all with cultural and linguistic 'maintenance'?

The answer to that is that British schools, explicitly or implicitly, have always been concerned with maintaining a language – English – and a particular culture – mainstream British culture. That this was and remains the dominant view is confirmed by a statement by Sir Keith Joseph shortly before he left the post of Secretary of State for Education: 'Our schools should transmit British culture, enriched as it has been by so many traditions . . . It would be unnecessary . . . and I believe wrong, to turn our education system upside down to accommodate ethnic variety or to jettison those many features and practices which reflect what is best in our society and its institutions' (reported in the *Guardian*, 22 May 1986).

The same is true of France, as we saw in chapters 2 and 4, and of most other Western societies. The question, therefore, is not *whether* schools should participate in cultural and linguistic maintenance, but *which* culture and language they are to maintain. This is not a matter that can be separated from social and cultural policy generally. It therefore obliges us to consider the kind of society we want to foster.

The Swann Report identifies three strands of thought which it calls 'assimilationist', 'pluralist' and 'separatist', placing its own thinking firmly within the pluralist camp. These categories must be treated as ideal-typical, and certainly not homogeneous. 'Pluralism' in particular can take many forms, and there is another stance which seems to come between the first two which I will call 'liberal integrationist', using the self-ascription of one well known advocate of this position, Robert Jeffcoate (though Jeffcoate 1984:xi, also calls himself an 'egalitarian').

I will not discuss straightforward assimilationism of the type represented by an eminent historian writing in *The Observer* in April 1984. Reviewing developments in the teaching of his subject in schools, he claimed that the syllabus had moved too far from the traditional constitutional treatment in the direction of social history. He wished further to have no truck with any kind of multicultural perspective – so far as immigrants were concerned the sooner they assimilated the better. Nor will I review the more strident views of Ray Honeyford, the Bradford headmaster whose articles in the *Salisbury Review* and other places led to a protracted, well-publicised, conflict with the parents of his mainly Asian pupils: 'Those of us working in Asian areas are encouraged, officially, to "celebrate linguistic diversity", i.e. applaud the rapidly mounting linguistic confusion in those growing number of inner-city schools in which British-born Asian children begin their mastery of English by being taught Urdu' (Honeyford 1984:30). I will also ignore entirely the 'rejectionists', as they might be called, who believe there is a simple solution to the entire problem: send them back whence they came. Here I confine attention to those who envisage at least some room for other cultures.

The key questions are: how much and what kind? Jeffcoate (1984:118), following Parekh (1974), contrasts 'full-blooded' and 'modified' pluralism, advocating the latter as he does not believe our society can or should tolerate or support every instance of cultural diversity: female circumcision, the subordination of women and *halal* meat are his examples (all Islamic ones). While he finds 'unexceptionable' (a favourite term of his) a set of aims issued for Bradford's schools which include, for instance, the right of children to wear ethnically specific school dress (1984:125), he draws the line very firmly at mother tongue maintenance, and any religious provision, in particular of Islamic doctrine – though he also describes Rastafarianism as 'atavistic obscurantism' (p. 133). He proposes to cope with the problem of religious education by abolishing it. In many respects Swann's pluralism is close to this 'weak' kind, as discussion of the language proposals will have shown. A similar 'weak' strain can be seen in the committee's assessment of multicultural education, though aspects of what they say here is 'strong' in another sense, and certainly not without value.

Here it is necessary to place Swann's contribution in a wider perspective. The Rampton Report was originally concerned with the educational underachievement, principally of young Black West Indians, and argued that quite fundamental to this was the racist nature of British educational institutions, and indeed of British society as a whole. Swann does not veer from this stance, and the point is documented in some of the most interesting – and terrifying – parts of the Report where it records the racist attitudes of teachers and pupils alike from schools in areas of both high and low concentrations of immigrants. Against this racist background Swann concludes that a multicultural perspective in education is thoroughly desirable for *all* pupils, not just something for Blacks or other ethnic minorities. Hence the title of the Report, *Education for all* (cf. pp. 318–19).

What is proposed under this slogan is a pluralist perspective throughout the curriculum, not to cater for the needs of specific ethnic groups, but directed towards all children, 'preparing *all* pupils for life in a multiracial society' (p. 199). Such a perspective would be 'across the curriculum' in maths, history, the performing arts, political education and in language (p. 329). It would not simply be incorporated, as is often the case now, as a token gesture towards Islam, Buddhism or Hinduism in religious teaching.

Although the broad aims are stated firmly enough, it is not clear what they might mean in practice. I doubt, for example, whether the Committee envisaged as thorough a reshaping of education as that proposed by Banks (1984) for 'multi-ethnic' education in the USA (though Banks's views are referred to approvingly by Swann (p. 322)). Nor indeed would Swann be likely to embrace what has been advocated in a recent British volume devoted to this issue (Straker-Welds 1984).

France, too, has seen some movement towards a multicultural perspective within education, though the debate has not been as important there as it has been in Britain. There is no French Swann Report, for example. One important contribution has come from the CEFISEM (Centre d'Information et de Formation de Personnels Concernés par la Scolarisation des Enfants de Travailleurs Migrants). The first was founded in Lyons in 1975 by the educationist Pierre Grange (see Grillo 1985), and by 1981 there were eleven. These are centres which offer short-to-medium term courses for teachers the content of which stresses the historical, social, economic, political and psychological background to migration. They thus inform the teacher about migration and the likely problems to be encountered in the teaching of migrant children. Pierre Grange and his associates, however, were originally interested in much more than this and in the mid-1970s were pursuing the idea of a bilingual and bicultural education involving children learning two languages in equal measure, with a curriculum (e.g. in history, geography and religious studies) which reflected a dual orientation (Grange and Cherel, 1975: 149–55, Colin, 1976). So far as I know, these ideas remained only matters for discussion. The work of CEFISEM does, however, enable teachers to deepen their knowledge and understanding of the migratory phenomenon and perhaps go on to convey that understanding to their pupils, French and immigrant. The intention of such courses is thus broadly similar to that of some of the proposals contained in the Swann Report (see, for example, Delrieu 1983:28).

My (pessimistic) prediction is that Swann's 'education for all' will suffer the fate of Bullock's 'language for life'. Many people will accept the proposals, most will do nothing about them. And in any event, those concerning language are inadequate to meet the educational needs of pupils or the social and cultural desires of parents. What is likely to happen is that among certain ethnic groups there will be increasing demands of a 'separatist' kind. Private Islamic primary schools already exist, and in a number of areas (e.g. Bradford, Brent, Ealing) Asian parents have been considering proposals to purchase schools and run them as part of the voluntary-aided sector as Muslim or Sikh schools (just as there are now Catholic and Jewish schools). Swann (p. 501 ff.) considered this option. The majority of the Committee were opposed to it – in line with liberal educational opinion which generally speaking favours secular, integrated schools for all; a minority of six entered a dissenting note (p. 515). That 'Swann is against' is likely to be used by the authorities when processing any future applications for voluntary-aided status.[4]

Though we live in a recognisably multiracial, multicultural and multilingual society, only a narrow range of cultural possibilities is still considered

---

[4] However, the 'opting out' provisions of the Baker Education Act may provide communities with opportunities for establishing ethnically specific schooling. Indeed a small number of such schools already exist.

legitimate and we are far from seeing multiculturalism as 'benefit and resource'. I am sure that Gellner would view this as a sad, though inevitable, outcome of the structural conditions which gave rise to the national imperative. Yet I am equally sure that the claims of multiculturalism – or perhaps the particularistic claims of cultural minorities – which have become increasingly loud and widespread in the last twenty years will not simply go away. Nor can they, in relatively free societies such as Britain or France, be readily suppressed. The continuing pressures *for* pluralism may well be seen eventually to have been the result, if not of an 'objective need' for heterogeneity, at any rate of a set of new structural conditions within which the legitimacy of heterogeneity once again became possible.

7

IMMIGRANTS AND LANGUAGE:
THE ISSUE OF COMPETENCE

'What's nice about it?'

TOWARDS the end of the previous chapter I outlined the case for encouraging pluralism in Britain, France and other societies of Western Europe. The type of pluralism advocated was 'stronger' than that approved by the Swann Report and writers such as Jeffcoate, offering institutional support for the mother tongue, or 'community language' of immigrant groups (what linguists usually call the 'L1'). But support for immigrant languages is only one side of the coin. The other side entails extending and/or consolidating competence in the *dominant* language, the language of the receiving society (the 'L2'). For the kind of pluralism that most people, including myself, envisage involves a significant degree of *integration* also. J. R. Edwards's phrase 'pluralistic integration' (1985:117) perhaps summarises this perspective.

This chapter, then, focuses on the relationship of immigrants to the dominant language (cf. Catani 1973). It also leads towards another set of issues concerning linguistic stratification, the hierarchical ordering of languages, and the relationship between language and class which forms the subject matter of chapters 8 to 10.

THE DOMINANT LANGUAGE AND ETHNIC ENCLAVEMENT

Let us start with the simple and obvious points that in the case of most immigrant workers and their families, at least those recently arrived, their mother tongue is not that of the labour-receiving society, and that collectively and individually they have knowledge of, and competence in, that language which varies from zero upwards. Let us explore this situation looking at causes and implications.

The first question is: does it matter? Who needs the language anyway? One could construct a model of migration under condition zero, so to speak, where the migrant has no language other than his or her native tongue, and has no need of any other. 'Separatist' models of labour migration, represented by certain 'guest worker' policies, in fact assume that migration is generally like that, or perhaps should be. But separatism need not only reflect such official policies. Consider the example of a male migrant – call him Ahmed – from a remote part of North Africa who has not been to school and who is illiterate in French, as well as perhaps in his own language, a dialect of Arabic or Berber. By day he is employed on a building site humping bricks in a work gang consisting entirely of other North Africans. By night he shares a room in a tenement occupied entirely by compatriots. He cooks at home with food bought from the local Algerian grocer. He intends to earn and save as much as he can in the shortest time possible and return for good to North Africa. In the meantime he spends whatever holidays he has back home. If he allows himself any luxuries it is the occasional coffee or meal in an Arab café or restaurant, or perhaps a visit to a cinema showing Arabic films (or more likely films dubbed into Arabic). What need does he have of the language?

This is a limiting case, and a number of restricting assumptions have been made. More could be added – for example. Ahmed might work as a dishwasher in one of the Algerian restaurants. But the point is that it is possible to conceive of immigrants – and indeed I knew a number myself in Lyons – who in some sense have no use for the dominant language. If this were generally the case, if the lives of all immigrants in Europe were like Ahmed's, we would have a system in which there was a high degree of what is sometimes called 'enclavement' as indeed occurs in many parts of the world. In such 'back-to-back' societies, as they have been called, there are separate ethnic blocks each with and within its own ethnically specific institutions, including often its own ethnically specific economy. With such a high degree of enclavement the need for access to the receiving society's language is minimal. Hong Kong Chinese in the restaurant industry in Britain come close to turning their back on the receiving society in this way, except in one important respect (Watson 1977).

In fact, in Britain, France and Germany that degree of enclavement for an ethnic group as a whole is rare, though it sometimes describes, if not the life of a group in its entirety, then that of a substantial section of it: for example Bangladeshi women living in Brick Lane in London. Indeed, among immigrants from Muslim countries the situation of women closely approximates to the enclavement model (see de Herédia 1983:115 for a description of the socially isolated, illiterate, monolingual immigrant woman in France). When the Swann Report opposed separate, single-sex schools for Muslim girls it was precisely the reinforcement of their segregation to which it objected.

A high degree of enclavement does not preclude all contact between communities. Chinese restaurants, after all, have to have British customers. And someone like Ahmed, assuming he is legally employed and resident, could not survive long in a country such as France without being obliged to make contact with the French bureaucratic system. That means forms, functionaries, offices in a society which makes few if any concessions to the non-French-speaking foreigner. How will he make out?

In any North African café in France there may be found someone, often sitting at the same table drinking endless cups of black coffee, who is from time to time approached, perhaps diffidently, by compatriots clutching bits of paper: a letter, perhaps, or a form. This is the solution, found in many cultures where the bulk of the population is illiterate, of the professional letter writer, the experienced form-filler, an expert, perhaps, in the regulations of the social security system. Lacking that expertise, Ahmed must put himself in the hands of someone else. When this happens in a regular and systematic way it means that the bulk of relationships between communities is *mediated* by go-betweens.

This kind of mediation is often called 'brokerage' by anthropologists, and when language is involved it is appropriate to call the mediators 'language brokers' (cf. Gumperz and Cook-Gumperz 1981). Where, as in Europe, there is a diversified language system, and language diversity is correlated with the differential distribution of, and access to, resources, their emergence is highly probable. Language brokerage of various kinds is widely found in immigrant societies. For example, immigrant men generally have greater knowledge of the dominant language than do women – not surprising if seclusion is practised. Thus the relationship of women to the receiving society may be mediated by men. Similarly, teachers in France frequently report that discussion with North African parents of their children's progress at school often takes place with the child acting as interpreter.

Brokerage is rarely, if ever, without cost, literal and figurative, economic, social and cultural. There may be a more positive way of interpreting this type of relationship (see below), but let us accept for now that many people will need and want to know the language for the most obvious reasons: to make their own way in the society in which they exist, in some cases in the hope that they can play a full part in it, in many others simply to survive. It is possible that before World War I knowledge of the 'L2' was less essential for survival and advancement, and this may still be true of certain sectors and occupations within the contemporary economy (see Brooks and Singh 1979:94), but generally, in highly industrialised, highly bureaucratised, highly institutionalised societies such as Britain, France or Germany survival is extremely difficult without considerable competence in the dominant language, and many adult migrants lack the wherewithal to attain that goal, and are thereby forced into an indirect relationship with the society in which they are implanted.

COMPETENCE

At this point, however, the notion of competence requires further consideration. Competence in what, of what, for what?

'Competence' is used here not in the technical sense proposed by Chomsky but as defined by the anthropologist Dell Hymes whose recapturing of the common-sense meaning of the term has become so widely accepted in the sociolinguistic literature, that, for example, a glossary in Ferguson and Heath (1981) defines it in his, rather than Chomsky's, way (see also Milroy and Milroy 1985:118 ff.). Hymes's usage differs from Chomsky's in that when Hymes talks of competence he means 'communicative competence': the 'ability to participate in (a) society as not only a speaking, but also a communicating member' (Hymes 1977:75). This encompasses not just linguistic but what Hymes sometimes calls *sociolinguistic* and at others 'interactive' competence (e.g. Hymes 1977:75, Cazden and Dickinson 1981: 463). To communicate as a member of the society one needs a great deal of cultural knowledge as well as knowledge of a kind that is specifically linguistic.

The following account draws on several papers in which Hymes has discussed the issue of competence (e.g. 1971a, 1971b, 1977). Hymes suggests that there are four aspects of competence which ought to be distinguished:

(a) *systemic potential*, whether and to what extent something is formally possible in a language – the sort of question with which Chomsky's notion of competence is concerned.
(b) *appropriateness* – 'whether and to what extent something is in some context suitable, effective or the like'.
(c) *occurrence* – is it actually done?
(d) *feasibility* – whether it is feasible with the means at hand.

Communicative competence involves both knowledge of these things, which in a native speaker may often be implicit, and the ability to put that knowledge to use, which may be a socially delimited ability. It is therefore concerned with a range of issues which Chomskyan linguistic theory deals with under the rubric of 'performance', if at all.

Communicative competence has nothing to do with cognitive capability, still less intelligence. Furthermore, it is not something one either has, or does not have in any simple way. There are degrees of competence, and ranges or fields of competence possibly varying by domain (buying goods in a market, obtaining a prescription from a doctor). And there are likely to be sets of competences which vary from group to group and individual to individual, which any description of competence among a population must take into account. Above all, competence is essentially relative, and can only be ascribed if we can specify in what kind of language or variety of language, in what situations, and for what purpose communication is taking place? Competence has to be measured against goals, and judged by reference to what may be quite arbitrary yardsticks (cf. Klein and Dittmar 1979:87, Milroy and Milroy 1985:139).

It is a complex matter simply to describe variation in competence in a population as substantial and as heterogeneous as that of migrants in Western Europe. We need to take into account the many different ethnic groups and their histories – for example in France the position of Algerians, Tunisians and Moroccans is in many ways very different even though all come from the Maghreb – their varied occupational and residential patterns, their different demographic structures and so on. A major difficulty is that for the most part the kind of French or German or Dutch or Swedish or English – the 'interlanguages' – actually spoken by migrants is poorly or only partially documented. For German, a good start has been made by Klein and Dittmar whose book *Developing grammars* explores the way in which Spanish and Italian guest workers acquire German syntax, and provides detailed descriptions of the language they use (see also Heidelberger Forschungsprojekt 'Pidgin-Deutsche' 1978, and Dittmar and Von Stutterheim 1983. Also Clyne 1984 for a general survey). The work on what might be termed 'pidgin French' spoken by migrant workers in France is much sparser.[1]

The one major exception is what is usually called Black English, or in the USA the Black English Vernacular (BEV), probably one of the best-studied minority languages. But applying a term such as 'communicative competence', with its apparent corollary of communicative *incompetence*, to

---

[1] See, however, de Herédia 1983, and some chapters in GRECO 13. There is, too, more recent, largely unpublished work on what is known as 'Beur' speech. There are also some accounts of 'foreigner talk', the language used by native speakers, say Dutch bureaucrats, when talking to foreigners (e.g. Snow *et al.* 1981).

Black English might on the face of it lead to deep and deserved trouble. The terminology risks serious and damaging misinterpretation. What is at issue at this point is the explosive subject of language deficit, or deprivation or disadvantage.

Bearing in mind the restrictions already put on the term, when one says that a Turkish speaker lacks communicative competence when interacting with a native German speaker, the meaning should be clear. After all, the person is a *Turk* with all that implies linguistically and culturally. He or she has his or her own native language which is by any standards rather different from German. To say a native German speaker is communicatively incompetent in Turkish should likewise pose no problem. However, what can it possibly mean to say that a *Black English* speaker manifests poor communicative competence when interacting with a *native* English speaker? That the Black English speaker is incompetent in his or her own tongue? It does not, or at least should not, though that was the accepted view of Black speech for many years in the United States and in this country. That interpretation is not intended here.

To make the point absolutely clear, let me add that the native speaker of Standard English is likely to be as incompetent in Black English as a speaker of the latter may be in the language of the former. For we are dealing at the very least with varieties or dialects of the same language, and the same statement could be made about the competence/incompetence of native English speakers using different English dialects, though this too may be open to misinterpretation (see chapter 9). Regarding Black English, however, some people would go further, arguing that it is a language or 'mother tongue' like Urdu or Arabic or Turkish, and should be treated as such.

None of this would matter – indeed the question probably would not arise – if we were dealing with populations which did not have to interact in a context in which languages and their speakers are hierarchically ordered (cf. Edwards, J. R. 1979:2). That is, where one language, dialect or code is in several senses dominant. Thus, although in interaction between two speakers there may be limited competence on both sides (or perhaps no overlap between two sets of competences), the incompetence of one party may well not be seen as incompetence at all. The incompetence of the 'other' – *your* lack of competence to talk to *me* – is what is at stake when interaction occurs in situations in which the dominant language or dialect or code prevails. You are disadvantaged because different – from *me*.

This reinforces the point that competence is no easy matter to describe, let alone *ascribe*, to any individual or group. However, it is equally clear that people are obliged to come out of the enclave, as it were, and interact directly with the receiving society on the receiving society's terms. Then the consequences of differential competences can be quite severe.

There are several domains in which this could be demonstrated. One is employment, insofar as it is not of the enclosed type mentioned earlier – and it should be said that the majority of migrant workers are not as ghettoised as is Ahmed in the example cited. The issues pertinent to this domain include not just the relationship between language competence, skill training and social mobility – what the French call *promotion* – but also the social linguistic aspects of all relationships found at work: between management and worker and between worker and worker in industrial disputes or in the day to day life of the shop floor (see Brooks and Singh 1979:94, 98). Another domain is interaction with the bureaucratic system, especially the state bureaucracy – what might be called bureaucratic encounters. Recent research in this field makes it a particularly interesting one to examine as it underlines the point about the complexity of the phenomenon of communicative competence, and also raises the more fundamental question of the significance or otherwise of language as such.

BUREAUCRATIC ENCOUNTERS

Some of the most detailed ethnographic studies of interaction between native and non-native speakers of English in bureaucratic contexts have been made by the American anthropologist John Gumperz and his associates (*Discourse strategies* and *Language and social identity*, both published in 1982). Their work has involved research not only in the United States but also in Britain and Norway, and in India.

Gumperz focuses on conversational interaction ('Discourse I'), the communicative processes found in discourse, and the communicative strategies that speakers employ (Gumperz 1982a, 1982b). In the 'Introduction' (with J. Cook-Gumperz) to an important collection of papers concerned with this research it is suggested that in contemporary bureaucratic society 'communicative resources . . . can be every bit as essential as real property resources were once considered to be' (Gumperz 1982b: 5). In certain kinds of speech event they could be critical: for example in exchanges between speakers of unequal status who come from different cultural and linguistic backgrounds, interacting in situations in which one party is a 'gate-keeper' with the power to 'decide whether the individual should have access to opportunities, resources, or facilities' (Jupp, Roberts and Cook-Gumperz 1982:249).

Gumperz argues that linguistic and cultural 'interference' – or perhaps what Hymes calls 'sociolinguistic interference' (1971b:288) – may affect the performance even of those with a high standard of formal competence in the English language, especially when they are under stress (in a job interview, at a committee meeting, or under cross-examination in a courtroom). Linguistic 'interference' here means the 'transferral of elements from one language to another' (Taeschner 1983:168). Cultural interference I would gloss as coding and decoding information in one culture by reference to cultural codes appropriate to another (what anthropologists call 'ethnocentrism'). In Gumperz's view the linguistic and cultural are intertwined in that the way discourse is organised varies from culture to culture. There are culturally distinct conversational conventions – for instance the stage in the proceedings at which speakers make their main point, or the use of prosodic markers to build and give coherence to discourse (Mishra 1982). Their employment by participants from different backgrounds gives rise to the drawing of incorrect inferences, to misunderstandings, and communicative breakdown.

A simple, even trivial, example cited by Gumperz illustrates the point about prosody. It concerns the word 'gravy'. He reports that at a major British airport, the Indian women workers in the staff cafeteria were thought to be sullen by their own supervisor and by the staff they served. In fact the servers and the staff came into brief contact only when the latter were queueing for their meals. Gumperz observed that while only a few words were exchanged they were often felt to be uttered in a hostile way. What was happening was that the Indian servers instead of asking a polite, English-style question: 'gravy?' (rising intonation), were making a polite Indian-style statement: 'gravy' (falling intonation) which was interpreted as surly, take it or leave it.

These points are further illustrated in some extremely detailed analyses of particular dialogues. One in particular concerns an interview between a British staff member of a counselling centre and an Indian teacher referred to the centre to seek advice on how to improve his language (Gumperz 1982: ch. 8; Mishra 1982a). In this interview it is clear that there is a total lack of understanding, on both sides, of the conversational conventions being employed. Both parties become more and more baffled as the 90 minute interview goes on, and the result is total communicative breakdown.

A similar picture emerges from the work of Dittmar and his associates on the speech of migrant workers in Germany in interaction with native German speakers (Dittmar and Von Stutterheim 1983). However, Dittmar would not want to suggest, as Gumperz at times appears to do, that communicative breakdown of this kind in any way engenders stereotyping or racial hostility. The causes are much more complex than that, though interaction can certainly reinforce discrimination or at least a sense of it, when one party is 'incompetent', or adjudged to be incompetent, in the language of the other. This research nevertheless reveals at what deep and hidden levels the barriers to communication are to be located, and as Dittmar and Von Stutterheim say, 'the notion of "L2" competence should go beyond the mere description of the respective linguistic devices' (p. 195). There may also be immediate practical consequences when what is at stake is some welfare resource, or a job or an apartment. The interlocutor (an employer, a social worker, a housing officer) may have a great deal of work to do to 'constitute the message' (Dittmar and Von Stutterheim 1983:209), and the applicant may simply not get what he or she wants.

Sometimes people *do* have the knowledge and ability to communicate under these conditions, but do not use it, as the work of Labov has shown (see also Hymes 1971b:276, and Cazden 1970 [1972]:308). Albert's research in Burundi (1972), which I could parallel from my own experience in East Africa, provides an interesting example. There, in a traditionally hierarchical society, a peasant is expected to bumble, speak incoherently, in the presence of an aristocrat. They are expected to be dumb, and act dumb. Sometimes, too, people have competence in a dominant language, but *refuse* to use it, deliberately employing some subordinate code to stress solidarity or distance or as a strategic or tactical political weapon (for instance, what Tom Wolfe calls 'Mau-Mauing the flak catchers'). In Britain children sometimes deliberately turn their back on the dominant code – social, cultural and linguistic – of the school. Hewitt's account (1982, 1986) of the use of West Indian Creole by white children in London comprehensives is one example, though recent writing on Black English (Sutcliffe and Wong 1986) suggests that the prevalence of Creole among Black teenagers is also evidence of a more positive project of cultural redefinition.

In a discussion of demands for mother tongue teaching in Britain, Roger Ballard (personal communication) has also suggested that these reflect positive attempts to create what he terms 'no-go' areas within the receiving society, seeking to maintain an enclave as an autonomous domain. Referring to 'the fiction of "Me no speakee Eengleesh"' he argues that an apparent lack of knowledge of the host language functions as a device which controls communication with the receiving society on the part of immigrants – by and for them. It obliges the host institutions (for example management in a factory) to operate through individuals designated as spokespersons by the immigrants themselves.

In some cases this may be so, but language brokers may not always be as innocent as this implies. In an industrial context the result might be the creation of pockets of solidarity of an ethnic kind which cut across other ties of solidarity that might be fostered between those who come from different ethnic groups. Once again the costs need to be taken into account.

IMMIGRANTS, EDUCATION AND LANGUAGE

Thus far the discussion has dealt mainly with male and female immigrants who entered Britain, France or Germany as adults without knowledge of the dominant language, or speaking varieties often thought by native speakers to be deficient in some way. Indeed they may be associated with communicative incompetence in the sense defined. Depending on their situation and needs in the receiving society, they will acquire knowledge of the 'L2', or their existing knowledge will deepen, though except for the work of Klein and Dittmar on 'developing grammars' there is little systematic information on how this happens and in what ways (see also de Herédia 1983 for France). There is, however, another section of the population which, as we saw in chapter 6, is of increasing importance: the so-called 'second generation'. What has been happening to the children?

The 'second generation' may be divided into two groups: those who came as children in the late 1960s and early 1970s, and those born and brought up in the receiving countries. I will concentrate on the recent past, and discuss what was happening to the first group in the mid-1970s, examining their experience of education.

First, France. Because of the way immigration developed in the late 1960s and early 1970s the demographic structure of the immigrant child population of France was rather skewed. There were relatively few of school-leaving age, rather more in the secondary age group, and a huge number moving through the primary schools. In the Académie de Lyon, for example, in 1975–6, there were roughly three times as many foreign children in primary and nursery schools as there were in secondary schools: 32,000 as against 11,000. Within the schools the proportion of immigrant children varied enormously between communes. In some areas percentages of 50% or more – even up to 100% – were not uncommon (see Grillo 1985). In those areas the high and increasing proportion of immigrants in the schools led many French parents to withdraw their own children from the state school system and place them in the private sector. This accounts in part for the vehement hostility with which proposals to reform that sector were greeted during 1984.

What progress were immigrant children making in school? At the secondary level the French system still retains a strong element of streaming. Although initially all children go to a 'CES' (what in Britain would be called a 'Comprehensive'), they are rapidly sorted into three tracks: one leading eventually to a lycée and the *baccalauréat* (roughly equivalent to what in Britain was the 'grammar school' stream), another to technical education at a 'CET', and a third confined solely to the CES. In the mid 1970s few immigrants were going on to the lycées, if they had any success it was in gaining entry to the technical colleges. The majority, however, continued at the CES, generally in the lowest classes, the 'CPPN' and 'CPA' streams. In the latter the curriculum consisted of reading, writing and maths (35% of the allocated time), training for a trade (23%), and sport (20%) They were known colloquially as 'the dustbin classes'. There was one further type of school to which children might be sent, the 'SES'. These *Sections d'Education Specialisée* were originally established for children with an 'intellectual deficit', but whereas North African children made up some 5% of the child population as a whole, they formed 20% to 30% of the SESs. In fact proportionately ten times as many North African youngsters were classified as subnormal in educational terms as were classified bright and sent on to a lycée. That this pattern was not confined to Lyons may be seen in the national figures cited by Charlot for the 1977–8 school year (1981:103), and a similar picture emerges from Germany and Scandinavia (Pfaff 1981, Rist 1978, Skutnabb-Kangas 1981, 1984, Willke 1975).

And what of Britain? There has been a great deal of research over the last twenty years on the educational performance of immigrant children in this country (reviewed in Tomlinson 1983, chs 3 and 4), reflecting the extent to which it has been a matter of concern to those involved. That concern led in 1979 to the establishment of the Rampton/Swann committee of inquiry which was asked to give priority to the case of children of West Indian origin. This they did in the 1981 interim report, concluding: 'While we accept that there will perhaps always be some children who underachieve and for various reasons will fail to reach their full potential, our concern is that West Indian children *as a group* are underachieving in our educational system' (Rampton Report 1981:10).

The evidence for this is complex and much debated, especially when it derives not from the 'objective' results of school performance but from special tests administered by researchers. Nevertheless, two things are quite clear. First, certain immigrant groups, notably West Indians, but also, for example, Bangladeshis (Swann Report 1985:163, and Annex C of chapter 3), emerge from British schools with fewer and poorer quality results in terms of examination passes than do other pupils. Thus a survey of six LEAs revealed that 'O' Level and CSE results for English and maths were much poorer for West Indians than for others (Rampton Report 1981:6–7). At 'Advanced' Level, whereas 13% of Asians and 12% of others obtained at least one pass, the figure was as low as 2% for West Indians (Rampton Report 1981:8). Further surveys cited in Swann (p. 60) showed that, taking children of working class background only, 'high performance' in form examinations was achieved by 9% of West Indians, 16% of Asians, and 18% of 'Others'. Low performers constituted 41%, 21% and 20% respectively. Although there is some evidence that performance is improving, it is not difficult to conclude with Swann (p. 60) that 'West Indian children are not doing at all well in the educational system'.

Secondly, where streaming occurs, immigrant children, again especially those of West Indian origin, are generally found in the lower echelons (Tomlinson 1983:38–41). In 1970, for example, at a time when selection procedures at 11 + were still general, national figures showed that whereas 20% of non-immigrant pupils were in maintained grammar schools, the figures for West Indians, Pakistanis and Indians were 1.6%, 2.5% and 3.9% (in Townsend 1971:57). Within secondary schools, there was a concentration of immigrants in the lower classes (Townsend and Brittan 1972:51–3, 151), and Townsend also recorded a 'considerable imbalance' among the children attending schools for the educationally subnormal: proportionately there were roughly three times as many West Indian children in such schools as might be expected (see Coard 1971). More recent research surveyed by Tomlinson (1983) indicates that the overall distributional picture changed little during the 1970s (cf. Edwards, V. 1979:4).

Neither in Britain nor France do immigrants perform *uniformly* badly, and there is some indication (see Tomlinson 1983:41–2) that the results for girls are better than those for boys, a fact which any explanation for educational underachievement must surely have to take into account. Nevertheless, this apart, and aside from the individuals who do better (or worse) than others, it is clear that particular groups of immigrants (West Indians in Britain, Algerians in France, Turks in Germany) do especially poorly in our schools.

EDUCATIONAL UNDERACHIEVEMENT AND THE PLACE OF LANGUAGE

Let us follow a 14-year-old Indian or Pakistani boy from the language centre to his secondary modern or comprehensive school. In the centre he has learned a certain amount of basic English and can hold a conversation, or at least answer questions: he can write the answers to questions, usually of the comprehension type on work he has read: he can write a connected description of something he knows well, such as life in his home village, and he can read fairly simple texts with reasonable fluency . . . When he arrives in his first class he is perhaps one of ten immigrants in a class of 30 pupils and the teacher sees his task as that of teaching Geography, Physics, Mathematics, or History rather than basic English. The new arrival is soon floundering in a world of contours, burettes, pentagons or Salic Law which must make him seriously doubt if in his preceding twelve months he really was learning English. (TOWNSEND 1971:47)

The reasons for the poor educational performance of certain immigrant groups have been the subject of an intense, at times extremely bitter, debate both in Britain (cf. Stone 1981) and abroad, notably the USA. In discussing this issue I will concentrate on the part played by linguistic and socio-linguistic factors in an immigrant child's educational experience. This does not mean language is the only important issue. Although it is undoubtedly a highly significant factor in a society which places such emphasis on verbal skills in its own tongue as, for example, does France, I share the view that there is no *single* explanatory factor.

Summarising the debate, Jeffcoate (1984) identifies eight types of explanation which have been proposed for underachievement:

(1) genetic endowment;
(2) material deprivation;
(3) inadequate upbringing;
(4) a fragmented cultural inheritance;
(5) cultural discontinuity between home and school;
(6) racism in school and society;
(7) informal teaching methods; and
(8) rejection of school values.

(JEFFCOATE 1984:71, *I have added the numbers*)

This omits specific mention of language, though it may be subsumed under (5), cultural discontinuity.

Several, though not all, of the factors these various explanations imply are likely to be significant, including (6) racism, which Rampton (1981:70) concluded 'does play a major part in the educational underachievement of West Indian children, without being its sole cause'. One, however, can be rejected out of hand.

Along with most contemporary commentators I would refuse any explanation which referred to genetic endowment, by which is meant inherited intelligence: the idea that certain groups are intellectually less well-endowed than others. The reasons for rejecting such an explanation are, or should be, well-known, though the Swann Report considered the arguments serious enough to commission a survey of the evidence. The results of that survey, and the very substantial literature on which it is based, should be examined carefully by anyone who entertains any doubts.

Among the other factors, it is significant that the schools which immigrants attend, certainly in France, are not well-endowed with resources, and not popular with teachers. In one immigrant area of Lyons, which had a dozen primary establishments with high proportions of immigrants, 52% of the staff had served less than one year in their school. The school must also be seen as a class, as well as a racial, institution, which in a real way reproduces certain social patterns of success and failure. Most immigrant children come from manual or semi-skilled working class backgrounds, and this obviously affects their educational performance, as it does that of indigenous White children. Finally, no explanation can confine itself to education alone. To explain what happens there, we need to have regard to the total social and cultural situation in which a group is located both inside and outside the school.

How does language fit in? In later chapters we shall see that this is a complex question, but in one respect the answer is obvious. Let us go back to the simple point that the dominant language (English or French) is not the mother tongue of most immigrant children, and trace the assessment of these children through the system. In France, streaming in the secondary schools is based initially on examinations taken in the final primary year, supplemented by teachers' reports. The tests consist of exercises in composition, dictation, vocabulary, comprehension of a text, grammar, conjugation, writing, and mathematics. A similar test in the secondary school to check the initial streaming includes numerical series, sets, diagrammatic difference tests, verbal analogy, meaning of proverbs, vocabulary, and verbal classification encompassing meaning and grammar. This implies considerable skill in the French language. When immigrant children lack this skill then it is obvious that they will face severe difficulties in making progress at school. Like the child envisaged by Townsend they will 'flounder'.

It is possible that in the 1980s, such children are a thing of the past, their situation characteristic of the early years of mass family immigration. In the 1960s and 1970s, however, the school authorities in Britain and France were faced with large numbers of children – in some areas overwhelming numbers – who had a severe language problem in that they had insufficient grasp of French or English to cope. In 1970, for example, according to Townsend, at a time when a significant 'bulge' of immigrant children was about to go through the education system, schools reported that some 43,000 pupils were so weak in English that they were 'unable to follow a normal school curriculum with profit to themselves' (Townsend, 1971:36). This figure represented 16% of all immigrant pupils, but in many areas, especially in the combinations of the Midlands and the North West, the figures were much higher (for example, 27% in the LEAs of Bradford, Leicester and Wolverhampton, 35% in Bedfordshire, 40% in Warley, see Townsend 1971:114–19). No systematic figures are available for France (or indeed for Britain after 1972), but certainly for children of North African and Portuguese origin the picture was very similar.

From the 1960s onwards in both Britain and France educational policy for immigrant children meant policy designed to cope with what was usually thought to be a short-term problem of a language gap. In France, although policy-makers in general saw immigrant culture as a whole as an obstacle to the successful participation of immigrants in the educational system, in practice, and perhaps fortunately, educational action concentrated on only one aspect of culture: language. Ignorance of French, which obviously creates severe practical problems for the teachers as well as for the taught, seemed to be the one problem open to practical solution; a technical matter with which the administration could cope. The main effort therefore went into the establishment of special classes aimed at children who spoke hardly any French at all, though classes were few and far between: 1 for every 1,400 foreign pupils in the Rhône (see Grillo 1985 and Charlot 1981).

In Britain, too, there was a history of special provision for the teaching of English as a second language ('ESL') for immigrant children (see *inter alia* Edwards, 1984a:50–7). In the early years, during what Swann calls the 'assimilationist phase' of policy, when, for example, various 'dispersal' or 'bussing' schemes to break up concentrations of immigrant pupils at certain schools were in vogue, this special provision took a variety of forms. There were some separate language centres attended on a full or part-time basis, but about half the LEAs preferred placing the pupils for part of their time in special language classes located within their own school, a system which Townsend (1971:44) equates with the 'withdraw classal', long used for remedial teaching. The use of such classes increased during the 1970s and the Swann Report cites a DES survey which showed that in 1983 they catered for 70% of the 104,000 children who were then being provided with additional language help.

Reviewing past and present policy, the Swann Report (pp. 389–92), which throughout sets itself against 'separatism', argues against the use of language centres which isolate the child from the mainstream school and curriculum. The committee also believed that there were educational and social arguments against withdrawal classes and came out in favour of 'integrated provision within the mainstream school' (p. 392). Following Bullock, they urge that 'the needs of learners of English as a second language should be met by provision within the mainstream school as part of a comprehensive programme of language education for *all* children' (p. 771). This view of 'language across the curriculum' would, however, require a radical reorientation, on the part of teachers, of their ideas and practices, as it affects everyday, routine classroom procedures.

That over 100,000 children in Britain are currently thought to be in need of help with English to the extent that they are dispatched to special classes shows that the problem is a considerable one that is likely to be around for some time. Not all would agree with that. Jeffcoate (1984:130–1), for example, comparing the present-day situation of South Asian immigrants with that of nineteenth-century Eastern European Jewish refugees, predicts that 'in the near future' the former will become like the latter are now, taking up English as their predominant language whilst retaining key elements of their religion and culture. Already, he suggests, 'most ethnic minority children are British born and speak English perfectly well' (p. 85). ESL is required only for a residual category of recent arrivals and those with special needs, and then on a short-term basis only.

Even if this were true, it would not affect the case for the radical reshaping of English language teaching attitudes and practices advocated by Bullock and Swann. However, I would agree with Verity Saifullah Khan that although in the *long run* a shift towards English as a first language is likely, that shift will not affect all minorities to the same extent or in the same way. In the case of South Asians, she says, 'the arrival of dependent wives and children, and the continuation of traditional marriage practices, will ensure contact and revitalization of the home-based dialect . . . (thus) *for several decades hence*, there will be many five-year-olds starting school with very little English' (Saifullah Khan 1980:83, my emphasis).

Other factors, such as degree of concentration and enclavement in neighbourhoods, work, school, and domestic and social relations, will also influence the extent to which English becomes the primary language of the children, and also *what kind of English is spoken*. It would be surprising if there were not to emerge several 'ethnic' varieties of English, alongside those of region and class, interacting with them in complex ways. Such varieties already exist and have long done so (see de Herédia 1983:122–4 for France). It is often taken as self-evident that anyone born in Britain will necessarily 'speak English perfectly well'. But what do terms like 'speak English' and 'perfectly well' actually mean? To explore this point further let us take the complex case of children of West Indian origin.

THE WEST INDIAN LANGUAGE ISSUE

In the 1960s, young West Indians were not seen as having a language problem, at least not of the same kind as that faced by children from South Asia. Townsend records that there were few West Indians in language centres and classes visited by his research team (1971:40), and those LEAs with large numbers of West Indians in their areas often reported fewer pupils with 'weak' English by comparison with authorities with substantial South Asian populations. This did not mean that West Indian children had no language problem. Townsend found that in many LEAs such children were quite often thought to have language difficulties, but they were generally placed not with other immigrants but with 'retarded English pupils'. This, he suggested, 'seems to stem from the belief that the West Indians' language difficulty is due to some kind of retardation or lack of ability; many teachers do in fact tend to regard West Indians as speaking English but speaking it badly, and this implies that what is needed is not language teaching but language correction' (1971:50). Townsend argued that West Indian pupils did have a 'special linguistic need', and unless provision were made to meet it their underachievement in education and at work would be unlikely to disappear (p. 110). During the 1970s there was increasing recognition that the problem resided not in the linguistic or intellectual 'deficiency' of the West Indian pupil, but in the 'difference' between their speech and Standard English. Viv Edwards, however, claims that by the time that this difference was officially recognised, the problem had disappeared, or at least changed as 'by the mid-1970s the majority had been born in Britain and could produce speech indistinguishable or at least close to the white norm' (1984:66). This was accepted by the Rampton Report which argued that whatever may have been the situation of those born in the Caribbean, 'We do not believe that for the majority of West Indian children in our schools, who were born and brought up in this country, linguistic factors play a part in underachievement' (p. 25), 'linguistic factors have been unduly emphasised and mask the more complex underlying causes of underachievement. We do not accept that, for the vast majority of British-born West Indian children in our schools today, language plays any part in underachievement' (p. 70).

However, Rampton accepts that the speech employed by West Indians is not always 'close to the white norm', and recognises two languages or varieties of language, both of which are used by West Indians: Standard English and Creole (see below). Thus the children 'need to be helped to understand clearly the differences and similarities between these two language forms, their relative values in different contexts, and the uses to which they should be put' (Rampton Report 1981:25). Hence their advocacy of a 'repertoire' approach, and 'the imaginative and constructive use of a child's home language' to assist the process of acquiring the ability to read and write Standard English. (See also the Swann Report 1985:419–25, and Annex G to chapter 7).

Rampton's point is not that West Indians or others born in this country can understand Standard English, and *therefore* no further problem arises, but that while many can produce Standard English, their mother tongue is something else (though essentially a variety of English) which among other things is undervalued *by both Whites and Blacks* (see Edwards, V. 1979, and Sutcliffe 1982 on this last point) with the result that the West Indian child's self-esteem is adversely affected. To the extent that this happens now there continues to be present a (socio)linguistic factor in underachievement.

The discussion of the West Indian language scene is complicated by at least two factors. One is a previous history of characterising West Indian speech as 'bad', i.e. 'deficient', English, in turn a sign of cognitive deficiency (an issue taken up in chapter 9). No linguist or anthropologist, and precious few educationists, give any credence to such a belief, though it is one that is probably still quite widely held in Britain. This historical legacy is such that sometimes any suggestion of *difference* is assumed to be a covert way of signalling *deficit*. Thus in the late 1960s and early 1970s when linguists in the United States were moving towards the position that the Black English Vernacular constituted a distinct linguistic system, it was suggested by some Black radicals that 'what is being promulgated as "Black English" is really a phenomenon out of the heads of a few white middle-class liberals' (cited in Labov 1982:178). By the late 1970s, however, the view that 'BEV has well-formed rules of its own, and forms a distinct linguistic system' (Labov 1982:178) was widely accepted. Of relevance and interest here is the so-called 'Black English' law suit (Labov 1982, Smitherman 1980a, 1984).

In the USA social progress often comes from citizens using the courts to secure or expand their rights, as in Lau v. Nichols cited in the previous chapter. The 'Black English' case concerned a number of Black children from a housing project in a mainly white suburb of Ann Arbor, Michigan, who attended the local Martin Luther King elementary school. The children were making poor progress at school, so their mothers, with the help of a law aid agency, took the school authorities to court asserting *inter alia* that the authorities had failed in their obligation under section 1703(f) of the Equal Educational Opportunity Act of 1974. The relevant section affirms: 'No state shall deny equal educational opportunity to an individual on account of his or her race, color, sex or national origin, by (f) the failure by an educational agency to take appropriate action to overcome language barriers that impede equal participation by its students in its instructional programs' (cited in Labov 1982). The judge accepted that there was a case to answer and that Black English, which the plaintiffs claimed was a distinct language and one spoken by their children, could constitute a 'language barrier' if it could be shown that the differences from Standard English were associated with a history of racial discrimination.

At the subsequent hearings the plaintiffs called a number of linguists as experts who demonstrated the differences between BEV and the standard language, and testified that attitudes hostile to Black speech on the part of teachers constituted a source of discrimination. It was also argued that although Black children of middle-class backgrounds might employ both BEV and Standard English, others 'not being adequate code-switchers . . . were . . . experiencing language-based problems in the school context' (Smitherman 1980a:30). The judge ruled for the plaintiffs and gave the authorities thirty days to come up with an appropriate programme. This they did with a proposal to enhance teacher training and change attitudes towards BEV.

In reviewing the case Smitherman argued that this policy was inadequate in that it tackled only half the problem – teacher attitudes – and more direct measures were needed to enhance the children's command of Standard English. She acknowledges, however, that the case was an important one which gave the Black community in the USA 'yet another weapon in our struggle to be free' (1980a:34).

The contrast between BEV and Standard English is similar to that made by Rampton/Swann between Standard English and Creole, but the linguistic situation is more complex than that as Smitherman's remarks about the codes available to working–class and middle-class Blacks suggests. In fact the sheer complexity of the language scene among West Indians in Britain is the second factor which complicates discussion.

Briefly, one way of conceptualising that language scene has been to view it as comprising not two contrasting languages (or varieties of English), but a continuum of linguistic variation. Strictly speaking, there are two inter-related continua: one in the Caribbean, the other in Britain, which together form a single linguistic (and social) field. West Indians in Britain may speak a form of language which is close to that also spoken in the Caribbean Islands and which is referred to as Creole or 'Patois' or colloquially as 'broken'. Creoles vary from island to island, but to take the case of that spoken on Jamaica, differences from Standard English are highly marked and include phonology, vocabulary, the formation of plurals, the use of pronouns, verbal forms, the absence of a passive voice, the use of copulas, morphology, negation and interrogation (see Edwards, V. 1979:22 ff., Sutcliffe 1982: ch. 5). To all intents and purposes it is a different language. In Britain, what is called Creole is a variant of the language spoken in the Caribbean. This, too, varies according to island of origin, but what Sutcliffe (1982) calls 'British Jamaican Creole' is spreading among young West Indians from other islands (Edwards, V. 1979:38). The current generation, 'although speaking the local variety of English to varying degrees, [they] are also able in the majority of cases to broaden Jamaican features in their speech to the point where it becomes Patois . . . At the same time this Patois differs from the original Caribbean variety' (Sutcliffe 1982:152, cf. Edwards, V. 1986:103).

It has also been suggested that as children grow up they may adopt 'broader' speech, whether consciously or unconsciously is not clear, to stress a Black identity (Edwards, V. 1979:38, Sutcliffe 1982:58 ff., Sutcliffe and Wong eds. 1986) thus emphasising solidarity (with peers) or distance (from authority) depending on the addressee and situation. British Jamaican, which Rosen and Burgess (1980:58) describe as 'a magnetic, political, social and peer group dialect', can in certain circumstances therefore become what Halliday (1978) calls an 'antilanguage', and may be used as such by *White* children (Hewitt 1982, 1986).

Against the continuum perspective is Viv Edwards's recent work. In *Language in a black community* (1986), based on a survey of young, British-born black people of Jamaican origin living in the West Midlands, she argues that there exists for them not a linguistic continuum but two 'model' varieties, English and Patois. Thus their situation resembles that of members of a 'bilingual community' (p. 48).

The issue between the continuum and the bilingual model is here less important than Edwards's demonstration that use of Patois varies situation-ally: generally little was employed in formal interviews (for example with the White researchers), a great deal in informal peer-group conversations. Nonetheless, a certain proportion of her informants (13%) consistently made extensive use of Patois in *all* situations while there was a similar number (11%) who employed it only in the most informal, intra-group contexts. Interestingly, Edwards suggests that these two groups may be characterised in the second case as generally female, with high educational aspirations, doing well at school, and in the first as male, educational underachievers (p. 116).

The extent to which informants were willing (and able) to use Patois is, argues Edwards, a function of their integration within the Black com-munity. The example of 'Don', whose life circumstances Edwards describes (p. 87 ff.), shows that some at least lead a life encapsulated within Black networks and institutions and employ a large proportion of Patois elements in even the most formal, 'White' contexts. This is clearly, as Edwards accepts, in turn a function of the social and economic environment which in certain areas encourages a high degree of enclavement.

That some, though by no means all, Black children are 'fully competent speakers' (Edwards, V. 1986:103) of both a variety of English and a form of Patois, and can therefore switch codes, apparently at will, is evidently what led Rampton/Swann to reject an explanation of West Indian scholastic underachievement by reference to what is called 'dialect interference', for example when a child reproduces in written work language forms which diverge from Standard English (see Edwards, V. 1979: ch. 4 and 1986:27 ff., Rampton 1981:24 ff., Swann 1985:421–2, and Sebba 1986 on code-switching). Nonetheless it is clear that unconscious linguistic, sociolinguistic and cultural 'interference', as that was defined in our earlier discussion of the work of Gumperz, does occur in the educational context, and not only in the case of West Indians or other immigrant groups (Cheshire 1982b:53). For example, as Viv Edwards points out 'The common assumption that West Indians speak "English" may lead both speaker and addressee to think that the message has been communicated successfully when this is not in fact the case' (1979:61). Driver's account of relations in the classroom between West Indian children and White teachers (1979) shows the significance of both linguistic and paralinguistic factors for the teacher's (mis)interpretation of the student's intentions. Research by Green (cited in Swann Report 1985:25, and in Annex B of chapter 2) which demonstrates the varied classroom experience of pupils of different ethnic origin also suggests that culturally distinct ways of organising discourse (e.g. in initiating questions and responses to questions) may play a crucial role in that as in other contexts of social interaction (cf. Gibson 1986:89 who lays greater stress than many recent researchers on the significance of the language factor in education).

CONCLUSION

Many of the questions raised in this discussion of the West Indian language issue – such as what constitutes 'speaking English' – take us well beyond those which can be readily accommodated within an analytical framework of cultural pluralism, nation and identity. They thus anticipate the material of the following chapters when the focus shifts from nation to class. However, let me briefly conclude the present chapter by stating agreement with Rampton, Swann and others who favour a 'repertoire' approach to language. Coupled with the perspective in which language is taught 'across the curriculum' it is likely to provide a way in which some of the educational problems of groups such as Algerians, Turks, South Asians (as well as West Indians) can be tackled. What this approach means, however, is that both teachers and taught will have to become keen practising sociolinguists. This brings us once again to policy implications.

The situation we are discussing cannot be seen primarily in linguistic terms, and any policy which identified the problem as solely linguistic, and proposed remedial action in those only, would be misplaced. This may seem obvious, but a consideration, for example, of French educational policy for migrants' children or for industrial language training would show that it is not. Nonetheless, there is an aspect to the situation which has centrally to do with language: it would be different if the language issue were not there.

Language problems do not, however, reside solely in what are tradition-ally thought of as linguistic factors, but in what Jupp *et al.* call the 'hidden process', 'the subtle and unconscious ways in which syntax, prosody and lexicon work together' (1982:248). Hence language policy must be based on a broad, social and cultural conception of linguistic competence. Such policy also needs to take into account the several ways in which competence in the dominant language and the mother tongues are linked. This in turn requires a revaluation of attitudes towards those languages. As we shall see in later chapters, attitudes towards language are a significant part of the problem. I fully concur that 'a speaker who is made ashamed of his own language habits suffers a basic injury as a human being. To make anyone, especially a child, feel so ashamed is as indefensible as to make him feel ashamed of the colour of his skin' (Halliday *et al.* 1964:105).

Revaluation has its dangers, however. A senior professor of education in London, a keen social observer with many radical sympathies, tells the following story against himself. Visiting a London comprehensive school to talk to the children he found in one class the usual mix, for London, of races and nationalities. He discussed with them their home languages, asking how many spoke West Indian Creoles. One boy put his hand up and said that at home his family spoke a French Creole. The professor, in an unguarded moment, replied 'That's nice.' 'What's nice about it?', answered the boy. Romantic celebration of the 'folk' language may mean little in the world of jobs and housing.

Finally we must abandon the idea that this is *their* problem, in which it is sufficient to introduce measures for them, but not for us (see Jupp *et al.* 1982). This is the lesson of the Rampton/Swann Report. Why should the onus be on *them* to become communicatively competent in *our* codes? After all, in some parts of the world multilingualism is the norm. I am not suggesting that everyone should learn Urdu or Arabic or Turkish – though for some people in some jobs that would seem crucial. What could be learned are skills of communicative decoding. In East African cities many languages are spoken as a matter of course, and people do not make as heavy weather as we do of trying to understand someone else speaking their language. The decoding of other people's discourse, a task which we and the French find so difficult, may be less of a problem than we think.

8

LANGUAGE AND SOCIAL DIFFERENTIATION

He walked into my oratory, without asking my permission, and recited first one verse, then another, then a third. He began to say the morning prayer and went right on to the end. When he had finished he picked up his cross and went away again. He spoke the language of the common people, his accent was poor and the words he used vulgar. It was not easy to follow what he was trying to say.

(GREGORY OF TOURS, *THE HISTORY OF THE FRANKS*, BOOK IX.6)

THE FOLLOWING chapters examine the relationship between language and class in Britain and France. This is a difficult subject because the analytical and theoretical problems raised by a consideration of the two phenomena separately, let alone in combination, are complex. Yet their interconnection touches on key issues for an understanding of industrial and post-industrial societies.

Many cultures have special preoccupations to which debate and argument return time and again. That the British, at any rate the English, are obsessed with 'class' (whatever we mean by that) is, among ourselves, a commonplace. A feature of that obsession, and one that can be traced continuously from at least the fifteenth century, is the belief that we signal class by grammar, vocabulary and perhaps above all accent. This belief is also held by European observers of the English scene. A Dutch colleague obtained a totally false impression of British anthropologists after meeting two whose accents were ripe examples of what is called 'Received Pronunciation' or 'RP' (see below). He himself claimed that in Holland there were only two ways of speaking (the regional dialects, based in the countryside, and the standard language, used in the towns) in no way connected with class, but employed as the situation demanded.

I do not know whether this view of the relationship between language and society in Holland is widely shared by other Dutchmen. Meeus (1979) certainly points to a class-related origin for Standard Dutch, and suggests that there is continuing class-linked variation in the use of dialect and standard in Holland. This is not the only European example. The observation of Gregory of Tours, who thought his own variety of Latin was 'provincial' (Lewis Thorpe in 'Introduction' to Gregory of Tours 1974, p. 39), was made in Merovingian Gaul in the sixth century AD, and earlier, classical, references to linguistic stratification could undoubtedly be cited.

In early modern and modern France, too, social differentiation through language has frequently caused comment, for example in Barère's remarks on 'aristocratic' usage cited in chapter 2. Nevertheless, since the Revolution, the issue of linguistic stratification of that kind has not been accorded the same priority as – the French obsession – the status of French, as a *national* language, *vis à vis* other languages and dialects in France and abroad. Similarly, a concern with language and ethnicity (or rather race) is a predominant cultural theme in the United States.

This is not to deny the existence of linguistic stratification in the United States, still less in France. The point is the degree to which such stratification is a cultural preoccupation. It is this preoccupation which underlies the following discussion. The present chapter documents the association between particular forms of the language and particular social classes, and includes consideration of the relationship between that association and the development of the standard tongues. Chapter 9 turns to an important ideological dimension of linguistic stratification: the idea that there are 'proper' or 'cultivated' forms of speech, and that languages and dialects may be hierarchically ranked. This leads, in chapter 10, to the implications of what I will call the 'hierarchical ordering of communicative practices' for the field of education.

LANGUAGE AND SOCIAL STATUS IN ENGLAND: THE EMERGENCE OF A STANDARD

First, some clarification of analytical and theoretical issues.

In English social linguistics – here I confine myself almost entirely to that – the terms 'language' and 'class' are used in a wide variety of ways. Some differences are marginal, others turn on alternative ways of constituting the datum of inquiry, deriving from quite different theoretical traditions and perceptions of what is expected of the relationship *between* language and class. Often none of these difference are made explicit, and many disputes arise from that.

Language and social differentiation

In this and later chapters I discuss and, where appropriate, draw on a number of different approaches. The first, which is all that will concern us in this chapter, is probably the foremost in terms of its general acceptance, for example in introductory textbooks. For this, the 'sociolinguistic perspective', what is significant is the relationship between hierarchically ordered social categories ('classes') and certain grammatical and phonological habits, themselves seen as hierarchically ordered.

'Class' here refers to 'status groups' in the Weberian sense, though the sociolinguistic conception of class as status probably owes little to Weber himself, and ignores most of his insights. It stems rather from the American (functionalist) sociological tradition from Thorstein Veblen onwards (cf. Burke 1987:6), though that tradition, indeed mainstream British or American sociology and social history generally, has had remarkably little to say about language. Sociolinguists usually take the status distinctions themselves for granted, rarely considering the criteria (income, wealth, property, occupation, type of housing, honour, or some combination of these) which might be employed, and have been employed in non-sociolinguistic social research, still less whose criteria they are. The status groups identified are no more elaborate than the Registrar General's occupational categories, or the advertising world's division of consumers. There is no theoretical limit to the number of strata which may be identified. It depends on how finely boundaries are drawn.

In this approach, language usually means grammar and phonology. Other features are ignored either because they are not thought proper to linguistics or because it is hoped by this to achieve sophistication through rigour. Higher order, macrostructural features, principally dialects and registers, are constructed from these microstructural linguistic elements, and the relationship between the social and the linguistic is conceptualised as a probabilistic correlation between the two: status group X is likely to speak dialect Y.

The perspective tends to be static, a-processual, and a-historical (though it need not be). It has a standard view of history – the accepted history of *the* standard. Interaction *between* classes/strata is dealt with cursorily, if at all – except perhaps in the institutional setting of education and in psychological accounts of the perception of accents. Then, the principal point made time and again is that a wholly irrational and unscientific conception of the value of one set of grammatical and phonological habits operates prejudicially against those who habitually use another.

In Britain the work of Peter Trudgill well illustrates its overall conception of British society. To convey the complexity of the contemporary sociolinguistic scene among English speakers in Britain, Peter Trudgill has on several occasions employed a diagram which may be called 'Trudgill's

153

Triangle' (see Figure 8.1). This illustrates sociolinguistic variation within a continuum, or rather within two inter-related continua. At the base are the regional dialects with no 'natural breaks' between one and another. These represent the English spoken typically in, say, Reading, Glasgow, Belfast or Norwich, to mention four areas recently studied by sociolinguists (Cheshire 1982a, Macaulay 1977, Milroy 1980 and Trudgill 1974, respectively). The vertical axis represents differentiation on lines of status, depending on difference/distance from Standard English. At the apex is speech closest in form to Standard English which is also spoken with RP.

This 'standard' or 'authoritative' way of speaking (and writing) requires closer attention. In chapter 3 I sketched the linguistic and political history of England to the point where in the period 1400–1600 the native tongue – English – became the official language of the crown, replacing French as the principal spoken language of the nobility. But what, at this period, was the native tongue? The development of Old English after the Conquest, whatever other changes of grammar or lexicon occurred, did not markedly disturb the outlines of the dialect map of England. There was probably considerable continuity between the four dialects of Old English and the five principal dialects which evolved in the Middle period: Southern (roughly in the area of Old English West Saxon), South Eastern (Kentish), Northern (Northumbrian), and West and East Midlands (the Mercian dialect divided), with East Midlands sometimes said to form Northeastern and Southwestern branches.

In the sixteenth century, George Puttenham in his advice to aspiring gentlemen authors (*The art of poesie* of 1589) commented that northern speech was 'not so Courtly nor so currant as our southern English is, no more is the far Westerne mans speach; ye shall therefore take the usuall speach of the Court, and that of London and the shires lying about London

Figure 8.1 'Trudgill's triangle' (after Trudgill 1984, p. 42)

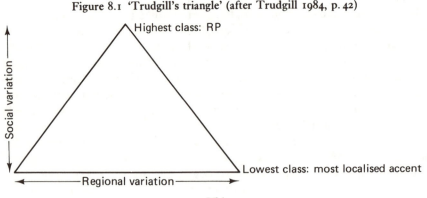

within LX myles, and not much more' (cited in Shaklee 1980:46, and elsewhere). For many years it was accepted that the east Midlands dialect of Middle English almost inevitably emerged, from the fourteenth century onwards, as a 'standard'. The region in which it was spoken was the most important in the country in terms of population and wealth, containing a major commercial and political centre, London, and the two main centres of learning, Oxford and Cambridge. Linguistically the dialect occupied an intermediate place between southern and northern English so that it could act as a sort of common denominator (Baugh 1957:231 ff.). And it was the dialect of Chaucer and other key literary figures of the period. Thus 'Out of (the) variety of local dialects there emerged towards the end of the fourteenth century a written language that in the course of the fifteenth won general recognition and has since become the recognised standard in both speech and writing' (Baugh and Cable 1978:191).

The process of dialect selection is now thought to have been more complex (see summaries in Price 1984:ch. 13, Shaklee 1980, Milroy 1984). There was, for example, a fair amount of writing in all the dialects during the thirteenth and fourteenth centuries, and the dialect of the London area was itself a hybrid drawing, via population movement and migration, on elements from Essex, Kent, Surrey, Middlesex, East Anglia, and perhaps most important of all the Central Midlands (Samuels 1972, 165–70, Shaklee 1980 and others propose a more northerly influence as well).

It has been suggested that an important contribution to the process of turning this London dialect into a *standard* was made by the clerks of Chancery. J. H. Fisher (1977) shows how the King's embryo bureaucracy, which in the fifteenth century formed a more or less permanent secretariat of about 120 clerks, began after *c.* 1420 to use English as the principal language of record and of written documents such as petitions. In doing so they regularized grammar and spelling, seeking uniformity and clarity. Thus the 'practice of the clerks' (Fisher 1977:898) gave the London dialect a particular direction, and 'It was the language of [the] professional clerks which circulated about the country and established the model for official English between 1420 and 1460 when English was being adopted for government use' (Fisher 1977:890–1). Baugh (in Baugh and Cable, 1978:194) seems sceptical of this, but Fisher's detailed analysis convinces me that the language of the élite, educated *bureaucracy* was as important an influence on standardisation as the work of the major literary figures such as Chaucer. The advent of printing, with Caxton's press from 1476 onwards, thus consolidated a process of standardisation which had already made some progress earlier in the fifteenth century.

Whatever the precise details, from the fifteenth century onwards England had, in the 'King's English', a literary, administrative and eventually educational dialect located originally in the political, commercial and social heartland of the country, and spreading outward from there. To use Anderson's terms (1983), the polity had chosen a particular 'print-vernacular' as 'language-of-state' whose pre-eminence became such that for long afterwards all other forms were of interest only to folklorists, and the history of 'English' became the history of this one dialect.

Regarding its dissemination in the sixteenth century, Dobson offers the following interpretation based on Puttenham:

the common people everywhere spoke dialect and the Standard language was the possession only of the well-born and the well-educated . . . in the Court and the Home Counties one might expect all well-born and well-educated people to use this Standard language, but beyond those limits, though one might still find men who spoke pure Standard English, the greater part of the gentry and scholars were influenced by the speech of the common people . . . in the far West and the North the Standard did not apply at all. (DOBSON 1956:33)

By the mid-sixteenth century, then, the standard language was well on the way to becoming what Wyld (1921:2–3) called a 'class dialect' of the well-born and well-educated, though the process was far from complete. As Dobson says, the gentry in the distant parts of the country had yet to 'learn' the language. That the standardised dialect was a model for admiration and imitation is, however, apparent from many of the contemporary writers on language, of whom Puttenham was but one (see Dobson 1968), and the period saw a rush of dictionaries and guides to correct usage. Interestingly, seven years after the Act of Union there appeared an English-Welsh dictionary and guide to English pronunciation (it is now an important sourcebook, Dobson 1968:11) which was probably intended for the Welsh gentry who aspired to the English language.

This does not mean that the form of Standard English was finally established by the sixteenth century, still less earlier. As Baugh, Dobson and others show, there was constant debate in literary circles on pronunciation, spelling, vocabulary and grammar through to the era of Johnson and Swift, who was closely involved with proposals for an English Academy on the lines of the *Académie Française*. These debates, however, themselves a kind of micro-politics of language, were increasingly internal to a class of *literati* who shared the assumption that there was a standard and disagreed only on what precise features should be included or excluded.

That the origins of Standard English are to be found in Chaucer, Chancery and Caxton (literature, bureaucracy and the media) suggests a formal, *written* standard. Puttenham's advice, however, indicates that the model he had in mind was a *spoken* language (he refers specifically to 'speech'). Some authorities suggest that in the fifteenth and sixteenth centuries the written and spoken languages were closer than nowadays. If so, the subsequent evolution of Standard English involved what I will call a 'double development': of an orthodox, 'grammatical', 'correct' style of writing and spelling, and of a way of speaking associated with a particular stratum of the population which might be close to the written standard in some respects but diverged conspicuously from it in others.

Strictly speaking there was a 'triple development' involving (a) the rise of a standard 'print vernacular'/language of state, (b) differentiation of the spoken language on class lines, and (c) in the non-English-speaking regions the consolidation of (a) and (b) at the expense of local languages and registers. Wyld (1921) partly recognised this, calling (a) 'Literary English'. Concerning (b): 'As regards its name, it may be called Good English, Well-bred English, Upper-class English, and it is sometimes too vaguely referred to as Standard English' (p. 2). He eventually settles on 'Received Standard English', identifying it with 'Public School English'.

This last connection is one widely made in the literature on English pronunciation. Thus Jones's authoritative work *An outline of English phonetics*, originally published in 1918, explains that the system of pronunciation he describes is 'based on my own (southern) speech, and is, as far as I can ascertain, that generally used by those who have been educated at "preparatory" boarding schools and the "Public Schools"' (1969:12, cf. Jones 1960 [1917]: xv–xvi, and Gimson 1980:89). More recently, Trudgill (1983:187) has identified the tiny proportion of the English speaking population (he puts it at 3%, Hughes and Trudgill 1979a:3) who use 'Standard English dialect' with RP as those 'educated at the large Public Schools or (having) acquired the accent as the result of conscious effort or training'.

The role of education in the formation of Standard spoken and written English (and *vice versa*) is discussed in later chapters, but we may note here that the relationship has long been important. The *literati* of the fifteenth and sixteenth centuries were, by definition, educated persons – that Standard English is sometimes called 'Oxford English' is no accident – and at least two of the influential sixteenth–seventeenth century writers on the English language, who encouraged increasing regulation in grammar, spelling and pronunciation, were important educators of their day: Richard Mulcaster, Eton, King's, Christ Church, and the first Headmaster of Merchant Taylors' School in 1561, and Alexander Gil, Corpus Christi, Oxford, and High Master of St Paul's from 1607–35, where one of his pupils was Milton (Dobson 1968:117, 131).

Historically, then, the double development entailed the emergence of two distinct though related standards, both of which, following Wyld, may be referred to as 'class dialects'. Neither should be confused with what most English people actually speak, which is likely to be a regional/social dialect which may differ considerably from the standard(s), though it may overlap with them in complex ways.

'THE BOY LINEKER DONE GREAT': THE STRATIFICATION OF ENGLISH SPEECH

Whereas 'upper class English' has generally been poorly described, and often we are left with the impression that it is no more nor less than an idealised version of the literary language, the English spoken by 'ordinary' men, women and children has been well documented in major surveys from the nineteenth century onwards. The earliest dealt mainly with rural dialects, remote (and dying) forms of the language, usually as far removed as possible from the language of the investigators. The more recent have tended to document the speech of the urban working and lower middle classes. One type of survey prominent since *c.* 1970 is that which follows, albeit not slavishly, the style of analysis pioneered by the American sociolinguist, William Labov. Jenny Cheshire's work in Reading (Cheshire 1982a) provides a good example of what this research sets out to do.

Cheshire's linguistic data are derived from 'natural conversational interaction between speakers of a nonstandard variety of English' (p. 1). Her sources were three groups or gangs of teenagers (one all female, two all male) aged between 11 and 17, whom she recorded in the public adventure playgrounds where they gathered. All the children lived on Council estates, and their parents worked in a variety of unskilled, semi-skilled and skilled jobs. They would therefore be generally agreed to be children of working class background.

Cheshire shows that the language of these children often differed significantly, but systematically, from that of Standard English in verb form, negation, clause syntax, and nominal and adverbial constructions (p. 26):

'We has a muck around in there.'	(p. 32)
''Cos I'm going on fucking holiday, in I.'	(p. 58)
'There wasn't no lights on.'	(p. 65)
'I talks ever so different to what they do.'	(p. 74)
'We was smoking up his nan's, right.'	(p. 77)

Each of these forms, which outrage traditional, prescriptive grammarians of Standard English, are part of a dialect widely used in Reading and indeed elsewhere in southern England. They are thus on a par with the football commentator's 'the boy done great' which achieved some notoriety during the 1986 World Cup.

Cheshire shows, however, that use of this dialect varies. Girls, for example, tend to use 'nonstandard features' less than boys (p. 86, cf. p. 109), but boys also vary amongst themselves in their use of such forms. There is a relationship between language employed and status within the gang, which in turn depends on the individual's standing by reference to what Cheshire calls 'vernacular culture' – 'skill at fighting', 'carrying weapons', (minor) 'criminal activities', having a 'tough' job, dressing in a certain style, and swearing (p. 97 ff.). The higher her informants were ranked in terms of this street culture, the more likely were they to use nonstandard language.

There are problems with Cheshire's data and analysis, stemming partly from the nature of her informants and the type of milieu they represent, but her attempt to link cultural and linguistic practices is an important one which carries the discussion some way beyond other studies in this vein. Taken together with the work of the Milroys (1978, 1980), which examines via the idea of 'social network' the relationship between language use (or rather the maintenance of particular types of language use) and socio-economic status in relatively closed urban working-class communities in Belfast, it shows that a genuinely *sociological* sociolinguistics is beginning to emerge in this country.

There are, however, two issues which Cheshire's study does not address, at least directly. The first, a relatively minor point, concerns the comparison that is made with Standard English. The language usages she describes are invariably identified as 'nonstandard' and, surely unintentionally, Standard English provides a kind of benchmark to which all must be referred: e.g. 'the tense of the verb in conditional sentences referring to past time is not the same in Reading English as it is in Standard English' (p. 49). In the context in which this type of research is produced this is probably inevitable. But it is not always clear what actually constitutes the 'Standard English' with which comparison is made (cf. Stubbs 1980:127). Cheshire is aware of the problem (p. 126), but it remains the case that she is obliged to compare one variety of the language which has been identified through ethnographic research with another which is essentially an idealised variant, the principal informants for which appear to be Randolph Quirk and the author herself.

The second, more important, issue concerns the definition of language on which this and research such as Milroy's is based. The principal features of speech which are investigated are those which pertain to linguistic differences (from Standard English) in matters of syntax and pronunciation. Vocabulary enters little into the discussion, though Cheshire does identify a short list of 'vernacular verbs' (*go* = to say, *leg it* = run away, p. 43) not found in the standard. Vocabulary lists of the kind beloved of traditional dialectologists (what they call a barn in Wessex, for instance, or a dozen ways of calling someone 'left-handed') are not the point here, however. Vocabulary is significant because it is one of the ways in which a world-view is signalled, and the world-view encoded in and through language is among other things what differentiates one class dialect (or rather discourse) from another. This may be illustrated by other ethnography.

One exception to the rule that upper class English has been poorly described is the popular work which followed from Ross's distinction between 'U' (i.e. Upper class) and 'Non-U' usage (1954). Some interesting data are to be found in K. C. Phillipps's *Language and class in Victorian England* which takes Ross's U and Non-U as its starting point. As his title implies, Phillipps's evidence is historical. It does not tell us how contemporary upper class speakers use the language, and in fact changing linguistic usage in the course of the nineteenth century is one of Phillipps's themes. The evidence is also inevitably literary, derived from that part of the written record which attempts, explicitly or implicitly, to reproduce in a text how the language was spoken. The earliest direct oral evidence for the language – the famous and now distorted recording of Tennyson reciting the *Charge of the Light Brigade* – was not made until well into the century. But Phillipps casts his net wide, catching not only the better known Victorian novelists but many minor figures as well as private correspondence.

Language in Victorian England was a decisive marker of social standing, 'a principal, precise, pragmatic, and subtle way of defining one's position, or having it defined by others' (Phillipps 1984:3). Phillipps discusses various ways in which grammatical usage (and changing usage) typified upper class speech. There was, for example, the use of the present tense to express future time, the past for the perfect, 'the absolute use of verbs where in object might be expected' (p. 71) – as in *to find* (a fox). Naturally enough he considers at some length too the question of pronunciation, again a subject of much discussion in contemporary books such as Savage's *The vulgarisms and improprieties of the English language*, published in 1833, and the many texts based on Walker's *A critical pronouncing dictionary and expositor of the English language* of 1791. In grammar and pronunciation there was at any one moment an accepted ('received') usage, though that usage might well be the site of a lively controversy, and change. The degree of tolerance of usages other than the 'received' varied according to the nature of the speaker (old, young, male, female, townsman, countryman) and the context or situation of the verbal exchange – what was permissible for a young man about town could not be allowed in a county lady.

That upper class speech diverged from the literary standard of the day (which in any case was not static) is clear both from the evidence cited by Phillipps and by his own comments. 'It would be wrong', he says, 'to equate upper class English with grammatical correctness' (p. 67), though his own sense of an idealised, 'correct', language is revealed in a remark on the speech of the East End of London where 'the errors of speech were not only numerous, but numerously varied' (p. 81). But if, in Phillipps's opinion (and indeed that of many of his 'informants'), working class speech was 'substandard' (pp. 70, 81), so was that of the upper classes. Indeed, divergence from 'grammatical', literary forms was sometimes quite consciously fostered. As Phillipps comments, 'it was not the part of a high-born lady to sound like a primly grammatical schoolmistress' (p. 40). Thus, for example, *ain't* was frequently used, if opposed by some of the many writers on 'correct' language use whom Phillipps cites. So, too, was *don't* for *does not*, an example of which (*it don't last*) Phillipps gives from a broadcast by Harold Macmillan in 1981.

Phillipps employs a much broader definition of language than that found in much contemporary sociolinguistics. He has many interesting things to say about loudness and silence in conversation (pp. 39–40), and more generally on the way in which discourse was organised around a 'studied casualness' (p. 40). He shows how fashions changed so that at one time it was appropriate to be brief and elliptic, at another long-winded and explicitly detailed (p. 34). He also considers the lexicon, showing that upper class usage – and surely that of other classes too – was distinctive in its combination of form *and* content: not just what one said and how one said it, but how one said what was said. Consider this commentary on the word *fellow*, cited by Phillipps from a book, *Manners for men* by 'Mrs. Humphreys', published in 1897:

In lowly circles a young man is called a *fellow*: young men *fellows*. So it is in good society, but with a distinct difference. It is not easy to make this difference clear. Young men of good position refer very commonly to others of their acquaintance as 'the fellows', but they would not use the word to describe young men generally. Women, young and old, of the lower classes speak of young men generally as 'fellows', but gentlemen never do so. A lady never uses the expression 'a girl and a fellow'. At the same time she may frequently speak of 'young fellows'. I am aware that there is a want of clearness in all this, but it is a matter among many others that can only be acquired by being accustomed to the usage of good society.

(IN PHILLIPS 1984:46)

Add the various ways of pronouncing the word (which unfortunately Phillipps does not discuss) and it is clear that 'subtle' is not too strong a term to apply to these practices (cf. Briggs's comment, 1960:69, on the Victorian idea of a gentleman).

This is one example from many illustrating the specificity of upper class discourse. Another where 'class language makes itself particularly clear' (p. 143) concerns mode of address (the use of Christian names, surnames 'Mr' and so on), and another was the language *of* class (Briggs 1960). For as Stedman Jones points out: 'One of the peculiarities of England has been the pervasiveness of the employment of diverse forms of class vocabulary' (1983:2). It was in such usages that boundaries of class and status were themselves marked out, and language signalled a set of class specific values.

The nineteenth century, however, was a period in which a considerable shift was taking place in the structure and composition of classes and in the relationships between them. To whom were the many anonymous etiquette manuals cited by Phillipps addressed other than the upwardly mobile? (E.g. *Hints on etiquette*, 1836, *How to shine in society*, 1860, *Society small talk or what to say and when to say it, by a member of the aristocracy*, 1879.) Unfortunately for the aspiring lady or gentleman, upper class usage, especially in matters of vocabulary, was constantly on the move too. There was, too, a constant appropriation of upper class usage by the middle classes and the 'lower orders' ('It is only washerwomen who call shifts "chemises" now', Mrs Gaskell in a letter of 1852, cited in Phillipps, p. 53). Fashions were always changing, and my impression from reading Phillipps is of a language in which as soon as vernacular speech threatened to converge on the 'received', the latter 'legged it', so to say, and redefined itself in another way. Indeed, eighteenth century and earlier debates concerning correct usage (through which agreement was reached on the inclusion or exclusion of particular linguistic features) were essentially concerned with the boundaries between classes and status groups in a changing society (cf. Baugh 1957:201, and Briggs 1960:70 on England in the mid-nineteenth century).

LANGUAGE AND CLASS IN FRANCE

It is interesting to compare some of these developments in the social stratification of English with what has occurred in France.

As we saw earlier, 'French' was a dialect of the *langue d' Oïl*, originally that of the Ile de France, the area around Paris. From the Middle Ages onwards it was the dialect spoken by the rulers of the most powerful kingdom in a region they came to dominate. In 1539, the Ordonnance of Villers-Cotteret made that dialect the official language of the multilingual

'Kingdom of France'. In the seventeenth century, that language, already a literary vehicle of considerable importance, was shaped by principles of 'good usage' into a formal literary language to serve as a model or standard.

Brunot (1930: 18–21) argues that French scholars in the early seventeenth century were still transfixed by Latin and played little part in the development of this standard. The lawyers, too ('the Palais'), offered little help. For although after 1539 the law was forced to look to French (not Latin) for its further development, legal language, with its fondness for archaisms, offered a poor model for literary endeavours. There were, in fact, several sorts of French, and in 1650 a contemporary observer, cited by Brunot (1930:28), identified three: that of the scholars, that of the 'vulgar', and that of the 'Purists', based on the usages of high society, though this ignores other registers, such as that of the lawyers. What was critical, a 'major event' says Brunot, was the emergence of what he calls a 'new language', a written standard guided by principles which were based by Malherbe, Vaugelas and others on the practices of the 'soundest part of society', namely the Court – the royal entourage, the government, and the dependent institutions of administration (François 1959, Pt. 1:95).

What was the nature of this written language? What was its relation to the spoken language? And what was the relationship between the literary language and stratification within the population employing the spoken tongue? The following discussion does not attempt to answer these questions systematically or in order, for the connection between the literary and spoken languages and linguistic stratification is a complex one, not easy to disentangle.

Once again, the idea of a double (or triple) development is useful. That is, from about the sixteenth century there was increasing differentiation in the spoken language which closely followed – and changed with – the shape of the class or more correctly status system. Simultaneously there emerged a relatively autonomous literary and administrative language. This is not to say that the written code is outside of the class system, indeed far from it. Nor was it entirely separate from the spoken system. Close to, but not the same as, one variety of speech, that of the upper classes, the written language influenced it in a number of ways, and throughout there was a dynamic relationship between the written and spoken form in all its class varieties.

This double development is disguised in France and Britain when upper class speech and the written language are seen as identical, and both taken as the 'standard'. That such conflation occurs may be seen in the terms which French linguists and historians of French themselves apply to both, often interchangeably. 'Standard' itself has only recently come into use (e.g. in Sauvageot 1972:177, Chervel 1977:111, and Lefebvre 1982, concerned with French-speaking Canada). More widely used over a much longer period are 'literary', 'written', 'cultivated', 'official', and 'bourgeois'. Opposed to these are *parler* (spoken language), 'popular', 'vulgar', 'low', and 'familiar'. Sometimes these terms are applied not only to the language but the people who employ it. Thus Brun (1931:16): 'There is a cultivated élite whose speech differs little from official French.' And the *populaire* of 'popular' French has to be understood as 'of the people' in a social and political sense.

The separation of the written from the spoken language, and within the latter an increasing diversification and stratification, had in fact begun in the sixteenth century. Evidence from writers such as Henri Estienne (1578), quoted by Sainéan, and by François (1959, Pt. 1:184) suggests that a linguistic stratification, of which the *literati* were conscious, already existed in Paris: 'What a pity it will be if we banish many words which we find in use among the people' (Estienne, in Sainéan 1920:6). By the seventeenth century we find a number of authors who (decreasingly) use the popular language, to create an effect, or because they are connoisseurs of popular speech and like to record curiosities (e.g. Oudin's *Curiositéz françoises* of 1640). Thus, according to Sainéan:

In the fifteenth and sixteenth centuries, the two idioms [i.e. the popular language of Paris and the literary language] were often intermingled . . . In the seventeenth century the boundary [between the two] became increasingly marked. The popular language was relegated to burlesque. That genre was itself a reaction against a literary tradition which was purified and far too solemn and serious.

(1920: 473)

Although, as Warnant (1973:111) points out, Vaugelas had accorded priority to *spoken* usage (i.e. of the Court) in setting standards for the grammar and the lexicon – an effort which culminated in the publication of the Académie's Dictionary at the end of the seventeenth century – the written language gradually became detached from the spoken. The model for writing became in effect a separate language – 'written', 'correct', 'classical', 'literary', 'official', 'academic' (Bauche 1928:17, cf. 189) – with its own special rules of syntax and vocabulary, punctuation and so on. This language is the basis of what Renée Balibar (1974) calls 'fictive French', a mode of discourse which encompasses much more than the grammar and lexicon, including, for example, a way of constructing sentences connected to a 'rational' mode of argumentation.

Balibar's formulation, to which we turn in chapter 10, implies a different way of looking at the relationship between language and class than is conventional in sociolinguistics. Nevertheless, the conventional picture of a correlation between language use and social status is valuable. In French, as in English, significant differences within the spoken language between the dialects of those at different levels of the social system cannot be ignored.

There are numerous studies of 'popular' French (e.g. Bauche 1928, Brun 1931, Guirard 1973, Sainéan 1920, Sauvageot 1972), particularly that of Paris. Some of these (e.g. Damourette and Pichon, 1968:45, Guirard 1973:8) employ the word *parlure* for varieties of speech associated with a particular stratum of society, e.g. 'parlure bourgeoise', 'parlure vulgaire', the latter identified by Guirard as 'the language of the people' (1973:9). There are also many studies of what is sometimes called 'regional' French (e.g. Lerond 1973), i.e. the French spoken outside Paris.

The connection between 'regional French' and 'popular speech' is not always clear. According to Brun, whose work on the penetration of French among the nineteenth century working class population of Provence was cited in earlier chapters, the dialects spoken by the 'people' of different regions, while sharing a range of grammatical practices which differentiate their speech from the official language, diverge considerably from each other in vocabulary, popular phrases and so on (Brun 1931:144–5, Guirard 1973:7). Brun argues that the language of the 'élite' does not differ greatly from region to region from 'official French', though Warnant (1973:116) says this is true only of the written language. This suggests regionally varied popular *parlures*, less varied 'bourgeois' speech. Sauvageot (1972), who uses transmissions of the radio station 'Europe l' as his principal source for popular speech, and who provides many interesting illustrations of current usage, ignores regional differences entirely, and it is possible that they have lessened since Brun's day. While recognising the importance of this regional dimension, I too will leave it to one side.

The general shape of contemporary popular speech can be seen in the following text transcribing comments by a skilled worker from the Paris area on a car accident:

Tu comprends, moi, j'roulais tout doucement, comme ça. Oui, sur ma droite. Devant, tu sais, y avait rien. C'est-à-dire que si, y avait de l'espace. Tout d'un coup, j'vois une bagnole qui s'amène. J'fais pas attention. Elle doublait le camion. Un camion, oh pas très grand, une sorte de camionnette, quoi. Y avait de quoi passer pour deux ou trois. Alors, brusquement, là voilà c'te voiture, qui se ramène sur moi. J'ai pas eu le temps de penser à rien. Oui si, j'ai compris; comme ça, qu'il fallait essayer de passer avant . . . oui, avant qu'elle se rebatte. J'ai accéléré . . . un bon coup. Heureusement. I' m'est arrivé dessus. Crac, i' m'a arrâché ma porte gauche et il a continué. J'ai freiné pile. I' s'est arrêté à son tour, derrière, loin. Il est sorti, avec

un des airs ahuris. Tu vois ça. I' se ramène et i' m'a dit: 'Excusez, c'est ma faute, j'
vous avais pas vu'. Tu t'rends compete, y avait bien dix mètres entre le camion et
moi . . .   (IN SAUVAGEOT 1972:173)

This text, discussed further in chapter 9, illustrates some, though not all, of
the differences between popular and 'correct' usage (e.g. je—j', the use of a
word like *bagnole*). Other features, often noted by the commentators,
include the ignoring of accord of number and gender (*ma femme est jaloux*, in
Guirard 1973:35), and the omission of *ne* in negative constructions (*je sais
pas* or more likely *chaipas*. A full discussion of such grammatical
'deviations', as they would usually be seen, may be found in the works cited
above (see, for example, Sainéan 1920:119–28 for an account of nineteenth
century popular Parisian syntax).

Some of these deviations are likely to occur in the familiar speech of all
classes, more so now, perhaps, than previously. But it would be a mistake to
confuse 'popular' speech with familiar speech as such. It would also be a
mistake to consider only grammar (or pronunciation). What strikes many
writers as a significant feature of popular French are differences of phrasing
and vocabulary compared with the 'cultivated' language.

The collection of lists of curious lexical items is as widespread a practice
in dialect studies in France as it is in Britain. These lists occasionally amount
to dictionaries (e.g. Bauche 1928:193–256). In some cases the words they
contain would be characterised as *argot*, slang, of which there exist a number
of dictionaries which are so styled. *Argot* had a precise historical meaning in
the nineteenth century, referring to the secret language of thieves (Sainéan
1920:41). This secret language from time to time penetrated what is
sometimes called 'low language' (*bas langage*) referring to the speech of the
'lowest' orders of Paris. Thence it extended to the 'popular' language at
large and occasionally penetrated literary discourse (see Edwards, A. D.
1976:22–6 for a similar process in Britain). However, during the nineteenth
century the term *argot* was applied to 'low language' itself, and even to
popular speech in general (Sainéan 1920:42), just as the 'dangerous class'
was sometimes identified with the working class as a whole. That this should
occur is a reflection of the way in which popular language was viewed (see
chapter 9).

Sainéan's account of the popular language of nineteenth century Paris
carefully distinguishes the various elements of which it was composed, and
argot, in the strict sense, was but one. He is particularly concerned to
document language use among the various communities and corporations
(in an occupational sense of trades and professions). The population of Paris
was, at least in the early years of the nineteenth century, composed of

numerous close-knit speech communities. Each of these (soldiers, sailors, butchers and so on) had a range of usage peculiar to themselves with the language employed closely reflecting the milieu of those who employed it. Despite differences in speech to be found in the urban villages which characterised nineteenth century Paris, there were similarities across the city. Sainéan notes, for example, the fondness for metaphor and irony in phrases such as *aller à la campagne* = go to prison, and *être à la comédie* = be unemployed. In the course of the nineteenth century there may have been increasing convergence of speech as new working-class suburbs (e.g. Belleville) developed on the outskirts, and there was an influx of population from the provinces, with immigrants making their own contribution to popular language.

The speech of high society was itself differentiated. The strictures of Barère and Grégoire on aristocratic usage are similar to those of a much earlier writer such as Estienne, who in the sixteenth century noted: 'you must always have on your tongue the words *infinitely* or *extremely* and say: I am infinitely obliged to you' (in Sainéan 1920:450). These remarks pertained to what was thought of as a 'ceremonious' style. It was contrasted with another more familiar and simple, as illustrated by two examples of Fénelon's (1713): 'Voilà une menuiserie bien travaillée', and, 'Voilà un ouvrage de menuiserie qui est d'un goût exquis et qui est exécuté dans la dernière perfection' (cited in François 1959, Pt. I:275).

In both speech and writing, a distinction was made between words, phrases, topics, ideas and styles appropriate to different genres and situations. There was 'A low style – highly expurgated – suitable for stories, satires and novels; a middle style for letters, for homely poetry, for simple speeches; a grand style, or noble style, for the major genres (real poetry, tragedy, epics, odes)' (Mornet 1929:310). 'Expurgated' refers to the excision of indelicate terms or those capable of evoking indelicate matters, i.e. 'low words' (Mornet 1929:309) – a word was considered 'low' if it suggested, 'directly or indirectly, a low or repugnant idea' (François 1959 Pt. II:90). Realistic or naturalistic terms, popular terms, insults, bourgeois words, words to do with trade and professions 'became outcast from the literary language' (François 1959, Pt. I:281).

When spoken, the ceremonious or noble style was produced through a type of pronunciation known as *soutenue* employed for theatrical performance, for singing and for public speaking. It had to be learned, through voice training. Thus 'a particular idiom', as François calls it, passed from the realms of literature 'to the conversation of educated persons and accentuated the distance between the popular and cultivated language' (1959, Pt. I:40, cf. Sauvageot 1972:117). The elevated pronunciation, by emphasising certain phonemes (e.g. the final *es* of *amies*) usually mute in 'ordinary' speech, produced utterances which were sometimes much closer to literary forms than were the utterances of 'familiar' or 'popular' speech (Chervel 1977:35).

Revolutionaries attacked this type of speech with only limited success. An early nineteenth century writer still had this to say:

> To achieve what is called *quality* or *supremely good form* one must above all speak in a mannered way, and affect the Parisian 'r'. One must adopt a haughty, resolute and arrogant appearance. One's conversation must be about oneself – one's excellence, one's knowledge, tastes and whims. One must speak of one's barber, one's tailor and one's bootmaker, of one's mistresses, of horses, the theatre . . . In short, everything which is ridiculous, extravagant, dull and feminine is brought together in what is called the *man of quality*. (IN SAINÉAN 1920:451)

As this suggests, it was not just a matter of vocabulary – though that was obviously important – or grammar or pronunciation which distinguished the 'well-bred person', but, as we saw in the earlier discussion of upper-class English, an entire way of comporting oneself in conversation, including precise ways of holding the body. The lexicon was also significant, and in the nineteenth century, at any rate in the more familiar registers of upper class speech, there was often a convergence between low-class language and that of high society, for example when the latter incorporated elements of *argot* (Sainéan 1920:452, Bauche 1928:22). Sainéan also notes the use of English words (at various times *dandy*, *smart*, *fashionable* and *snob*) and the speed with which words came into fashion, were current for a period, and were then dropped: e.g. *chic* and its various synonyms such as *choc*, *pschutt*, *tchink*, *tschotte*, *vlan*, *zing*, some invented by an attendant society press.

This type of language not only served to mark status, and presumably did so in as subtle a way as did language in England, but it, too, diverged from 'correct', 'cultivated' usage.

And somewhere in between the language of high society, in all its registers, that of the 'people' (in all its grades), and that of cultivated, literary discourse, came something else.

LANGUAGE, STATUS AND VOICE

Wyld's *History of modern colloquial English*, first published in 1920, distinguished 'Received Standard English' from 'Modified Standard', which is neither regional dialect nor received:

> These forms of Modified Standard may, in some cases, differ but slightly from Received Standard, so that at the worst they are felt merely as eccentricities by

speakers of the latter; in others they differ very considerably, and in several ways, from this type, and are regarded as vulgarisms. It is a grave error to assume that what are known as 'educated' people, meaning thereby highly trained, instructed and learned persons, invariably speak Received Standard. Naturally, such speakers do not make 'mistakes' in grammar, they may have a high and keen perception of the right uses of words, but with all this they may, and often do, use a type of pronunciation which is quite alien to Received Standard . . . These deviations . . . may be shown just as readily in over-careful pronunciation, which aims at great 'correctness' or elegance – as when *t* is pronounced in *often*, or when initial *h* is scrupulously uttered (wherever written) before all personal pronouns, even when these are quite unemphasized in the sentence – as in a too careless and slipshod pronunciation – as when *buttered toast* is pronounced *butterd tose* or *object* is called *objic*. (1921:3–4)

Wyld castigates those who use this type of language, 'the more or less educated Middle Class of the South', (p. 7), 'shopwalker words' (p. 17), 'a loutish awkwardness which springs from an ignorance of how to behave' (p. 20), 'sham refinement in pronunciation and vocabulary' (*ibid.*). 'Such are among the chief vices of Middle Class English at the present time, and such they have always been' (*ibid.*). A similar perception is revealed by Bauche, who identifies a type of speech midway between popular and correct French 'remarkable not for its faults as for the fact that it consists of a set of phrases and a type of pronunciation (of ideas too) which do not belong to the usual speech of people of good society' (1928:24). This is the speech of those whom the bourgeois call 'common'. Typical of their thinking, according to Bauche, is that 'for them the word *bureaucrat* is not used ironically or unfavourably, but as a term of approbation' (p. 25).

Relevant to this discussion of 'middle class' language (or if I interpret Bauche's tone correctly, what might in Britain be termed 'lower middle class') is Trudgill's comment that there is in England a 'more or less regionless' (Trudgill 1983:187) Standard English dialect which he associates, generally speaking, with 'educated people' (cf. Leech, Deuchar and Hoogenraad 1982). Both Trudgill and Stubbs define this dialect in grammatical terms, associating it most strongly with forms found in the written language, though it is spoken, and has both casual and formal styles. Stubbs (1980:126) actually defines Standard English as 'that variety of English spoken by educated middle-class people in most parts of Britain'. Its speakers – especially when they come from the South of England – are often described colloquially as 'accentless', though as Trudgill (1983:187) points out, 'most . . . speak it with a (usually not too localized) regional accent, so that most educated people betray their geographical origins much more in their pronunciation than in their grammar or lexis'.

Many readers of this book probably speak thus, as does Trudgill himself, and the present writer. For while RP and upper-class English are confined to a tiny minority of the population, this 'middle' style of speaking the language is quite widespread, as is the equivalent style in France. In a survey of London schoolchildren, Rosen and Burgess (1980) found that some 16% of pupils were identified by their teachers as speaking Standard English in 'stronger' or 'weaker' forms. It is also the predominant style nowadays of the 'media', i.e. radio and television: 'Home Service' or Radio 4, rather than 'Third Programme' or Radio 3. (In the early days of wireless the BBC adopted a particular style of pronunciation close to RP – what became called, in fact 'BBC English'. In the 1930s there was, apparently, some concern that this style of speech was distancing the medium from its audience. During the War the BBC took the then daring step of recruiting a Yorkshireman to read the news. His 'Good neet' was for a time a national sensation, cf. Stubbs, 1980:126 ff.)

The examples of 'middle-class' English and (lower middle-class?) French usage cited earlier show how important it is to broaden the discussion of linguistic stratification to encompass not only syntax and accent or even vocabulary, but culture in general as coded through language and language use, and consider also interaction between strata or classes. This has a bearing on the phenomenon known as 'style-switching'.

The extent to which those in the middle 'betray' (or display) their regional and/or class origins in their speech varies considerably. One prominent academic of Yorkshire origins, whom I have frequently heard speak, reveals only slight signs of his regional background by occasionally allowing an *s* to become z-ish in, for example, 'uz'. Other Yorkshiremen – Harold Wilson or Roy Hattersley for example – can become 'broader', seemingly at will, depending on context and situation. This is similar to the accent/dialect range deployed by West Indian speakers who, it will be recalled, 'are able to broaden Jamaican features in their speech to the point where it becomes Patois' (Sutcliffe 1982:152). In like manner, says Trudgill, 'Southern English speakers . . . often command a range of the social dialect continuum and, as it were, slide up and down it according to social context' (1983:190).

Studies of dialect- (or style- or code-) switching often suggest that many speakers have a 'repertoire' of styles at their disposal. That speakers may thus 'command' a variety of linguistic resources should not, however, lead us to suppose a 'free market' in style-switching. The extent of 'active competence' (Trudgill 1983:10) in 'other' dialects and accents does not appear to be well documented, but Trudgill's work suggests that 'it is a rare speaker who acquires or imitates a dialect other than his own vernacular perfectly' (1983:29). Trudgill's formulation here and elsewhere poses a problem. A person's 'own vernacular' presumably means, in some sense, the 'mother tongue'. This, Trudgill seems to imply, is the 'real' accent which neither social nor geographical mobility allows one to lose in entirety. This in turn raises the problem of *sincerity*. Many people feel that style-switching is 'insincere', a 'betrayal' of origins in a different sense. Nonetheless, it is certainly true that the skills displayed by mimics, actors and con men are not widely distributed. Style-switching can be more, or less, well done, more or less convincing.

In addition, styles are not value- or judgment-free. At the very least in Britain and in France they are ranked in terms of their prestige and may also be thought to signal varying degrees of 'intelligence' (see chapter 9) or authority, or distance or solidarity. For example, Milroy (1980:60) records that on one occasion a teenage informant switched from his normal working-class Belfast voice into something approaching the standard: 'His tempo and loudness range levelled out, some vernacular phonological features became less evident, and he self-consciously fingered his hair and straightened his clothes.' He was immediately teased by his companions for putting on airs: 'Come on, you're not on television you know.' Thus, although in both Britain and France certain ways of speaking (e.g. RP) have considerable prestige, they are not always universally admired or respected.

Some styles which are non-standard have, in certain contexts, a prestige of their own, what is sometimes called 'covert'. Once, in a bank on a university campus, I stood in line behind two male students who were conversing in a style which approximated in its grammar, accent, and vocabulary to what is often conceived of as working-class speech. On reaching the cashier one of the students said in perfect RP: 'I believe my mother has forwarded my allowance.' Style-switching of this kind, which may be compared to what Bakhtin calls 'juxtaposition of voices' (cf. Hill and Hill 1986:388), suggests the inadequacy of simple correlations between class and speech form. The phenomenon requires a much more dynamic analysis than correlational studies allow.

This suggestion is taken further in later chapters, but for the moment let me note the following. First, the potentiality for, and actualisation of, styles switching may vary from one class to another. Adopting Le Page's notion of *focusing* (Le Page 1979), Milroy suggests that the type of social structure, including type of (close-knit) social network, which characterises certain levels of British society has fostered 'highly focused language varieties' (i.e. varieties which are stable, regulated and controlled, in form and presumably in use). These are to be found 'at the highest and the lowest strata' (p. 180). This does not mean that style-switching never occurs in these strata – there are, after all, *within-strata* stylistic varieties – but suggests that switching to styles which are associated with another stratum – *between-strata* style-switching – is likely to be closely monitored and controlled.

Secondly, and following from Milroy's formulation, there is likely to be greater variety, diffusion, and indeed confusion, among groups subject to different social conditions. Increasing social and geographical mobility, coupled with the widespread availability of education and literacy, have not only changed the shape of the stratification system in both France and Britain, but also shaken up the connection between speech and class. Milroy's image of working-class life in close-knit inner-city communities points to a conjunction of residence, occupation and culture which is decreasingly typical in Britain, especially in the south. The 'more or less educated Middle Class', to whom Wyld referred disparagingly in the 1920s, now form a substantially greater proportion of the population, and it is their voice which is the dominant one in the media, the office, the school, and factory. It is the 'managerial voice' in broader and narrower senses. Here again, of course, there is a multiplicity of within-stratum styles, but it is significant that for Wyld, Trudgill and others the outstanding feature of this dialect, at least in its more formal register, is its convergence with the *grammatical standard*.

Thirdly, what happens within a stratum may be less important than what occurs between strata. The absence, for the most part, of serious consideration of the linguistic aspects of interaction between strata or classes reveals limitations of contemporary sociolinguistics, though Trudgill (1978: 17–18) seems to want to make a virtue of the methodological practice of confining attention to the usages of one stratum of the population at a time or in isolation. The approach which stresses the vernacular, the speech of 'speakers from the lower end of the socio-economic scale who will use nonstandard linguistic forms most consistently' (Cheshire 1982a:6) tells us much, but by no means everything, about language in *a* class, little about language and the changing composition of classes, or language and mobility or language *and* class, or language and power.

9

'BARBAROUS TONGUES':
THE HIERARCHICAL ORDERING
OF DIFFERENCE

No language . . . has been shown to be more accurate, logical or capable of expression than another.

(EDWARDS, J. R. 1979: 73)

BARBARISM, VULGARITY, AND DEFICIT

A BASIC premise of modern linguistics is – and remains despite the strictures of John Honey (1983) – that all languages are equal (see Kingman Report 1988:43). Just as anthropologists refuse to judge the relative worth of cultures, linguists believe that 'one language is as good and adequate as any other' (Trudgill 1983:205). This does not preclude critical comment on particular linguistic or cultural practices, especially if they contravene the basic premise of equality.

In many societies, however, languages and cultures are routinely evaluated. Linguistic, social and cultural stratification is the norm. The social, economic and political framework within which such stratification occurs in Europe has been sketched in the preceding chapters. Here I examine an important ideological motif which frequently accompanies it, the idea that certain subordinate languages and their speakers exhibit a 'deficit'.

A great deal of evidence, drawn from a wide range of contexts, and from many different times and places, shows that an integral feature of the system of linguistic stratification in Europe is an ideology of contempt: subordinate languages are despised languages. From at least the sixteenth to the eighteenth centuries the word 'barbarous' and its derivatives was one of the commonest epithets employed in Britain and France by speakers of the dominant languages and dialects to refer both to subordinate languages themselves and their speakers. The argument could work two ways: the relevant population was barbarous or savage, and therefore so was their language; or the language was barbarous, and therefore so were the people.

The assignment of barbarity to speech and population is, of course, of classical origin. The word 'barbarian' (*barbaros*) is Greek, and represented the unintelligible sounds (barbarbar) which passed for communication among outlandish people. It is not surprising that, in the British context, it was Scots Gaelic, Irish and, to a degree, Welsh (described in 1681 as the 'gibberish of Taphydom', cited in Morgan 1983:48), to which the epithet was applied.

A similar perspective on the regional languages of France is revealed in the use of the word 'barbarism' and its complements and oppositions (savage/cultivated) and in terms such as *jargon, baragouin, charabia*, etc., applied to subordinate languages and dialects. Again the letters received by the Abbé Grégoire in his survey of the patois provide valuable evidence. Thus, a memorandum from the Société des Amis de la Constitution de Limoges:

> The peasant whose ideas are very restricted will be continually cut off from education so long as he does not know the language spoken by educated persons. If he knows how to read and write, he will be instructed and rid himself of prejudice, communicate his thoughts, and will be less easily led astray and tricked.
>
> (IN GAZIER 1969: 170–1)

> We do not have any desire to hold to our patois. You may, if you wish, take it away. We will not mind. It seems to us that French is better suited to praying to the supreme Creator and singing his praises. We feel that our patois is too stupid and coarse. It is not worthy of God. It seems to us to encourage sloth, monasticism, superstition and the inquisition. The destruction of our patois can only be pleasing to God.
>
> (LES AMIS DE LA CONSTITUTION D'AUCH, IN GAZIER 1969: 94–5)

> A coarse language keeps a population coarse and ignorant.
>
> (IN GAZIER 1969: 258)

Barbarous speech, barbarous people.

But it was not only the Celtic languages, or Breton, Basque and the dialects of the *langue d'Oc*, which were thought of in this way. In the sixteenth century, the French language itself was considered 'barbarous', by the Italians. Alexis François's history of 'cultivated French' (1959 Pt.

1:122) cites a number of contemporary protests against this view, including Du Bellay's 1549 defence of French which has a section entitled 'Que la langue française ne doit être nommé barbare'. François suggests that sixteenth-century French writers felt that one of the reasons why their language was described as barbarous was that it lacked regulation – a point to which we will return. (German was similarly conceived to be unsuitable for lofty thought: Blackall 1978:3–4).

'French', too, had its savage varieties. François (1959 Pt. 1:94) cites this apology from a thirteenth-century poet, Jean de Meun:

> Si m'excuse de mon langage,
> Rude, malotru et sauvage,
> car nés ne suis pas de Paris.

And François reminds us (1959 Pt. 1:267) of J. L. Balzac's dictum of 1636: 'All (usage) which is not that of the Court is called barbarous.' A long tradition in Britain, also, represented dialects other than the dominant or standard as 'barbarous'. Dobson (1956:29), for example, cites a sixteenth-century reference to the 'barbarous speech of your country people', and in the seventeenth and eighteenth centuries, one of the aims of those engaged in forming and shaping the literary language was to rid it of barbarisms. Thus Johnson's purpose in compiling his dictionary was 'to refine our language to grammatical purity, and to clear it from colloquial barbarisms, licentious idioms, and irregular combinations' (cited in Baugh and Cable 1983:271).

Although the term *barbarism* was frequently applied in England in the eighteenth century and earlier to refer to words of foreign origin (Leonard 1962:36), many examples of its application that he cites show that it had a wider connotation. Thus *Government* for *the Government* is described in 1779 as 'an expression of great barbarism'; *Tis* was 'a barbarous contraction of *it is*' (in Leonard 1962:38). In 1762, Lowth, following Johnson, deemed *lesser* 'a barbarous corruption of *less*, formed by the vulgar from the habit of terminating comparisons in *er*' (in Leonard 1962:113).

'Vulgar' itself was used in a similar way to refer, as one eighteenth-century writer put it, to 'impure, or debased language, such as is commonly spoken by the low people' (in Leonard 1962:175, for use of such terms in France see Guirard 1973:52, Sainéan 1920:26, Sauvageot 1972:133). It was 'the depraved language of the common people' (*Art of Speaking* of 1708, cited in Leonard, p. 170). Johnson's favoured term 'cant' was interpreted, according to one critic, as referring not to hypocritical sentiments but to words 'belonging only to the vulgar; and which therefore have no certain origin nor precise meaning' (John Horne Tooke, in Smith 1984:125). They were words without history:

Of the laborious and mercantile part of the people, the diction is in great measure casual and mutable; many of their terms are formed for some temporary or local convenience, and though current at certain times and places are in others utterly unknown. This fugitive cant, which is always in a state of increase or decay, cannot be regarded as any of the durable materials of a language, and therefore must be suffered to perish with other things unworthy of preservation

(IN THE PREFACE OF JOHNSON'S *Dictionary*, CITED IN SMITH 1984: 14)

Olivia Smith sums up the eighteenth-century perspective on popular speech as follows:

'The vulgar and the refined', 'the particular and the general', 'the corrupt and the pure', 'the barbaric and the civilized', 'the primitive and the arbitrary' were socially pervasive terms that divided sensibility and culture according to linguistic categories. The baser forms of language were said to reveal the inability of the speaker to transcend the concerns of the present, an interest in material objects, and the dominance of the passions. Those who spoke the refined language were allegedly rational, moral, civilized, and capable of abstract thinking.

(1984: 3)

These ideas concerning barbarous or vulgar speech are not characteristic of an earlier era and have long since been abandoned. (An instance of the use of 'barbarous' occurs in a 1980 quotation cited by Milroy and Milroy, 1985:9.) It is still widely believed that distinctions may be made between languages and dialects, for example in terms of their inherent aesthetic properties. Trudgill (1983:212, cf. Trudgill 1974) cites two informants in a contemporary survey of Norwich as saying:

'I talk horrible, I think. But BBC announcers and that, they really sound nice when they talk.' (HOUSEWIFE, 45)

'I think the Norwich accent is awful – but people you hear on the wireless, some of them have got really nice voices.' (NIGHTWATCHMAN, 57)

As Trudgill says, such widely reported ranking of one's own accent and those of others is 'the result of a complex of social, cultural, regional, political and personal associations and prejudices' (p. 214). So too are those judgments, again widely reported (e.g. in Giles and Powesland 1975), according to which speakers of Received Pronunciation are said to be more 'intelligent' than speakers with regional and/or lower class accents. The same content is evaluated differently according to the accent of the speaker. 'Careless' or 'slovenly' speech – for which read speech which is non-standard – are thought to reveal a slovenly mind. (See Leonard 1962:82, 183, on the use of 'slovenly' in England in the eighteenth century, and Trudgill 1975:60, Stubbs 1980:137, 1983:25, for more recent references.

See also Orwell 1946 [1970]: 157.) A 1921 Report on *The teaching of English in England* attributed such slovenliness to 'lip-laziness' (Newbolt 1921:96), arguing that 'It is emphatically the business of the Elementary School to reach all its pupils who either speak a definite dialect or whose speech is disfigured by vulgarisms, to speak Standard English, and to speak it clearly' (p. 65). And one of the witnesses referred to 'guiding the child to that refinement of speech which, in a subtle manner, is an index to the mind, and helps to place it beyond the reach of vulgarity of thought and action' (p. 67).

In one respect, to say 'barbarous' or 'vulgar' or 'savage', as opposed to 'civilised' or 'cultivated', is simply to employ a label with no purpose other than to distance and put down. Any sort of practice, irrespective of the content, could be so labelled, and indeed probably has been (cf. Kroch 1978:19). But to say 'all usage not of the Court is barbarous' is to associate what 'they' do – whatever they do – with savagery and indeed animality. It is thus an ideological motif underpinning a system of stratification which happens to encompass language as it also encompasses (in the British case) religion (Protestantism versus Catholicism, established church versus nonconformism).

The barbaric epithet may also signal a more specifically social linguistic commentary in two ways. The first, and perhaps less objectionable, refers to 'access', or rather the lack of it, and appears in a discourse of 'backwardness'. Given an existing correlation between the distribution of resources (economic, social, political and cultural) and the distribution of populations and languages, those who do not know the dominant tongue are placed in a disadvantageous position. Grégoire's correspondents felt this particularly strongly, as did the Welsh education Commissioners. Thus Henry Vaughan Johnson:

> For secular subjects they have neither literature nor a language ... They are compelled to employ two languages, one for religion and domestic intercourse, another for the market, in the courts of justice, at the Board of Guardians, and for the transaction of every other public function; and to increase their difficulties the latter language remains, and must continue an unknown tongue.
>
> (KAY-SHUTTLEWORTH 1847, PT III, p. 61)

Compare also the remarks of Lingen, cited in chapter 5 ('all the world about [the Welshman] is English'), and Nicolson's comment on the Hebrides and Western Isles where 'the general ignorance of the English language constitutes a special and powerful obstacle to the progress of improvement in the district' (1866:90). Without the dominant language the population lacked access to what was thought to be a decent education, and like modern migrant workers were forced to accept the lowliest occupations.

Related to this is the connection between the regional languages and religion. The Welsh Commissioners agreed that the Welsh language had evolved a highly elaborate discourse for handling theological subjects, but 'its resources in every other branch remain obsolete and meagre' (Pt. III, p. 59). The language was 'undeveloped' as that term is used by modern linguists, 'not . . . employed in all the functions that a language can perform' (Haugen 1972:244). However, if in some instances it was thought that the regional languages were suitable for religion – and perhaps only for religion – in other cases, as Grégoire's correspondents reveal, it was believed they encouraged an inappropriate or lesser type of faith, one imbued with superstition and irrational practices (see in Gazier 1969:288). French, after all, was the language of *Reason*.

French and English were also the languages of literature – the high culture – and of science. For Johnson, who was one of those who rejected the Ossianic epic as spurious, it was the absence of a literary tradition which put Gaelic and its speakers beyond the pale:

When a language begins to teem with books, it is tending to refinement; as those who undertake to teach others must have undergone some labour in improving themselves, they set a proportionate value on their own thoughts, and wish to enforce them by efficacious expressions; speech becomes embodied and permanent; different modes and phrases are compared, and the best obtains an establishment. By degrees one age improves upon another. Exactness is first obtained, and afterwards elegance. But diction, merely vocal, is always in its childhood.

(1971 EDN, P. 115)

Whether or not this fairly represents the differences between non-literate and literate peoples (or at any rate those possessing a high literate culture of the kind envisaged by Johnson), the idea that those without one, or without access to one, lack something has been, and still is, widely held. The Italian Marxist, Antonio Gramsci, perhaps reflecting on the situation of those from a background similar to his own – he was a Sardinian – remarked 'Someone who only speaks dialect, or understands the standard language incompletely, necessarily has an intuition of the world which is more or less limited or provincial, which is fossilised and anachronistic in relation to the major currents of thought which dominate world history. His interests will be limited . . . not universal' (1971:325).

In one respect Gramsci's point, and Johnson's too, is only about *access*. In so far as what Gramsci says is correct, it is not self-evidently a function of the intrinsic properties of dialect as a form of language, but of the social distribution of dialects and standards, of the domains with which they are associated, and the issues which they address. For social and political reasons some languages are much less 'developed' than others or rather –

and the case could certainly be made for the Gaelic literary tradition – have not been *allowed* to develop as have others. Because 'undeveloped', such languages and dialects may well be 'inadequate'. As Chapman comments on Scots Gaelic: 'Its suitability for scientific and business use is a matter for doubt, not surprisingly since it has been attenuated by disuse in the very areas of vocabulary it would require' (1978:108, cf. 142, 168, and Mackinnon 1977). The speakers of such a language, unless bilingual, have at the very least a momentary disadvantage, though it may well be only momentary as the reforms implemented in other languages (e.g. Arabic, Hebrew) would indicate (cf. Calvet 1974:129). With dialects which have only marginal grammatical differences from the standard language the problem may not in theory exist. Thus Trudgill (1975:27) argues that 'there is no reason why nuclear physics should not be discussed in Cumberland dialect', illustrating his point with a translation of a piece from an introductory text in Social Anthropology! (cf. Smitherman 1980b).

But Johnson's point about Erse was, after this and because of this, that its speakers 'conceived grossly too'; for Gramsci, the dialect speaker's 'intuitions' were 'more or less limited'. This leads to a quite different perspective, concerning what might be termed the 'relative cognitive power' of particular languages and dialects. Certain languages, as it were, 'generate' barbarousness of thought and deed.

'DIFFERENCES' AND 'DEFICITS'

In both Britain and France the ascription of some form of inadequacy to subordinate languages and dialects, with implications for the cognitive potential of their speakers, has had a long history. In the modern era one focal point for discussion of this issue has been the debate about linguistic 'deficit', which in Britain at any rate has become entwined with discussion of the relationship between language and class, notably in the writings of Basil Bernstein and in commentaries on his research.

In chapter 8 I argued that in both Britain and France there occurred a 'double development' involving on the one hand a differentiation of speech along class lines, and simultaneously the emergence of a (written) standard for each language which is somewhat apart from the spoken (class) dialects. The difference between these varieties is not confined to their formal linguistic properties (grammar, vocabulary, pronunciation) but includes a wide range of linguistic practices (for example the use of the paragraph in writing, in speaking the form of a conversation – indeed the very idea of a 'conversation'). Following Hymes, I call these 'communicative', rather than 'linguistic' practices, and argue that each language variety, in English and French, entails a distinct set of communicative practices. The purpose of this section is to consider the relevance of the debate about 'deficit' to the hierarchical ordering of these different sets of communicative practices.

Earlier I referred to a basic premise of modern linguistics that all languages are in some sense equal. Languages may differ, phonetically, grammatically, and in their vocabulary, but not, formally, as 'vehicles of conception', to use Geertz's phrase (1964:59). This 'difference' position on language is contrasted with the 'deficit' perspective whose application to class dialects is summarised succinctly by Dittmar as the view that 'the speech of the lower class is more limited in its competence than the speech of the middle class' (1976:4). According to Gordon (1981:61), it is the view that success or failure at school, say, is attributable to the 'intrinsic nature' of the type of language the child employs. That this perspective takes us into difficult and dangerous terrain may be appreciated if, as happens, such a sentiment is expressed in a comparison not of classes but of different cultures or races.

In its modern application to varieties of class speech, deficit theory is usually traced to research in the USA in the 1950s (*viz* Schatzman and Strauss 1955; see Atkinson 1985:54, Bernstein 1974:16, Dittmar 1976:42, Edwards, J.R. 1979:31). It is usual also to point to the Sapir-Whorf hypothesis on linguistic relativism and the determinism of the 1930s for the assumptions concerning the relationship between language and thought which the deficit perspective shares. In fact, something similar to a deficit theory may be found earlier, in the work of the turn-of-the-century French grammarians, Damourette and Pichon, who wrote that 'In general, cultivated people and those whose intellectual life is relatively refined have a form of speech which is linguistically more interesting because richer in syntactic and semantic nuances' (1968:50). And from the evidence cited previously, the notion is of much older vintage. The traditional discourse of barbarism and vulgarity and the modern discourse of deficit to say the least overlap.

It is frequently implied that the work of Basil Bernstein suggests a connection between forms of speech, modes of thought and social categories (i.e. class) of a deficit kind (see Gordon 1981). Rightly or wrongly – and the facts of the matter are complex[1] – criticism of Bernstein on this and other

[1] Bernstein's own defence is presented in 1974:81, 128, 243, and in 1985b. His cause is taken up by Halliday (1973, 1978:86–7), and Atkinson (1985). Criticisms are to be found most famously, or notoriously, in Labov 1972a, and Dittmar 1976, Edwards, A. D. 1976, Edwards, J. R. 1979, Gordon 1981, Jackson, 1974, Rosen 1972, Trudgill 1975, 1984a, and many others. François (1980a, 1983b) and Bautier-Castaing (1980) present a French view. For an assessment of the argument see Burton (1983) and Stubbs (1980, 1984). Historical accounts of the development of deficit theories may be found in Atkinson (1985), Lawton (1968), Edwards, A. D. (1976), and Gordon (1981). Interestingly, Bernstein receives no mention in the Kingman Report (1988). Part of the problem is defining what constitutes a deficit theory.

counts has led Trevor Pateman to conclude that 'Bernstein-type accounts are . . . pretty much in tatters' (1980:150). Despite the cogency of the arguments of his opponents, Bernstein's ideas deserve the closest attention. Even Gordon, a severe critic, notes that among teachers he interviewed many 'felt that Bernstein's theory, or at least aspects of it, articulated something that they had encountered in their own experience' (1981:137).

One attraction of Bernstein's ideas is that, irrespective of any 'deficit' implications, his approach points to a way of conceiving the relationship between language and class which goes far beyond that found in much conventional sociolinguistics, and which in fact makes a significant contribution to the study of the hierarchical ordering of communicative practices (see Atkinson 1985 for a defence of Bernstein on other grounds). It is undoubtedly difficult to elicit that contribution from the corpus of Bernstein's own writings in which he appears so often to shift his ground and change his terminology, and in this account I make no attempt to disentangle what he has to say in its entirety.

Let us begin with Bernstein's work of the late 1950s and early 1960s which as he himself says was undertaken in the context of a debate about the then prevailing system of secondary education in Britain (Bernstein 1964b:55, 1985b, Rosen 1972:2–3). That system was highly selective, making extensive use of intelligence testing. All the evidence suggested that working-class children had less success within this system than did their middle-class counterparts (see Jackson and Marsden 1962). Bernstein's research was directed towards understanding the reasons for this.

Pointing to earlier findings which had revealed different 'language habits' in children of different social backgrounds, Bernstein argued that 'the measurable inter-status linguistic differences between lower working-class and the middle-class, rather than reflecting differences in innate capacity, result from entirely different modes of speech which are dominant and typical within these strata' (1964a:251, cf. 1974:61). Via a distinction between what he termed 'highly-coded' and 'now-coded' utterances, Bernstein went on to contrast two 'pure forms' of language: 'public' and 'formal':

Public language is a mode of communication, which is marked off from other forms of speech by the rigidity of its syntactical structure and the limited and restricted use of structural possibilities for sentence organization. It is a form of condensed

---

Gordon's extremely wide definition includes 'any theory that seeks to explain differential educational attainment and its social distribution to any significant degree in terms of dichotomous types of language or language-use, with unequal access to both' (Gordon 1981:86). By this definition Bernstein's ideas could well be interpreted as falling into the 'deficit' camp, as could much else. This formulation is too broad to be of value. 'Deficit' is best restricted to those theories which attribute disadvantage to the intrinsic nature of a language, a definition which Gordon in fact employs elsewhere.

Table 9.1. *The properties of formal and public languages (after Bernstein)*

Public language	Formal language
Short, grammatically simple, often unfinished sentences with poor syntactical form	*Accurate grammatical order and syntax regulate what is said
Simple and repetitive use of conjunctions	*Logical modifications and stress mediated through complex grammatical sentence construction, use of range of conjunctions and subordinate clauses
Little use of subordinate clauses, adjectives and adverbs	*Use of prepositions indicating logical relationship, temporality, and spatial contiguity
Dislocated informational content	*Frequent use of impersonal pronouns
Rigid and limited use of adjectives and adverbs	*Discriminative selection from a range of adjectives and adverbs
Infrequent use of personal pronouns as subjects of conditional clauses or sentences	*Individual qualification mediated through structure and relationships between sentences
Frequent use of statements where reason/conclusion confounded to produce a categoric statement	*Expressive symbolism discriminates between meanings
Use of phrases which reinforce previous speech sequence	*Points to possibilities inherent in a complex conceptual hierarchy for the organising of experience
Repetitive selection from a group of idiomatic phrases or sequences	
Language of implicit meaning	

speech in which certain meanings are restricted and the possibility of their elaboration is reduced . . . *formal* language . . . is one in which the structure and syntax is potentially less predictable for any one individual. The formal possibilities of sentence organization are used to clarify meaning and make it explicit.

(1964a:252–3, cf. 1958, 1959)

It is the formal language which is 'considered the dominant and typical speech form of the middle classes' (p. 253). Its distinguishing features are set out in the accompanying table (9.1) drawn from Bernstein (1964a:253, cf. 1959).

In a 1962 paper (reprinted in Bernstein 1974:76–94) and in a 1964 revision of a previous essay (Bernstein 1964a) the terminology changes. The public/formal distinction becomes the subsequently better known one between *restricted* and *elaborated*, and they are termed *codes*. The contrast between these codes lies in the way in which they 'orient their users' (1972b:164) towards different orders of meaning, namely 'particularistic' and 'universalistic'. Their properties are summarised in Table 9.2.

There are four issues to be examined in this chapter and the next, not

Table 9.2. *The properties of restricted and elaborated codes (after Bernstein)*

Public/restricted		Formal/elaborated
particularistic	*	universalistic
condensed symbols	*	articulated symbols
implicitness	*	explicitness
metaphorical	*	rationality
context-dependent	*	context-free
communalised roles	*	individualised roles
social intimacy	*	social distance

necessarily in the following order: the meaning of the term 'code'; the nature of the difference stated to exist between elaborated and restricted codes; the evaluation of that difference, and the relationship, if any, between code and class.

ELABORATED AND RESTRICTED CODES

In his early writing (e.g. a 1960 paper reprinted in 1974:61–7), Bernstein referred to 'modes of speech' 'associated with' or 'found within' social classes. This seems to suggest that 'modes' (later 'codes') are styles, and the contrasting features of 'formal' and 'public' languages certainly look, for the most part, superficially like stylistic variations (see Table 9.1). Thus Bernstein has been taken as implying that there is a formal style, in Standard English, associated with middle-class speakers, and an informal style, in dialect or vernacular, associated with the working class.

Lindenfield (1972) and Van den Broek (1977) have pursued this line in attempting to verify such a contrast for languages other than English. Lindenfield investigated two groups of French speakers – one working-class, consisting of skilled and manual workers, the other middle-class with teachers, a lawyer, a psychologist and a bank manager – and examined the 'syntactical complexity' of their speech in formal and informal contexts. 'Syntactical complexity' referred to the use of subordination, relativisation and nominalisation; formal meant asking informants to imagine 'talking to an audience of 100 people assembled in a conference hall' (Lindenfield 1972:80) on the subject of education or their work; informal meant getting them to talk about their summer holidays. Here are some samples of the speech she elicited (pp. 89–90):

Middle-class, formal style: 'Quand on vous donnera une dissertation littéraire à écrire, comment l'entend-on? Il est difficile bien entendu de donner des conseils généraux . . . et théoriques. Néanmoins, je pense que . . .'

Middle-class, informal style: 'Et . . . nous avons rencontré . . . une belle Americaine . . . qui faisait beaucoup d'sensation . . . dans l'bateau. De loin on lui donnait 16 ans mais quand on approchait, on s'rendait compte qu'elle avait bien au moins 60 (Rire)'

Working-class, formal style: 'Une fois que les plans sont tirés, les dessinateurs euh ont le schéma; et quand ils construisent euh soit un immeuble, ils se basent euh sur ce dessin pour leur construction'

Working-class, informal style: 'Quand i f'sait beau on allait s'baigner. Le soir, on rentrait, on préparait l'diner; et ensuite euh y avait des . . . un genre de crochet dans un p'tit . . . café'

Lindenfield concluded that in syntactical complexity there was a significant difference between middle-class and working-class speakers in *formal*, but not in *informal*, topics. This conclusion was supported in Van den Broeck's study of Flemish, which showed a convergence of styles in informal situations. He argued: 'If Bernstein *et al.* had studied informal instead of formal speech, they would probably have had no linguistic foundations for restricted–elaborated code theory' (1977:166). Differences in syntactic complexity 'do not signal differential abilities in logical analysis or conceptual thought', claims Van den Broeck, they are simply 'differences of style' (1977:175). It could be said, therefore, that Bernstein is not comparing like with like.

However, even if Bernstein was simply concerned with style, to have pinpointed two distinct 'modes of speech' would itself have been an achievement at a time when analysis of that kind of sociolinguistic variation was in its infancy. Further, the whole tenor of Bernstein's work is to show not only that these styles are different, but that they are ranked, and not everyone has equal facility in, or access to, each mode. The 'speech economy', to use a term associated with the ethnography of speaking, is not a free market.

Bernstein himself, however, soon replaced 'modes of speech' with 'codes' and later asserted: 'It is a travesty to relate the concepts of elaborated or restricted codes to superficial stylistics of middle-class and working-class forms of speech, as implied by Labov [1972a] . . . I was not essentially concerned with dialect or so-called non-standard speech' (1974:241–3). I take his word for it (see also Bernstein 1985b), though comments like the following from an associate, Denis Lawton, suggest that in the work of those influenced by Bernstein there is a closer association between dialect, code and class than Bernstein himself would allow. Discussing differences – in this instance 'output' (= length) – between essays written by a sample of boys of middle-class and working-class background, Lawton remarks:

The most likely explanation of these differences in output is that for a *Restricted Code user* expression of ideas in writing, especially in the formal medium of an essay, is much more like an act of translation than is the written expression of *middle-class boys.*

(LAWTON 1968:106, *My emphases*)

Labov, in his celebrated rejoinder to Bernstein, was responding to that school of thought which developed in the United States, and which, unfortunately for Bernstein, drew on the latter's work to demonstrate the validity of the deficit hypothesis in its application to working-class and Black speakers. The proponents of this view were, argued Labov:

giving teachers a ready-made, theoretical basis for the prejudice they already feel against the lower-class Negro child and his language. When they hear him say *I don't want none* or *They mine*, they will be hearing through the bias provided by the verbal deprivation theory: not an English dialect different from theirs, but the primitive mentality of the savage

(1972a: 206–7)

i.e. a 'barbarous tongue'. He is quite right, but in so far as Bernstein's own writings are concerned, rather than those of some of his interpreters, Labov's fire was misdirected (see Stubbs 1983:79, and especially the discussion in Atkinson 1985). For it is clear, as Bernstein, Halliday, Hasan, Hawkins and Atkinson argue, that 'code' is *not* a style or dialect, but a more abstract notion (see also Trudgill 1975:92–4). That Bernstein links 'codes, ideologies and economic structure' (1974:28) shows at what level he locates the term. Indeed, A. D. Edwards (1976:94) argues that the abstraction is such that the codes are 'beyond observation, beyond proof or disproof, and so outside the domain of social science'.

Halliday's distinction between 'code (ii)' – a speech code or style – and 'code (i)' – 'a principle of semiotic organisation' (Halliday 1978:69) is useful. As Atkinson (1985:68) succinctly puts it, Bernsteinian codes are 'regulative principles which are realised through *different possibilities of selection and combination*' (his emphases). They are 'dominant cultural principles' (Bernstein 1975:24) which in the context of a discussion of educational curricula he calls 'basic organising principles' (see Bernstein 1974:202 ff., 1975:ch. 5, and Atkinson 1985 for similarities between Bernstein's use of code in his linguistic and pedagogic analyses). Elaborated and restricted codes 'entail qualitatively different *verbal planning orientation*' (1974:92, my emphasis) which respectively *'orient their users* towards universalistic . . . and particularistic meaning' (1972b:164, again my emphasis). Halliday (1978:111) calls them 'types of social semiotic', and provided the result were not simply to substitute one ambiguous term for another, I would suggest that Bernstein's work is concerned essentially with *two distinct modes of communicative practice.*

185

Bernstein's argument depends on a connection between the form of language used (language consisting of 'relational elements and syntactic devices', and 'vocabulary' (1964b:55)), and the principles which underlie the form of usage (i.e. codes). Let us, first, look more closely at the content of the elaborated and restricted codes, as set out in Tables 9.1 and 9.2, based largely on Bernstein's own words. My basic argument is as follows. The criticism that Bernstein is not comparing like with like is substantially correct. The language in which the restricted, 'public' code is realised corresponds closely to informal, spoken language; what French linguists would call 'familiar' speech. The elaborated code is realised through a 'formal' language which corresponds closely to the *literary* language, *la langue cultivée*.

The elaborated code produces speech – or writing – which is grammatically 'accurate', syntactically complex, and lexically varied. Lexical selection is 'discriminative'. No wonder that at this point many of Bernstein's critics throw up their hands – especially when he contrasts this formal language – 'accurate grammatical order and syntax regulate what is said' (1964a:253) – with public language which has 'short, grammatically simple, often unfinished sentences with a poor syntactical form', and which is 'the major speech form of the lower working class' (*ibid.*). As anyone who has transcribed a taped conversation will know, and as Lindenfield's and Van den Broeck's research reveals, the casual speech of most classes most of the time takes that form. What Bernstein is describing as the product of the elaborated code is, undeniably, *formal* language, as he himself obviously recognised by the choice of that term in his early work.

It has been suggested elsewhere that the formal language associated with the elaborated code corresponds closely to the canons of *literary* production (Stubbs 1980:111, Street 1984:24, François 1983a:18, and Atkinson 1985:96–7 for a sceptical view). In similar vein, the Milroys (1985:146 ff.) draw attention to the contrast often made between 'planned' writing and 'unplanned' speech. I do not want to suggest an equation of elaborated code = written language (even if the latter is restricted to non-fictional prose, where the connection is perhaps closest), but simply that formal language and written language, in English and French, are of a generally similar kind. That the formal language shares the properties and values attributed to written language may be seen from a glance at what is commonly said about such language when it is contrasted with speech (cf. Brazil 1983, Brown 1983), and both formal and written language are likely to follow closely the canons of *Standard* English (or French or Dutch). 'Accurate grammatical order and syntax' means here *standard* grammar and syntax.

It might have helped Bernstein's argument on educational implications if he had acknowledged that one of the two 'languages' he identified – that produced by the elaborated code – was in effect Standard English. However, as I have said, the distinction formal/public or elaborated/restricted resides not only on the surface, in the speech produced, but at a second, deeper level of different underlying principles, specifically *planning* principles. What these are can best be seen by examining what they achieve. Five points may be emphasised.

(a)   The elaborated code is associated with *explicitness*. What needs to be said to make the meaning clear is said through the language. The context is not taken for granted.

(b)   It is associated with language which is *propositional*, rather than *performative*. Bernstein draws attention on a number of occasions to Malinowski's 1923 article on phatic communion, and suggests that a 'pure form' of the restricted code would be found in 'ritualistic modes of communication' (1964a:259). Hence the association with metaphor and condensed symbols. In consequence, that code is associated with 'position', i.e. social position or status, and thus characteristic of 'closed' societies or groups based on 'mechanical' solidarity. (Here Bernstein follows Durkheim, though he might equally have cited Tönnies.)

(c)   The elaborated code is *universalistic*, an idea Bernstein (1974:2) takes from Parsons. It refers to the way in which 'principles and operations controlling object and person relations are made explicit through the use of language' (1974:197). This universalistic principle is realised through 'metalanguages' (1974:196, 1972b:163) including those of 'control and innovation' (1974:196). Adlam makes a slightly different point by linking universality and explicitness. Thus, in particularistic speech 'only particular others – those of whom the speaker has knowledge . . . – can fully decode the message' (Adlam 1976:15). Universality is in turn linked to *consciousness*.

(d)   The elaborated code involves an 'extensive self-editing process' whereas with a public language 'speech does *not* become an object of special perceptual activity, *neither* does a theoretical attitude develop towards the structural possibilities of sentence organization' (1964a:254, cf. 1974:134).

(e)   Whereas restricted codes 'draw on metaphor' (1972b:164), elaborated codes draw on *rationality*.

It is not clear what Bernstein intends by rationality (his acquaintance with

Weber seems slight, see 1974:120). His meaning may be inferred from his comparison of public and formal language (see Table 9.1, especially items 2, 3, 5, 7 under 'Formal', and 3, 4, 7 under 'Public'); from his reference to 'the need to make explicit through syntactic choices the logical structure of the communication' (1972b:165); and from his comment that in speech associated with the restricted code 'the thoughts are often strung together like beads on a frame rather than following a planned sequence' (1974:134). Thus rationality appears to refer to organised planning, logical arrangement and overall cohesion (Cook-Gumperz 1972:138). In connection with the latter Sauvageot's comment on the text of colloquial French cited in the previous chapter may be cited:

In the story, cohesion is obtained only through the delivery, the tone, the mimicry, the gestures . . . The sample contains nothing particularly trivial, no trace even of *argot*. What characterises it [i.e. as *langue parlée*], other than the pronunciation and the shape of the delivery, is the lack of articulation of the discourse, and even of the sentences.   (SAUVAGEOT 1972:173–4)

In sum, the elaborated code is associated with explicitness, propositionality, universality, consciousness, and rationality, which entails planned, logical, coherent structure. These principles guide the way language is organised. The elaborated code is, as Trudgill (1975:100) points out, 'a matter of language *use*' (his emphasis). It is not essentially related to any particular form the language takes at the level of accent, grammar or vocabulary. Indeed, in a personal communication to Lawton (1968:98) Bernstein suggested that 'very elaborate speech' (N.B. 'elaborate', not 'elaborated', he cites the example of a religious text) might well be formed according to principles associated with the restricted code (cf. Bloch 1975a). In the next section I will develop the point that there is an important similarity between what is said to be associated with the elaborated code and what is said to be associated with what was called historically the 'cultivated language' (cf. Milroy and Milroy 1985:147). There was a discourse of 'cultivated speech' of which Bernstein's ideas are a subset.

THE DISCOURSE OF CULTIVATED LANGUAGE

The excellence of a work is constituted by the accuracy of its thinking and the manner of its organisation. That is where one finds reason. That is where one finds eloquence.   (LAMOTTE-HOUDART, CITED IN MORNET 1929: 186)

Commenting in 1930 on the 'national French language', Dauzat remarked that it represented 'the language of cultivated Parisian society which, since the Renaissance, by eliminating or modifying a number of innovations in popular speech, by adopting or adapting others, has become a highly developed tool quite different from what the language would have become if left to its own devices' (1930:544). In both Britain and France there was, by the eighteenth century at least, a clear vision that the respective languages were developing in this way, and that there was a type of language appropriate for writing – and to a certain extent speaking – on the part of those who in terms of class or caste occupied the higher echelons of the society. In France among the terms used to describe such a language by contrast to the 'vulgar' or 'popular' speech was *la langue cultivée*. What was the nature of this 'new language' that emerged in the early seventeenth century?

Some of its features are revealed in a comparison made by Pierre Guirard (1973) between it and the 'popular' language. The difference between the two, he says, is like that between Art and Nature (p. 11). Cultivated French as it developed between the sixteenth and eighteenth centuries was, Guirard argues, a learned language which was normalised and stabilised, often arbitrarily, under the influence of the grammarians. Its use was characterised by 'a heightened grammatical and etymological consciousness, and submission to rule and the authority of the author' (1973:10). Underlying its transformation were principles of logic and 'a rationalism which strives for analysis which is meticulous, detailed and *clear* in thought and expression' (1973:10, his emphasis). In the words of Vaugelas, 'If one rereads a sentence two or three times, it ought to be for the purpose of admiring it . . . not because one has to try to understand what the author meant' (in Brunot 1930:690).

The principles which regulated this cultivated language were very similar to those which Bernstein has attributed to 'formal' language and the elaborated code. Both the principles and the type of language they generated were, as Smith (1984) argues, 'hegemonic': they constituted the dominant discourse of language of their period, and in many respects, as this chapter and the next will seek to demonstrate, they do so still. To substantiate this point let me first follow certain themes in the development of *la langue cultivée* in France.

For Alexis François *la langue cultivée* is the language of 'high culture' in all its manifestations: 'dictionary, grammar, rhetoric (or stylistics), as well as its systems of versification, spelling, pronunciation and delivery' (1959 Pt. 1:xiv). It is thus not something confined specifically to writing or literature, but consists of a range of communicative practices which, however, have special application to the written word. In speech, the principles were still operative, but might be modified. An extract from Bellegardes's *Réflexions sur l'élégance et la politesse du style* (1965), cited by François, illustrates this:

One must never employ unpleasant words or phrases because it is easy enough to fall into the habit of speaking badly and one has a great deal of difficulty in ridding oneself of this unfortunate practice. However, one should not inconvenience oneself in familiar conversation nor speak in lengthy sentences. Over-organised speech inconveniences both speaker and listener. Low, easy, familiar terms may be tolerated in conversation which would find no place in a written work of consequence. One may essay words which have only recently come into being provided that one does so without affectation or in expectation of applause for having uttered a new term.   (IN FRANÇOIS 1959 PT. I: 389)

Cultivated language was *studied* speech or writing, and thus subject to the type of thinking which Lévi-Strauss contrasts with *la pensée sauvage*. It is language (Lévi-Strauss says 'mind') which is 'cultivated or domesticated for the purpose of yielding a return' (1966:219). Such domestication can be a feature of any language, as is shown in accounts by Keenan of Merina (Malagasy) oratory, and by Strathern of 'veiled talk' among New Guinea Big Men (both in Bloch 1975b). In France, and in Britain, however, from the seventeenth century onwards there was a period of *heightened* domestication, and of domestication which took a particular direction. Some indication of the direction given to *la langue cultivée* was provided in chapter 8, and here I amplify some of the points made then.

A major feature of the domestication of French was the provision of that regulation, which for Dauzat, Guirard and many other commentators was one of the key characteristics of the cultivated language, but which the sixteenth century language was said to lack. That century saw the production of a variety of treatises on grammar, spelling and pronunciation, and of dictionaries. François (1959 Pt. I:152) cites a poem by Marot (1496–1544) which dealt with one knotty problem: the rule of the agreement of the past participle. It was at this time, says François, that 'the grammatical corset began to squeeze the literary language' (p. 153). This tendency culminated in the Académie Française, the Statutes of which, devised by Richelieu, identified one of its major tasks as 'providing the language with exact rules, rendering it pure, eloquent and capable of dealing with the arts and sciences' (in Brunot 1930:35).

Why was this development thought necessary at this time? The historians of the Académie are curiously unhelpful. Certainly Richelieu himself was devoted to literature and to *reason*, for as he said in his *Political testament*: 'Si l'homme est souvrainement raisonnable, il doit souvrainement faire régner la raison' (in 1947 edition:325), and why should language escape (cf. Boissier 1909:10)? Tapié, however, suggests that 'he desired to discipline language and thought in the interests of good order and for political considerations' (1974:273). The latter would have included the prospect that French was to be the official language of an empire stretching far beyond the Hexagon, as France is sometimes called, and would achieve a status in Europe similar to that formerly held by Latin. Richelieu was also a great administrator, and the language needed to be shaped and regulated, 'cleaned up' (Brunot 1930:34) to suit the needs of a centralising bureaucracy. Unfortunately, the role of the bureaucracy in the development of French has not been accorded the attention it deserves. It would be interesting to see a study such as Fisher's (1977) applied to France, and in that connection it may be noted that most of the original members of the Academy were officials 'whose claims to literary distinction were moderate' (Perkins 1908:312).

Although regulation was one of the primary aims of Vaugelas and Malherbe, during the seventeenth century insistence on the usage of the Court as the arbiter of the rules gave way to the application of a more abstract principle, that of reason itself: 'the court was replaced by Logic' (Mornet 1929:315). Reason and logic (the two seem to have been used interchangeably) were certainly not entirely absent from Vaugelas's scheme (François 1959 Pt. 1:325, Mornet 1929:315), and certainly reason, or the desire for rationalisation, had a key role in Richelieu's thinking, but it was only later in the seventeenth century that it became a central preoccupation in discussions of language, and then perhaps in a different way.

Crucial here was the publication in 1660 of the Port-Royal Grammar, or *Grammaire général et raisonnée contenant les fondements de l'art de parler expliqués d'une manière claire et naturelle* to give it its full title. *Raisonnée* meant that the rules had to be justified not by reference to usage but to 'the logical agreement between the rule and the requirements of the mind' (Mornet 1929:314). The devotees of *grammaire raisonnée* took on all aspects of the language (vocabulary, grammar, etc.) and subjected them to logical principles. One example was once again the agreement of the past participle – 'fixed logically in the eighteenth century and eventually represented as a masterstroke of the language, a touchstone of intelligence' (François 1959 pt. 1:326).

The wider implications of the Port-Royal Grammar, of which much has been made by Chomsky (1972), are not our concern. I merely note it as an example of the application of reason to language, and of the view that reason was found *in* language, or in language of a particular kind. Between 1680 and 1750, says Mornet, classical French literature was gripped 'by a sort of rationalist fervour . . . by a sort of mysticism of logical clarity' (1929:91). Descartes, who figures prominently in Chomsky's account, certainly had a hand in this, though Mornet (1929:60 ff.) shows that his influence on literature is not easy to trace. Nevertheless the 'spirit of geometry' ruled the day (Mornet 1929:91). Language was seen as a kind of mathematics.

Rationalist fervour led to a search for the best possible way of ordering the language, especially one which lacked the declensions of the classical tongues. Thus:

The subject is brought close to the verb, the past participle is brought close to the auxiliary verb; the complements are brought close to the noun or adjective on which they depend. The subject tends to be placed at the beginning of the sentence. The direct object is never placed at the beginning of the sentence; the indirect object is also relegated to a position after the verb at least as clarity demands.

(MORNET 1929: 296)

Crucial in this was the *phrase logique*, the basic unit of discourse which François (1959 Pt. II: 153) describes as one of the 'masterpieces' of the language. The flow of speech or writing was to be constituted by logical building blocks linked together to form the phrase, the sentence, the paragraph, the work as a whole. Throughout there had to be a logical transition from one part to the next. Influential here was J. L. Balzac. 'To speak Balzac' meant to abandon the lengthy Latinesque periods which characterised earlier prose and employ shorter phrases in which primary and secondary ideas were placed in a clear relationship (Mornet 1929:291).

Order, linkage, above all clarity, were the basic principles of *la langue cultivée*. Clarity entailed transparency of meaning. To achieve this there had to be order, but the elements from which order was constructed had themselves to be 'clear' or 'pure' (Mornet 1929: 39). There was, for example, a careful selection of vocabulary: 'clear and exact terms for clear and exact ideas' (Mornet 1929: 308). Ambiguity was abhorred, and so was metaphor. The taste for images was said to be an 'illness'. Only 'logical' images were tolerated. Thus one could not *envisager les périls* because dangers (*périls*) do not have faces (*visages*) (Mornet 1929: 306–7).

Many commentators on *la langue populaire* (e.g. Sainéan 1920:367) remark its penchant for metaphor and expressive language, none more so than Guirard:

There is a sort of exaggerated affectivity in popular thought and expression, though doubtless it would be more exact to say that there is an exaggerated intellectualism in the thought of cultivated people . . . This exaggerated expressivity which one finds in certain people (certain women especially) and in certain styles (lyric poetry, familiar conversation) is quite general in popular language of which it is a specific feature.

(1973: 82)

Many of the ideas which guided the development of *la langue cultivée* were also influential in eighteenth-century England where the prevailing – Smith (1984) would say 'hegemonic' – view of language assumed 'the power of reason to remould languages completely and appeal[ed] to various principles of metaphysics and logic' (Leonard 1962:13). 'Reason and analogy' (the latter referred to parallel instances in the language) determined correct usage: '[*Either*] relates to two persons or things taken separately, and signifies the one or the other. To say "either of the three" is therefore improper' (Murray 1807, cited in Leonard, p.75).

Choice of vocabulary, too, was guided by logic. Leonard refers to one authority's 'carefully minute distinctions among such words as *abandon*, *forsake*, *leave*, *relinquish*, *desert*, and *quit*' (1962:108) – cf. Bernstein's 'discriminate selection from a range'. The goals were 'purity, propriety and precision' (Blair 1783, in Leonard 1962:146). Hence, once again, an objection to metaphor as an instance of 'vulgarity' (pp. 172–3). As in France, too, considerable attention was paid to the order of words, the structure of sentences, and their connection (see Leonard 1962: chapter VI). As Smith (1984:23) shows, the 'connective particles' (prepositions, conjunctions, and certain adverbs) were thought particularly important. She too cites Blair writing in 1780: 'The more that any nation is improved by science, and the more perfect their language becomes, we may naturally expect, that it will abound with connective particles; expressing relations of things, and transitions of thought, which had escaped a grosser view' (in Smith 1984:23). Compare Bernstein on formal language: 'use of a range of conjunctions and subordinate clauses . . . of prepositions which indicate logical relationships' (1964a:252). And conjoined with these forms was a lexicon which was not only 'rich' and used discriminatingly, precisely and non-metaphorically, but one which was shorn of 'barbarisms', 'vulgarisms', 'improprieties', 'cant', 'low terms'. A 'noble' vocabulary was required for the fine ideas which this language conveyed. In France, the use of 'vulgar' words to describe 'noble' things was in fact given a special name: it was called 'burlesque' (François 1959 Pt. II:272).

Aside from the noble lexicon, however, *la langue cultivée* shares many features with formal language/the elaborated code: explicitness, rationality, propositionality, universality, self-consciousness, 'accurate grammatical order and syntax', 'discriminative selection' of vocabulary and so on. And both are legitimated by a discourse of rationality which appropriates rationality to itself. This does not mean that the cultivated language/elaborated code are exactly the same nor that the latter is merely a descendant of the former. Nonetheless the comparison provides us with a different perspective from which to appreciate the strengths and weaknesses of Bernstein's ideas, in particular his and other sociolinguists' consideration of the relationship between language and class.

10

LANGUAGE, CLASS, POWER, EDUCATION

There are two facts (and possibly only these two) which are not in dispute. Fact (A): the language of working-class and middle-class speakers is different. Fact (B): working-class children do less well at school than middle-class children. (STUBBS 1980:149)

LANGUAGE AND CLASS AGAIN

THE MATERIAL on language and class surveyed in the two previous chapters covered a complex range of interrelated social linguistic phenomena. Much written on these topics deals selectively within that range, and confusion arises because scholars sometimes assume they are dealing with the same issues when they are not. Nowhere is this complexity and confusion more clearly demonstrated than in the discussion of language and class in education, as the account of the work of Basil Bernstein and his critics will have illustrated.

One source of confusion in Bernstein's work is his concept of code (dialect? style? semiotic principle?). Another is his conception of class and class relations: what kind of statement is he making about the connection between class and language?

In so far as Bernstein, in his early work, specifies a connection it is an indirect one. Codes are relatively autonomous ('restricted codes are used by all members of a society at some time' (1974:128)), but may be 'associated' with a particular class through a complex linking of occupation, education, community structure, family organisation and processes of socialisation. Thus: 'The normative system associated with the middle-class and associated strata are likely to give rise to the modes of an elaborated code whilst those associated with some sections of the working class are likely to create individuals limited to a restricted code' (1974:135).

A major critic of Bernstein's has been Harold Rosen, who accuses him of basing his ideas on 'an inadequate concept of class', presenting a 'stereotyped view of working-class life in general and its language in particular', and attributing 'to middle-class speakers in general certain rare and remarkable intellectual virtues' (Rosen 1972: 13). Much of this criticism is well-taken. In so far as Bernstein's analyses represent a form of correlational sociolinguistics (class A/B associated with code X/Y) then his formulation, by reducing the complex range of possible social groupings and language varieties to two in each case, clearly oversimplifies.

Rosen wants to differentiate much more finely within the 'working class' and the 'middle class', and also to extend the analysis to include language use in contexts other than those of the home and the community, notably work and the media (pp. 7, 9). However, Bernstein's concern with language is not of this correlational kind, and strictly speaking Rosen's remarks (p. 9) on the language of dockers, miners and railwaymen are irrelevant, as there he confuses code with dialect or register (and, in passing, 'articulate' with 'elaborated' (p. 16), as indeed does Labov). Nonetheless, Rosen is correct to say that Bernstein's concept of class is decidedly limited, and Rosen himself points to an alternative approach to the relationship between class and language in the following passage:

Much of the language which the working class encounter in their daily lives is transmitted to them through a variety of agencies not under their control which deploy a language designed to mystify, to intimidate and to create a sense that the present arrangement of society is immutable. Certain strata of the bureaucracy acquire this language as a vital part of their formation. (1972: 6)

This suggests that the crucial point is not that category X 'speaks' variety Y, but that speaking Y forms a part of the relationship between X and some other group, X2.

At this point it might help to note that in the background to both Rosen's and Bernstein's discussion is a perspective on class very different from that which derives from Weber or from American sociology. It comes from Marx, and refers to position in the system of production, distribution and exchange. The key distinguishing criterion is *ownership* of the means of production, etc. and by extension position in the labour market, though this may be represented in a rather different way so that class and class relations are seen as generated by the logic and operation of a particular 'mode of production'. Traditionally this model has identified not a multiplicity of strata but a duality of classes within society, though here too there has been a proliferation of terminology to bring out nuances of class position.

Grammar, phonology, and the macrostructural concepts of dialect and register have not figured prominently in this type of analysis. Where they do, as for example in Renée Balibar's account of the evolution of French during and after the Revolution, the tendency is to relate such developments to the logic of the mode of production. Language, dialect and register stem from and reflect what are ultimately material forces. Great attention, however, is paid to meaning, and the lexicon, which has a small part to play in the sociolinguistic perspective, begins to come into its own. This is not a matter of the vocabulary lists beloved of folklorists (fifty ways of saying 'apple' in Normandy; cf. Lepelley 1973) which if analysed at all lead to dialect and register. Nor does it primarily involve the language *of* class, though that has received some attention from social historians, Marxist and other. Nor does it entail the approach central to anthropology whereby the lexicon is the basis for an analysis of 'world view' or 'conceptual system'. This perspective is concerned with world view, but as 'ideology', and at its simplest the relationship between language and class is conceived in terms of what is known as the 'dominant ideology thesis' (cf. Marx and Engels 1965). Language is seen as an important vehicle for the transmission of ideology, as something through which ideology is embodied, and in which, more problematically, it is embedded.

Something of this emerges in a more recent paper by Bernstein (1981) which is indubitably one of his most obscure. It is full of gnomic utterances ('the subject is established by the silence through which power speaks', p. 338) which mean anything or nothing and which drive commentators to despair. There is, however, a detectable change of emphasis from his earlier work. This stems from his reading of Althusser. For in the opening paragraph 'class' now becomes 'class relations' defined as 'inequalities in the distribution of power and in principles of control between social groups, which are realized in the creation, distribution, reproduction, and legitimation of physical and symbolic values that have their source in the social division of labor' (1981:327). Code is still a principle of semiotic organisation, to repeat Halliday's gloss, which 'regulates the *what* and *how* of meanings: what meanings may legitimately be put together and how these meanings may be legitimately realized' (p. 342).

How, then, is the relationship between code and *class relations* formulated? Bernstein tries to specify a complex chain of linkages between codes (and ultimately specific types of text), their hierarchical ordering, the distribution of power, and the division of labour (see Figures 3, 4 and 5 in the 1981 paper). Taking the hypothetical (and it has to be said suspect) example of a 'peasant' and the 'patron' on a sugar-cane plantation, Bernstein suggests that their different 'locations' in the division of labour 'generate different interactional practices, *which realize different relations to the material base* and so different coding orientations' (p. 337, his emphasis). It is implied, though not stated, that the one orientation would be 'restricted', the other 'elaborated' (see also Bernstein 1985b where he goes over the same hypothetical example). At the same time – and this is Bernstein again wishing to have it both ways – 'coding orientations are not intrinsic to different positions' (*ibid.*) nor are particular types of coding such as the elaborated code specific to particular modes of production or to complex societies (see Bernstein 1981:355, footnote 6).

Although sceptical about much of what Bernstein says in this paper, I believe it contains valuable insights which may be linked with what a number of other writers, including Rosen, want to say, and helps us identify potentially fruitful ways of constructing the relationship between language and class. The rest of this chapter explores this issue within the institutional context of primary and secondary schools. First, I go back to the material and ideas encountered in chapter 8, that is the approach concerned with class (or rather status) as a social category, and language as dialect: 'X' speaks 'Y'. This is followed by a section in which the focus shifts to material drawn from what is known as the 'ethnography of the classroom', and considers what contribution discourse analysis can make to our understanding of language and class. 'Discourse' here is used in the conventional linguistic and sociolinguistic sense of verbal exchange of conversation – 'Discourse (I)'. The later parts of the chapter shift the focus yet again, and building on what has been said earlier about the work of Bernstein and Rosen develops the notion of 'communicative practice', outlined in chapter 1, applying it to an analysis of the relationship between language and class in education.

CLASS/STATUS:: LANGUAGE/DIALECT

Stubbs's remark cited earlier suggests that two 'Facts' pertinent to our inquiry into the relationship between language, class and education are well-established, but that their significance is a matter of considerable controversy. What kind of connection exists between language (=dialect) and class (=status) in the institutional complex known as the school?

The relative lack of educational success of working-class children in Britain and France – their educational underachievement – is so widely documented as to need little further comment. For Jeffcoate, whose *Ethnic minorities and education* we considered in chapter 6, working-class underachievement is of far greater significance than that of ethnic minorities, and indeed the two cannot properly be considered in isolation. Equally well-documented are the differences between middle- and working-class speech, though the actual distribution of class dialects within the school population is not well described.

Some indication is found in Rosen and Burgess's pioneering study in

Table 10.1. *Children and their language in London (1977–8)*

	% in population	% with 'difficulties' Reading	Writing
Strong SE	5.9	4	5
Weak SE	9.7	6	9
Weak London	35.7	15	19
Strong London	31.7	22	27
Other British	1.8	17	24
West Indian	8.2	19	23
Other	7.0	28	33

London in the late 1970s (see Table 10.1, derived from Rosen and Burgess 1980:84). This survey asked teachers to classify children by various criteria which attempted to locate the child's basic language or dialect. Omitting West Indians (the majority of whom were said to speak London Jamaican), and speakers of languages other than English, less than a fifth (18.3%) were said to speak Standard English. These figures only provide a rough and ready indication of the overall language profile of the London school system – all else considered the profile varies considerably from one school to another – but they reinforce the point made by Rosen and Burgess that 'Linguistic diversity as a phenomenon has always been present in our schools. There is scarcely an issue raised by the [contemporary] richer diversity of languages and dialects which was not there before' (1980:3).

Rosen and Burgess also had teachers assess which children were having 'difficulties' with reading or writing, and comment:

There is an unmistakeable tendency for Standard speakers to be estimated much more highly as readers and writers . . . pupils who were Standard speakers converging on London speech [i.e. 'weak' SE] tended to be estimated less highly than speakers of full Standard . . . and full London speakers less highly again than those London speakers for whom dialectal features are less marked.

(pp. 7–8)

This raises the question whether educational underachievement (of which having difficulties with reading or writing might be a symptom) is a function of the linguistic practices of the children and/or the school, or whether it is a result of something else, say the attitudes of teachers.

In the case of language attitudes do play a major part. Brazil (1983:150), in a paper published originally in 1969, provides an illuminating example of a poem written by a rural secondary pupil. Version A is what the child wrote, Version B is Brazil's 'translation':

(VERSION A)
The Balte of Wacster

I wos on my hase the Balelt begun someone Bule of a derteygrat gun.
my mate was hit in the are and. the hed and he fell to grawnd. and
ofcuse he was ded a nuther was het with a flipping grat stik a nuther was
hit and a nuther was Hit

(VERSION B)

I was on my horse and the battle begun;
Somebody blew off a dirty great gun.
My mate was hit in the arm and the head,
And he fell to the ground and of course he was dead.
Another was hit with a flipping great stick,
Another was hit and another was hit.

Brazil used this example with student teachers. Their comments ranged
from 'poverty of language' and 'slovenly speech' to 'strongly developed
sense of the rhythmic potentialities of the language'. By the late 1970s at
least one student would also have mentioned 'dyslexia'. The divergence of
opinion is important, but the fact is that for many years, and still for many
teachers, Standard English in its formal style (grammar, vocabulary,
pronunciation and the full etiquette of writing conventions) has been the
dominant language of the school and of the teaching profession. Rosen and
Burgess again:

Universal education may have been the most potent force in making people lose
confidence in the language they speak (p. 30) . . . Incalculable pupil–teacher hours
have been expended to banish 'ain't', 'we was' and the so-called double negative, all
to little or no avail except perhaps to implant doubt and even shame where none
existed before.   (p. 130)

To what avail we will see in a moment. The point here is shame.

In *Accent, dialect and the school*, Trudgill (1975) argues that social
attitudes towards language are crucial to any relationship between class,
dialect and educational failure. The child may react against the teacher's
language – the language of the school – as 'posh' (p. 60), and the teacher's
constant denigration of dialect may make the child 'inarticulate, hesitant
and resentful' (p. 62). 'Linguistic insecurity' (p. 68) may create in children a
reluctance 'to say anything lest they reveal their "inability" to use language.'
This leads Trudgill, reared in a tradition which rejects notions of linguistic
superiority, to advocate 'a society free from dialect prejudice' (Trudgill
1975:69), and policies of the kind which were later taken up by the Swann
Report (see especially Trudgill 1975: ch. 4, and Stubbs 1980, 1983). *On
dialect* (Trudgill 1983) later shows how hostile reactions to the earlier book

revealed the strength of unfavourable attitudes towards the vernaculars (see chapter 11). Is it, then, only attitudes which create educational disadvantage for those with different language or dialect backgrounds?

In one sense, yes, but in a more complex way than has so far been indicated. In his excellent account of the problem, Stubbs argues that opposition to theories of (linguistic) deficit and deprivation depends on a relativist argument, familiar to anthropologists, that language and cultures must be understood on their own terms. Certainly no culture or language could be said to be absolutely deprived or in deficit, but as Stubbs points out, it is important not to confuse 'the inherent value and complexity of some culture or language variety, with the social value attached to it' (1980:154). Languages and their speakers cannot be treated as if isolated from an existing world of jobs, housing and education. Thus 'If a group is denied access to power, knowledge or resources which are available to others in the wider community . . . they are deprived of benefits which others have, deprived of access to "mainstream culture"' (p.154, cf. Edwards, J. R. 1979:26).

'What's nice about it?'

Thus, Stubbs believes, the educational system sets up a series of 'sociolinguistic barriers' comprising 'the pervasive language environment of the school; the difficulty of separating conventional styles of language from the content of academic subjects; the complex relationship between language, thinking and educational success; and the power of social attitudes to language' (1983:21). One of these barriers derives not from the way that dialect as such is despised, but from the very fact that the practices of the school are usually in a dialect different from that of the majority of pupils. These dialect differences are often described as 'slight', but Cheshire (1982b) shows that they may often lead to considerable confusion on the part of pupils and hence to educational difficulties. What occurs is comparable to the 'linguistic interference' which Viv Edwards and others (e.g. Driver 1978, Wight 1983) say is experienced by West Indian Creole speakers (see chapter 7). Thus Wight (1983:229) concludes 'it would not be un-controversial to suggest that the greater the distance between a child's spoken English and the written English he has to learn, the longer it will take for that child to achieve literacy'.

It is easy to exaggerate the potential confusion. Trudgill, who concentrates on pronunciation, spelling and grammar, implies that most of the differences between dialect and Standard English ('the dialect of the school', 1975:46) give rise to difficulties which are at the most 'short-lived' (p. 54). And the continuing problems faced by dialect speakers (such as those documented by Rosen and Burgess for reading and writing) he would attribute solely to attitudes. Trudgill is right, of course, to say that such problems are sociolinguistic rather than strictly linguistic in nature, but the gap (or 'space' as Wight calls it) between the spoken language of the home, say, and the language of the school, is undoubtedly greater for some children than for others, and this bears on their response to the school's linguistic practices, and hence their progress in education.

On this point, Lawton's evidence on the form and content of middle-class and working-class boys' essays is interesting, even if we limit interpretation of the results to matters of stylistic difference. Consider, for example, the following opening sentences of two essays on 'My life in ten years' time' (given in Lawton 1968:112–13):

I hope to be a carpenter and do a ton on the Sidcup by-pass with a motor-bike and also drinking in the Local pub.

As I look around me and see the wonders of modern science and all the fantastic new developments I feel a slight feeling of despondency.

No prizes for guessing who wrote which essay or what consequences are likely to follow from the consistent use of one style rather than the other, at least in a traditional educational institution.

Young people's essays are also cited by Nancy Martin (1967:67) to show the problems some children have with 'the form of the written language':

(A) Only an hour to go before I leves to cattes the train which will take ms to portmouth with a thunded other fellows, Going to the same place.

(B) I do not like to hurry unduly. When I get up in the morning, I dress in a leisurely fashion. Not for me, a cold vest, thrown over the shoulders; or my shivering skin exposed to chilly bedroom air.

She comments:

In crude terms the picture at fifteen to sixteen years looks something like this: a few pupils can manage all modes; many can handle narrative and descriptive and personal experiences well, but fail dismally in the impersonal uses; many can really only write down speech with a greater or lesser degree of control of the technical forms of the written language; and when, in speech, they want to engage in argument or impose a logical order on their ideas, they fall away into narrative or become inarticulate.

Martin's remarks pose a number of problems (for example the meaning of 'inarticulate'), but to write as she does is not necessarily to subscribe to a 'deficit' theory if by this is meant a theory which attributes inarticulacy to the inherent properties of a language (Gordon 1981:60). Nor is it in any simple way to 'blame the victim'. A. D. Edwards (1976:132) criticises critics of deficit theories of the 'intrinsic' kind, which Edwards himself rejects outright, for failing 'to distinguish between *absolute* linguistic inferiority and an inferiority relative to some of the communicative demands and expectations encountered outside the particular sub-culture'. It is undoubtedly the social system whose values the educational institutions reflect which makes of difference a deficit, but equally undoubtedly this leads to real disadvantages for the child. The system is to blame, and in the long run the system must be changed, but it is utopian to suggest that meantime there is nothing to be done, and that measures aimed solely at minimising damage and equalising opportunity are simply to be condemned (cf. Edwards, J. R. 1979:141, and for France Bautier-Castaing 1980:9).

CLASS/POWER::LANGUAGE/'DISCOURSE I'

This view of the relationship between language and class in education, which treats 'class' as a category of the population, and 'language' as a dialect which that population speaks, does not, however, reveal the full story. The study of class and language within the school must move beyond a conception of language in terms of grammar and accent to consider ways in which linguistic practice as a whole is organised.

One approach is through what conventional linguistics calls 'discourse analysis'. There is now a growing ethnography of the classroom (though in 1983 Stubbs called for more) focusing on interaction between teachers and pupils in the context of teaching itself. Stubbs (1983: chs 6, 7) surveys a number of such studies, in particular that of Sinclair and Coulthard (1975, cf. Coulthard 1977, Brown and Yule 1983, Edwards and Westgate 1987).

Sinclair and Coulthard examine the minutiae of verbal exchanges to reveal the structure of the dialogue between teachers and taught, and the 'function' of, or part played by, utterances of different kinds in the dialogue's development. Central to their analysis is the concept of 'move', or linguistic gambit, and discourse is seen as consisting of a sequence of 'moves'. One such sequence has become known as 'IRF': Initiation, Response, Feedback: 'A typical exchange in the classroom consists of an *initiation* by the teacher, followed by a *response* from the pupil, followed by *feedback*, to the pupil's response from the teacher' (Sinclair and Coulthard 1975:21):

I. (Teacher): 'What is one name we give to these letters? Paul.'
R. (Paul): 'er, vowels.'
F. (Teacher): 'They're vowels, aren't they.'

(FROM TEXT OF A PRIMARY CLASS IN SINCLAIR AND COULTHARD 1975: 64)

The teacher's domination of the classroom is expressed in and through this structure which 'giving the teacher the last word, allows him to recast in his own terms any pupil response' (p. 130):

R. (Pupil): 'There's two haitches.'
F. (Teacher): 'Yes, some of them are duplicated, aren't they.'

Sinclair and Coulthard add: 'Pupils acknowledge this domination by choosing elliptical responses, and by avoiding initiating' (p. 130). As Sara Delamont remarks, 'unsolicited pupil responses are disruptive in most classrooms' (1976:101). The discourse is highly controlled, not to say orchestrated, and the way language and speakers are organised through the IRF structure reveals a great deal about the system of power and authority that prevails in the education system, and the values which underlie the social relationships enacted within the classroom.

The quasi-ethnomethodological, interactionist approach adopted by Sinclair and Coulthard does not make it easy for their analysis to move beyond the minutiae of the classroom. As Sara Delamont argues 'classroom processes' have to be studied against 'the organizational and educational background in which they are embedded' (1976:40). A further drawback to their work, which in the 1975 book is based on what happens in a primary school, is their emphasis on the overarching form of discursive practice, and their failure to comment on whether they find significant differences in the language actually used by teachers and pupils. An earlier, and in some respects more illuminating, study which tackles both discursive structure and language difference is Barnes (1971), reviewed by Stubbs, but also the subject of considerable comment elsewhere (e.g. in Edwards, A. D. 1976).

Barnes's work and that of Rosen (1967, 1971) are on the same ground as Bernstein, though the conclusions that Rosen draws are quite at odds with those adduced by his colleague at the London Institute of Education. Rosen opens his 1967 paper on 'The language of textbooks' with a quotation from the psychologist Jerome Bruner ('Concepts and the language that infuses and implements them give power and strategy to cognitive activity'). He comments: 'You are almost certainly having difficulty in making sense of that sentence . . . if you are, then console yourself, your difficulty . . . should give you greater insight into the linguistic-intellectual bafflement which besets children in school, particularly in the secondary school and more particularly in "subject" learning' (Rosen 1967:100). The form of the language is one in which meaning is encoded through abstractions which are themselves built on abstractions. The tone is highly formal, the language is 'highly compressed' and impersonal, 'as far from a spontaneous spoken utterance as the statutory provisions of the Education Act are from two boys having an argument in the school playground' (p. 101).

Following normal usage, Rosen describes such language as a 'register' (he also calls it a 'kind of discourse') whose features are characteristic of the language employed in secondary school textbooks, e.g. 'The climate of more than half the continent is thus marked by the aridity and the high range of temperature experienced', cited in Rosen 1967:104. Rosen was writing in the late 1960s, and his comments may not apply to textbooks of the 1980s, but at that time, at any rate, Rosen felt that such textbooks used language 'at the furthest pole from the pupil's own' (p. 105), which 'looks at children across a chasm' p. 111). And for some children the chasm is so great that for them 'the textbook is mere noise' (p. 111).

Barnes extends the analysis from the language of textbooks to that of the classroom teacher, finding the oral register similar to that identified by Rosen. Further:

[It] has much in common with the language . . . of official publications, of almost any printed document that sets out to discuss a topic in an impersonal public way, and indeed with the language in which this paper is expressed. [It] overlaps still more with the language of public debate and discussion in which the business of the community is carried on, in meetings and committees of greater or less formality.

(BARNES IN BARNES, BRITTON & ROSEN 1971:53)

Barnes is not specifically concerned with 'subject' registers: the specialised languages of chemistry, history, geography or mathematics. Each of these has a distinctive vocabulary often quite different from that of every day (see Barnes's description of a geography lesson in which the teacher seeks to elicit the 'correct' technical term 'crescent' used by geologists to describe the shape of sand dunes, in Barnes 1971:42, and comments in Edwards, A. D. 1976:153). Edwards himself does not believe that subject registers differ much beyond vocabulary, but clearly they also have distinctive styles for oral presentation and for written work. Compare essays on 'The Battle of Worcester' likely to be required by teachers of history or English, and both with the chemist's 'A large amount of hydrogen is made to combine with nitrogen to make ammonia' (cited by A. D. Edwards, 1976:151).

Each subject register, however, is a sub-register of the broader discourse of secondary education – in turn a sub-register of formal language – characterised by a stress on generalisation and explicitness. These are sometimes believed to reside in the subject's specialised vocabulary, and a feature common to the communicative practices of all subject registers is a concern for teaching and learning jargon: 'The technical term is often taken to have a value of its own, and its substitution for an alternative formulation is sometimes taken to have the weight of an explanation' (Barnes in Barnes, Britton & Rosen 1971:51). Thus:

204

T: 'Now can anyone remember the other word for windpipe.'
P: 'The trachea.'
T: 'The trachea . . . good . . . After it has gone through the trachea where does it go then? . . . There are a lot of little pipes going into the lungs . . . what are they called? . . . Ian?
P: 'The bronchii.'
T: 'The bronchii . . . that's the plural . . . what's the singular? What is one of these tubes called? . . . Ann.
P: 'Bronchus.'
T: 'Bronchus . . . with 'us' at the end.'
(BARNES IN BARNES, BRITTON & ROSEN 1971: 49)

Barnes calls this 'presenting' the terminology. Not only must the terminology itself be correct, however, but the language accompanying it must be 'appropriate'. Rosen (1967: 101) cites a geography essay in which the pupil wrote: 'An erratic is quite an exciting result of glaciation.' The teacher red-ringed 'exciting' and commented: 'No need to get excited. "Spectacular" a better word to use here.' This is a world, as Rosen points out, in which one does *not* get excited about erratics.

Specialist language is not always 'presented' in such explicit fashion. Degree of presentation may vary from one subject register to another (for example between 'scientific' subjects and the humanities). What is *not* presented is language which is non-specialist but which still forms part of the distinctive secondary register. To illustrate this Barnes cites the following explanation by a teacher:

They were called 'city states' . . . because they were complete in themselves . . . They were governed by themselves . . . ruled by themselves . . . they supported themselves . . . These states were complete in themselves because the terrain between cities was so difficult that it was hard for them to communicate . . . Now because these people lived like this in their own cities they tended to be intensely patriotic towards their own city. Now what's patriotic mean?
(BARNES IN BARNES, BRITTON & ROSEN 1971: 55)

Barnes comments that some 'technical' words or phrases (in this case 'city-state') are 'presented', that is explained to the pupils, through the use of other phrases which in Barnes's view 'exemplify the language of secondary education', but which are themselves taken for granted: 'one set of counters is being substituted for another'. However,

in learning such essential concepts as 'tendency', which form part of no specialism, the child is given no support from school, which tacitly assumes he comprehends them. Children whose home life does not support such language learning may feel themselves excluded from the conversation in the classroom.   (P. 55)

205

No child who cannot learn to manage [this register] . . . can hope to take much part in secondary education. (P. 60)

But what prospect is there of learning to manage it (rather than – attentive and retentive – reproduce it) if the 'conversation' in classrooms is orchestrated in the way that Sinclair and Coulthard's discussion of the IRF mode suggests?

The reasons for suggesting that Barnes and Rosen were at least 'on the same ground' as Bernstein should now be clear. A further similarity (but also a difference) between the two perspectives is found in a distinction that Rosen makes between two aspects of the secondary register: the 'linguistic conventional' and 'linguistic intellectual'.

In his 1967 paper Rosen questions the need to use the impersonal, formal, specialised register. What difference does it make if the child emerges from the biology lesson's discussion of trachea, etc. with 'it's got a lot of tubes in its body'? (This happened in the lesson cited above, Barnes in Barnes, Britton & Rosen 1971:70–1.) In Rosen's view much of the language of textbooks and subject registers is no more than 'conventional', not essential, intellectually, to the discourse. However, 'within these conventions . . . there is also language which has been perfected to embody rational thought, ultimately at its highest level' (1967:105) – a remark echoed in the conclusion to Rosen's critical review of Bernstein: 'I do think there are aspects of language usually acquired through education which, given favourable circumstances, give access to more powerful ways of thinking' (1972:19).

Barnes's gloss on this distinction identifies 'conventional' with 'sociocultural' and 'intellectual' with 'conceptual'. Conventional language has a sociocultural, 'performative', function, possibly that of signalling a boundary between disciplines, or, more generally, between educated and non-educated persons. It connotes group identity (cf. Edwards, A. D. 1976:151). An intellectual–conceptual, 'propositional' function, on the other hand, may reside in the precise, rigorous, vocabulary of substance and processes in, say, chemistry. Such language, according to Edwards, is denotative.

The distinction between 'conventional' and 'intellectual' is relatable to one advanced by Gillian Brown (1982) between 'message-oriented' and 'listener-oriented' language (cited in Milroy and Milroy 1985:119). However, the line between the two may be quite fine. For example, is the chemists' 'a large amount of hydrogen, etc.' simply 'saying': 'This is an impersonal and hence objective statement and shows we are *scientists*', or is the form of words essential? Is it an intellectually necessary component of the objectivity which the discipline requires?

How does this link with Bernstein? Lawton (1968:77) seems to suggest that the language of teaching and school textbooks is 'in' an elaborated code, and indeed the register discussed by Barnes and Rosen is close to what Bernstein had earlier called 'formal' language. Barnes himself says that the register is not 'coterminous' with the code, though he also agrees that the language of secondary teachers will 'tend towards it' (p. 60). Once again there is a danger of confusing 'code (i)' and 'code (ii)'. It would be more appropriate to say that an elaborated code or cultural principle *underlies* the discourse. Be that as it may, it is apparent that there is a discourse ('register', 'language', set of communicative practices) and a dialect, Standard English, characteristic of education, and that there is a significant gap between that discourse and that in which most children are enmeshed most of the time in their everyday lives. How, then, does this relate to class and class relations?

CLASS/POWER::LANGUAGE/'DISCOURSE II'

The evidence on the significance of status-related dialect differences for educational progress cited earlier came entirely from Britain. Although research on links between status, dialect and education in France has been less extensive, and perhaps less intensive, sufficient has been done to show that the position is in broad terms very similar (for example, Bautier-Castaing 1980, François 1980b, 1983c, Marchand 1972, and Jones and Pouder 1980 on classroom discourse). On the other hand, compared to what is said about the situation of speakers of the minority languages, orthodox linguists and sociolinguists in France do not appear to be as strongly critical of the educational dominance of the standard language as do their English counterparts (but see Fabre 1983 and the references cited). Comments are generally much more cautious than those one finds in, say, the work of Stubbs or Trudgill. Sauvageot, for example, merely notes that the spoken language is usually ignored in the teaching of French, and suggests that 'it is useful for teachers to have some notion of what actually happens when they speak and when their pupils speak' (1972:184), leaving the teachers to draw their own conclusions.

There is, however, another critical tradition in France with an important direct and indirect bearing on what we are discussing. It reflects the second perspective on language and class outlined earlier, and deals with the relationship between class, power and language as 'Discourse II'. The work of Renée Balibar (1974, and Balibar and Laporte 1974) provides a valuable point of entry, *inter alia*, for an understanding of the history of French education.

Balibar is concerned with 'linguistic practice', the social activities through which language is produced, and how these are labelled and organised. *Les français fictifs* (1974) is specifically concerned with linguistic practice in education, that is within the context of a related set of practices which are of the school: *pratique scolaire* (Balibar 1974:24). Her basic argument is that within post-Revolutionary schools there were – and are – two sorts of linguistic practice which were/are hierarchically ordered. Both involve 'fictive' French. By this she does not mean that they are 'false', nor does the term imply 'literary' languages as such, with specific grammars and vocabularies. These are 'constructed' languages whose mode of organisation set them 'at a distance from the utterances which are exchanged in practice' (p. 40). They are artificial codes deemed appropriate for writing.

The existence of two sorts of fictive French had the consequence 'of reserving the full exercise of reasoned French for the ruling classes at the same time as obliging the population as a whole to know enough grammatical French to understand the French of the fully educated classes' (Balibar and Laporte 1974:39). Nonetheless these are not to be seen as two separate languages or dialects – a bourgeois French on the one hand and a proletarian French on the other, to use her terms – but *'different ways of practising the same language'* (p. 27, her emphasis). In France, as in Britain, there is a *common language* which at one and the same time is a force for unity, but also because of divergent practices, a force for division.

Balibar's argument requires amplifying and modifying: with what kind of linguistic practices are the two sorts of fictive French associated? How were (are?) these realised in schools and classrooms? Have they changed in any way? If so, with what historical periods can various practices, and changes in practice, be associated? And what is the social or political significance of one kind of practice as compared with another?

Balibar insists on a fundamental difference between what she terms 'monarchic' French, prior to the Revolution of 1789, and the 'Republican French' which followed it (p. 58). By comparison with the French of the Ancien Régime, Republican French was 'unmarked socially'. This refers to three things. (a) In theory, French was the 'national' language, the property of no one estate or class; (b) in terms of usage, the Revolution attacked the linguistic distinctions employed by the aristocracy, creating a kind of classless French (p. 239); (c) in literature – principally descriptive prose – it is the usual practice to eradicate all kinds of vernacular or regional forms, and to write in a standard which cannot betray the origins of the author. In certain nineteenth-century novels this practice extended to dialogue. Thus the peasant woman Félicité in Flaubert's *Un coeur simple* speaks a classless, regionless French (Balibar 1974:130 ff.). However, the idea of a common, unmarked, national language, a standard available to all, is also *fictif*, not because the differences between the spoken language of one class and another continued to exist, albeit in a changed form, after the Revolution, but because after 1789 the Court and the aristocratic salons 'ceased to exercise their ancient domination of the "language", which was then taken on by "literature"' (p. 59). And through literature, education. In Balibar's view a major new form of differentiation emerged from the school, finding expression in what after the Revolution came to be called education of the primary and the secondary 'degrees'.

Revolutionary language policies incorporated a call for universal primary education wherein the people of France were, according to Balibar, to be 'trained, on the basis of equality in the national language' (p. 126). Eventually the system provided *elementary* French, a 'primary school French', for everyone. But there was unequal access to, and provision for, training in *secondary* French, which Balibar defines as 'rhetorical and grammatical techniques which allow one to obtain the effects of verbal creation by way of the national language' (p. 126). There is a linguistic and ideological 'trench' (p. 281) separating the two degrees. On one side the 'elementary grammatical primary degree', where French, 'the only language which is taught, is realised by way of rules acquired by rote learning', and on the other, the secondary degree where 'elementary grammatical French is reconstructed through the diverse forms of French appropriate to translation and literary discourse' (p. 143). Thus (p. 244):

> The end result, but to be expected in our class society, is pregnant with conflict. All the French speak French. That is they possess a linguistic weapon–cum–tool for the defence of their interests which is legally common to all. But only the most educated are in possession of advanced essay-writing and compositional skills (de la Rédaction intégrée à la Composition-Dissertation) and thus exercise linguistic domination.

In evaluating Balibar's distinction between primary and secondary practices it is well to remember that until far into the nineteenth century the provision of even elementary education was extremely poor through much of France, and for many if not most people (Cherval 1977: 142 ff.). In Furet and Ozouf's examination of variation of educational provision – between North and South, town and country, rich and poor regions and strata, and for boys and girls – what stands out, generally, is the total absence of it. Where it did exist the provision could be skimpy and haphazard. Teachers came and went, most had few if any qualifications. What can an educational language have actually meant in a situation like the following?

> Some time after our arrival in Mes Gourmelon (1818), we went to a school run by M. Preau, a customs officer at Laber . . . When M. Preau left for Camfront, we

remained for some time without going to school, except for our Aunt Marie-Renée, who taught us to read. Later there came to Laber a drunkard by the name of Couer who taught us when he wasn't too plastered; he didn't stay long. Then came M. Grinet, who was an intelligent man for his time . . . When M. Grinet left for Kerhouan, that was the end of school. Finally, M. Toussaint came . . . So we were back to school again . . . Then he too left, and that meant that the only school there was was with Aunt Marie-Renée.

(CITED IN FURET AND OZOUF 1982: 106)

Compare the hedge schools and itinerant teachers of Ireland and Wales.

For most people education was precarious, poor or non-existent, at least until *c*. 1850. It was only in mid-century that 'classes' and the so-called 'simultaneous' method of teaching became common (Furet and Ozouf 1982:133), and the school house emerged as a building in its own right, providing a home for a distinct, *localised* set of practices of which the outward signs were 'books, the blackboard, slates, exercise books and pens' (Furet and Ozouf 1982:248).

This does not affect Balibar's point as she is concerned less with provision than with aim and content. In *Le Français national* she argues that even if the Republic, in the years following the Revolution, had not the wherewithal to implement an educational policy, that policy established a *model* of education *à degrés* – basic, elementary for all, advanced for some – which dominated thinking over the next hundred years, to be realised after the Jules Ferry Reforms in the last decades of the nineteenth century (Balibar and Laporte 1974:127 ff.). Certainly within existing provision a distinction between elementary and advanced was implemented, and although Furet and Ozouf do not deal directly with this, they show that the extent of provision varied with the wealth of a region or locality. Access to provision was thus almost certainly linked to occupation and status.

Early in the nineteenth century the basic skills taught in elementary education were elementary indeed. So far as there were established educational practices, teachers retained the method favoured under the Ancien Régime of a division of learning into three stages: reading, then writing, then arithmetic (pupils' fees were set accordingly). In writing it was the technique, the physical skill, which was taught (Furet and Ozouf 1982:76–7), usually on an individual basis. André Chervel, who bears out many of Balibar's contentions, comments that:

If, for the more advanced pupils, one of the favourite exercises was the copying out of contracts, private agreements, model receipts or acknowledgements of debts, it was the case that for many the use of writing in adult life did not extend beyond this limited range of practices. If composition was unknown and remained so for a long

210

Table 10.2. *Language instruction in French primary schools, 1834, 1868 by age group*

	6–8	8–10	10+
1834	Correct pronunciation, memory exercises.	French grammar, dictation.	Rules of syntax, grammatical and logical analysis, composition.
1868	Elementary spelling, simple dictation.	Spelling, dictation.	Reasoned application of rules of grammar to classic texts. Simple exercises in composition.

time, it was because the kind of writing taught to working-class children was thought of as a servile form of writing, a form of imitation closely linked to existing models. (CHERVEL 1977: 144)

At this stage the gap between the practices of elementary education and those of the secondary level, based in the classics and offering an abstract, literary and philosophical training, could not have been greater (cf. Balibar and Laporte 1974:149). As the formal, institutional system of education took shape, however, differentiation by level was built into the evolving primary syllabus which in its later stages began to overlap with that of the early stages of secondary education. The 1834 curriculum for primary schools, laid down by statute, included provision for moral and religious instruction, arithmetic, geography and history, drama and singing, and three linguistic elements: reading, writing and the French language (Furet and Ozouf 1982:137). The syllabus for the latter was set out for the different age groups as follows (Table 10.2, from Furet and Ozouf 1982:137, 140. The provisions for 1868 are those for the Seine Department).

There is nothing surprising in the progression indicated in the syllabus: how would a six-year-old make out with 'classic texts'? However, Chervel's account of the nineteenth-century school grammar books indicates (1977:149–50) wide acceptance of the view that the teaching of grammar should be divided into analysis of 'first', 'second' and 'third' levels, each with their own textbooks, etc. These were later reduced to two: 'grammatical' and 'logical'. Chervel comments that this graduated method of teaching grammar, orthography and punctuation remained in force through the nineteenth century, and survived to modern times: 'Thus was initiated the practice of beginning with the analysis of words, grammatical analysis, restricting logical analysis only to the most advanced pupils' (Chervel 1977:150).

Balibar's analysis of elementary French emphasises certain grammar books widely used through the nineteenth century. One of these was Lhomond's *Elémens de la grammaire française* published before the Revolution, in 1780, but which won a competition for textbooks to be used in the post-Revolutionary system. Lhomond's book presented a simple grammar in a simple way, in the style of the catechism – Lhomond also wrote a textbook on *Christian doctrine* for school use (Chervel 1977:67): 'The verb is a word which is used to express that which is or that which does' (cited *ibid.*). Later texts such as Larive and Fleury's *Grammaire préparatoire* an edition of which was adopted officially after the Jules Ferry reforms, were, according to Balibar, largely based on Lhomond. She comments:

Elementary French Grammar became *what it still is now* [my emphasis]: too detached from the terminology and sentence structure of Latin to prepare the way for grammatical and logical analysis and for the type of discourse characteristic of the second degree; too attached to that terminology to acquire the rationality required by the widespread, national practice of French. The most tangible result was and *still is today* [her emphasis] the holding back of three-quarters of French citizens in the exercise of French at primary school; the closing of the passage from one degree to the other. (BALIBAR 1974: 146)

Though Lhomond's book went through several hundred editions up to 1893 (Chervel 1977:63), there were other, in some respects more influential, competitors. One was Noel and Chapsal's *Nouvelle Grammaire Française* of 1823, the 1826 abridged version of which was specifically aimed at primary schools (Chervel 1977:102). Chervel calls it 'the fundamental work of French school grammar in the 19th century' (p. 100). It was favoured by the 1830s education reforms, went through multiple editions, and made Chapsal himself a millionaire.

The importance of this work in Chervel's opinion was that it provided teachers and pupils with a complete and up to a point unambiguous set of rules for the construction of 'good', 'correct' sentences, resolving a number of problems left over from the previous century. (Anyone in doubt of the 'fictive' nature of French should read Chervel's account of how nineteenth-century school grammars treated the 'problem' of the agreement of the past participle.) Noel and Chapsal also provided a solution to the practical difficulties posed by the demands for mass instruction in French by offering a large number of 'exercises' which could be used in class after class, year after year. In certain respects, however, the approach underlying 'chapsalism' as Chervel calls it was fundamentally different from the rote-learning of a catechism assumed by Lhomond.

Chervel traces a connection between Noel and Chapsal and eighteenth-century ideas of analytical grammar through the importance attached to the *phrase*, conceived simultaneously as a grammatical and logical unit. The *phrase* or sentence consisted – or should consist – of a proposition or series of principal and dependent propositions (Cherval 1977:131–2). Thus grammatical analysis entailed – in theory – logical analysis (p. 133, cf. François 1959, Pt. II:166). It might seem, therefore, that Noel and Chapsal bridged primary and secondary education, in some respect anticipating the principles inculcated in the latter (see Balibar 1974:110). This, I think, is what Balibar means when she says that elementary French is 're-elaborated' at the secondary level (p. 143). In reality, Noel and Chapsal provided only mind-numbing exercises. The vast majority of pupils found 'grammar' stultifyingly boring (see Appendix 1 in Chervel 1977).

THE LANGUAGE OF THE 'TWO DEGREES'

The position Balibar takes on the language of the two degrees is not unique. Shorn of its Althusserian associations, her concept of secondary French is not far removed from the much simpler notion of *la langue cultivée* developed by Alexis François, which he expressly distinguished from a literary language (1959 Pt. I:xiii). It is also at the very least on the same ground as Rosen's and Barnes's concept of the 'language of textbooks', just as they in turn are on the same ground as Bernstein's elaborated code, and the latter has much in common with *la langue cultivée*.

Her work also deals essentially with the period when most pupils finished schooling at the elementary stage. Until well into the twentieth century (compulsory) elementary education was the only education available to most people, and not every pupil completed that. Only relatively recently have all children normally gone on to some form of secondary education, as the history of changes in the school-leaving age shows. But the kind of distinction she makes carried over into the modern system of secondary education via streams of schools or classes.

Let us recall that linguistic-educational practices encompass grammatical, lexical and phonetic usages employed and/or encouraged or discouraged, implicitly or explicitly, within the school ('slovenly speech', the 'language of textbooks', the use of commas), and 'higher' levels of linguistic and socio-linguistic organisation oral and written (a 'lesson', a 'seminar', a 'lecture', a 'tutorial', 'note-taking', 'essays', 'a paper', 'a book', the IRF structure). Linguistic-educational practices differ from those which characterise the everyday life of pupils (and teachers?) – hence the 'chasm' of which Rosen writes so eloquently – though in certain respects they resemble those of formal public life generally.

In Britain, the existence of differences *within* schools, according to the 'level' of establishment or pupil, is indicated by Sinclair and Coulthard's evidence (for primary schools) and that of Barnes and Rosen (secondary). Barnes's evidence also suggests a difference within the latter sector, with less use of explicit presentation and in general a preponderance of the language characteristic of secondary education (in Barnes, Britton & Rosen 1971:54) in what were the selective (grammar) schools compared with others. Balibar's work is not directly comparable with this as she is not concerned with the form of classroom discourse or, at least directly, with the 'language of textbooks', but with the different kinds of production, especially written production, which the pupils are taught and encouraged to learn.

In France, elementary educational practice instructed pupils how to produce simple, grammatically 'accurate' sentences. The linguistic emphasis was 'microstructural' and 'textual' (Bautier-Castaing 1980), concerned with the linguistic environment of the word or phrase, and confined to the sentence. The *phrase* was the largest linguistic segment thought to be within the competence of nineteenth-century school grammars (Chervel, p. 131). Little attention was paid to the extra-linguistic features of language use, and 'macrostructural' features of language organisation – the discursive level – were ignored except for the production of simple 'narrations'. This, as Weil points out, isolates 'as the only possible form of verbal expression' a type of discourse which is only one of many actually available to the child, and thus in effect reduces the child's 'global expressive potential' (1972:93). Yet in contemporary schools, says Bautier-Castaing, what distinguishes between pupils – in addition to differences in 'lexico-syntactic repertoire' – is precisely the degree of mastery of discursive organisation (1980:11). She argues that it is in these higher orders of language use – which she claims linguistic research in education has generally ignored – are to be found the linguistic sources of educational underachievement (1980:16).

Whether pupils, especially those from the working class, for whatever reason have difficulty in mastering the kinds of discursive practices that the school ultimately favours, or whether – as Balibar might put it – streaming is 'arranged' in such a way as to deny working-class access to those practices, is not the issue I propose to discuss here. More important for the moment is the nature of these practices and the fact that they are accorded very high value.

Bautier-Castaing's paper, which examines how written work is assessed by teachers in contemporary secondary schools, sets out some of the criteria by which work is judged (1980:13). The desired features include a proper introduction and conclusion, an argument which is coherent, the use of 'appropriate' arguments, their degree of abstraction and generality, the presentation of an objective opinion, and the degree of 'maturity' which the piece reveals. Above all, perhaps: 'The realisation of a discursive plan, a macrostructure involving a dissociation between the author and the actor in the events under discussion' (p. 14). She provides the comments of one teacher on an essay judged 'Mauvais':

(Handling of the theme): 'You have brought out the basic issues but you deal with them without much thought on your part and without sorting clearly the arguments for and against.'
(Plan): 'No rigorous plan, mostly a succession of remarks without any link between them.'
(Language): 'Too imprecise.'

(Rather like comments I find myself making on my own students' essays!)

Further illustration of the type of practice which contemporary secondary French seeks to cultivate comes from research by Frédéric François (1983b), which asked people from different backgrounds to define words. Two interviewees responded as follows to *hammer* and *wizard* (in François 1983b: 139).

Hammer: (1) tool; (2) tool comprising a handle and a mass of metal which is used for knocking. Wizard: (1) predicts the future; (2) mythical character with evil power who appears in legends and children's stories.

(1) is a 'peasant', (2) a doctor. François's comment on their different definitions is that in the doctor's we find 'much wider lexical and syntactic knowledge, a class-based practice in handling abstraction, cultural reference (historical reference too so far as the wizard is concerned), an "ease", as opposed to a strategy of minimal discourse'.

François's paper is in fact about 'complexity' in language and how that might be defined. In a further test respondents were asked to paraphrase a speech by the then Justice Minister, reported in *Le Monde*, which François himself judged to be 'complex' (p. 142) because of its abstract nature, its presentation of an argument between two points of view, its use of technical and rare words, and its syntactic complexity (use of subordination, coordination, chains of complements, use of connecting words, cf. Kingman Report 1988: 34). If this sounds familiar, it is. For with François's account of this text we come back to Bernstein.

François himself has evaluated and criticised Bernstein's work in a number of papers (1980a, 1983a, 1983b). On the whole I concur both with the reservations he expresses and his ultimate judgement that Bernstein's work represent a significant shift in focus from the microstructural features

215

of language to the macrostructure of discursive organisation. However, like Rosen, François believes that the relationship between class and the type of language which might be called complex or elaborated is far more diffuse than Bernstein's earlier work at least allowed. This brings us back to the theme with which this chapter started and to the question posed in the subsequent discussion of Balibar's work: what is the significance (political, social and intellectual) of the hierarchical ordering of the communicative practices we have identified?

11

AUTHORITATIVE DISCOURSE

LET US accept that there is a type of discourse – call it elaborated-formal – which has no connection with any superior form of cognition. Let us further accept that the relationship between this discourse and the dialect or language through which it is realised is an arbitrary one. It could, in theory, as well be through Cockney or Gaelic as through Standard English. That any language or dialect has this potential is illustrated by the fact that features of linguistic practices associated with the elaborated-formal discourse are found in French and English, and may be observed in many other European languages.

Let us also accept that any connection with class (= status) is indirect. The elaborated-formal discourse is best treated as an ideal-type (cf. Bernstein 1964a: 252). It cannot be identified in a straightforward way with the speech of any individual or group, nor is it necessarily (or even usually) characteristic of the language of Mayfair or the Faubourg St Honoré. Nonetheless, as discussion of the principles which underlie this discourse will have shown, it represents ways of ratiocinating associated with the dominant culture and mode of organisation in Europe (cf. Bernstein 1975: 22–4). This need not imply that such ways of ratiocinating are dominant because they are *intrinsically* more powerful. They seem more powerful, and in a real sense *are* more powerful, because they are dominant.

Rosen's criticism (1972) that Bernstein's original discussion failed to make that kind of connection is certainly justified. Bernstein's predilection for Durkheim – and later for the most functionalist of Marxisms – obscures some of these issues in his own writing (see Atkinson 1985 for a defence of the Durkheimian influence in Bernstein). A brief reference to Weber (Bernstein 1974: 119–20), on the other hand, suggests ways in which Bernstein's own ideas could be developed, and the discussion of 'legitimacy', in the 1981 paper, begins to illustrate the potential (see also Bernstein 1985a).

Legitimacy is crucial. Elaborated-formal discourse is authoritative, having in Weber's terms legitimate power. It is 'hegemonic'.

There are, however, several ways in which discourse may be authoritative, several kinds of authoritative discourse. Each has a contextually or situationally defined legitimacy (e.g. in religion, science, politics, literature, and consider the idea of 'appropriateness' in sociolinguistics).

In 'Discourse in the novel', the Russian literary critic M. Bakhtin (1981) draws a distinction between what he terms 'authoritative' and 'internally persuasive' discourse. By the former, all that concerns us here, he means an 'external' or 'prior' discourse which speaks with authority, as for example 'the word of a father, of adults and of teachers' (p. 342):

The authoritative word demands that we acknowledge it, that we make it our own; it binds us, quite independently of any power it may have to persuade us internally; we encounter it with its authority already fused to it. The authoritative word is located in a distanced zone, organically connected with a past that is felt to be hierarchically higher. It is, so to speak, the word of the fathers. Its authority was already *acknowledged* in the past. It is a *prior* discourse. It is therefore not a question of choosing it from among other possible discourses that are its equal. It is given (it sounds) in lofty spheres, not those of familiar contact. Its language is a special (as it were, hieratic) language. It can be profaned. It is akin to taboo, i.e. a name that must not be taken in vain. (p. 342)

The discourse to which Bakhtin refers is a special case, associated with what Weber called 'traditional' authority. The formal language of oratory and ritual in many societies is often authoritative discourse of the kind that Bakhtin has in mind (e.g. 'its semantic structure is static and dead', p. 343, cf. Bloch 1975a). Though the elaborated-formal discourse may now sometimes (perhaps often) appear 'static and dead', its authority is in theory at least what Weber called 'rational-legal', or at any rate grounded in an ideology of rationality now hallowed by tradition.

How did this particular form of discourse acquire authority in those settings and institutions where it has possessed it? One reply might be that the question is irrelevant. Any form would do so long as it was 'theirs' and so long as it could connote the boundary between one class and another. It is not the form which is important, but its function. Does this mean that there is no relationship whatsoever between *this particular form* and other features of social, cultural, economic, or political organisation?

If the elaborated-formal discourse is associated with 'rationality' as a principle of organisation – and we have to be careful here because this element of its form is one which the discourse claims for itself – then it could be said that it embodies principles which underlie the linguistic and other practices of bureaucracy, science, technology and the industrial order. It is the code of the dominant institutions which provide the framework for, and are at the heart of, a 'modern' economic and political system. This is the crux of Gellner's point in a discussion of the role of rationality in entrepreneurial and bureaucratic activities where he links economic and what he calls 'cognitive' growth (1983:23, 77–8) – though 'transformation' would be preferable to 'growth'. Making a connection with the 'elaborate code' [*sic*], Gellner argues that the potentiality of language for 'formal, context-liberated use . . . comes into its own, and . . . becomes indispensable and dominant' in an industrialised society 'based on a high-powered technology and the expectancy of sustained growth, which requires both a mobile division of labour, and sustained, frequent and precise communication between strangers involving a sharing of explicit meaning, transmitted in a standard idiom and in writing when required' (1983:33–4).

Gellner's remarks remind me of the many claims often made for literacy, claims which, as Street (1984) has shown, must be subjected to the closest scrutiny. Nonetheless the interlinking at an ideological and practical level of rationality, discourse and standard language in what may be called 'techno-literate' societies provides a major contrast between them and their 'agro-literate' predecessors.

Whether or not elaborated-formal discourse is indeed more 'rational' and hence more 'powerful' in its own right is a difficult point (see Street's discussion of the alleged relationship between literacy and rationality, 1984:19 ff.). Linguists would affirm that 'what can be said in one language can be said in another'. True, though this may beg the question of the meaning of 'what can be said'. It also begs the question whether what is at stake is language in the linguists' restricted sense. Bakhtin, for example, views language not as 'an abstract linguistic minimum of a common language, in the sense of a system of elementary forms', but as 'ideologically saturated . . . a world view . . . insuring a maximum of mutual understanding in all spheres of ideological life' (1981:271).

Some of the problems might be surmounted by putting it this way. There may be communicative practices, in the broadest sense, operating at the discursive level, which *given certain organisational goals* achieve those goals most effectively. Moreover, such practices need not be *inherent* in any language or linguistic structure, but potentially available to all. They constitute machinery for speaking and writing, and thus a socio-technical phenomenon (like bureaucracy of which they are an integral part) which come into their own in particular kinds of society.

Whether or not such a case can be made, the relationship, if any, between discourse, language of articulation, mode of organisation, and the economic and political system, is by no means a simple one.

First, it is possible to 'locate' the elaborated-formal discourse in historical terms and make a connection with the development of science, technology and bureaucracy, and the industrial order. Nonetheless, just as Bakhtin (1981:271) traces the unitary literary language back to Aristotle, we must recognise that the discourse has long formed the basis for language deemed, in a European context, appropriate for 'ideas' (cf. Lukes 1982: 298, fn. 95). As such it antedates the rise of science and so on.

One implication of a historical language of 'ideas' is that those who do not employ this form of speech are not engaged in the discussion of ideas, or rather what are thought, by the culture, to be ideas. However, since the sixteenth century, approximately, there has been a conscious harnessing of the principles embodied by this language to the social, economic and cultural order (cf. Lukes 1982:298) in ways which have made it a fundamental feature of dominant ideology and practice – if not exclusively of the dominant.

Secondly, the elaborated-formal discourse transcends national languages, in a similar way to that in which, argues Bakhtin, there is a relatively unified and centralised literary language in Europe. The relationship between the discourse and a particular mode of economic production and social relations such as capitalism should not therefore be taken for granted. It may be present in *any* type of 'complex' industrial-scientific-bureaucratic order (cf. Bernstein's comments on the 'pedagogic device' in 1985a). It thus cuts across the boundaries of capitalist and non-capitalist, though not necessarily pre-capitalist, systems (cf. Bloch's discussion of formal language from this point of view, 1975). Strict adherence to a Marxist definition of class, and the search for a relationship between type of discourse and a specific (capitalist) system of production relations, both of which characterise the work of Balibar, preclude the possibility of seeing this.

Thirdly, for reasons connected with their socio-economic base, certain languages such as English and French (or German), and within these certain dialects, have become associated with the elaborated-formal discourse. The way in which processes such as the rise of the nation-state and of the technical-scientific-bureaucratic order have impacted on society has meant . that the dominant language or dialect has incorporated the elaborated-formal discourse within its domains. Dialect and discourse overlap, and the 'ability' to actualise the elaborated form is thought to reside in competence in the specific language with which it is associated. Hence that competence may both denote and connote the holding of society-wide power. Thus lack of command of the language or dialect which actualises the discourse excludes the speaker from the domains in which power resides, and thence from direct participation in the dominant system. In this respect he or she may be rendered powerless (cf. Baric 1979). Kress's account (1979:62) of a dialogue between a speech therapist and a child illustrates this at the micro-level (cf. Mueller 1973:44 ff.).

CHALLENGING THE DISCOURSE

None of this is to say that the system is immutable or unchallengeable. In Britain, and in other European countries, there have frequently been challenges to the supremacy of the elaborated-formal discourse, some attacking its form or content, others the language or dialect in which it is actualised – occasionally all of these simultaneously. In different ways, perhaps, a literary and artistic movement such as Romanticism has been part of the challenge, as have been various kinds of anti-seriality in music, film, novels and painting.

This is a vast field, worthy of study in its own right, and here I consider only three examples relevant to the social linguistic themes of this book. The first represents a strategy of 'adoption', the second one of 'reclamation', the third one of 'counter-proclamation'.

One difficulty with correlating discourse and class is that the elaborated-formal discourse and its associated language or dialect is potentially available to *any* individual or group, including those formally outside the established power system. Anyone may adopt its communicative practices as their own.

An illustration of this is the widespread use within the British labour movement of Citrine's rules for the conduct of meetings (1952), based on Erskine May's *Parliamentary practice*. Consider, for example, what Citrine has to say about 'Points of order':

Points of order must deal with the *conduct* or procedure of the debate. The member rising to put the point of order must prove one or more of the following: (a) That the speaker is travelling outside the scope of the question, (b) that he is using unparliamentary language, (c) that he is transgressing some rule of the society, or (d) that he is infringing standing orders . . . If the Chairman finds a member continually rising on frivolous points, he should check this firmly . . . Brevity and directness are the soul of points of order.　　(CITRINE 1952: 201–2)

An extended example of this strategy of adoption is provided by Pratt's account (1979) of the language of adherents of the Italian Communist Party (PCI), in particular the party leaders.

Pratt begins by discussing the language of informal public conversation (between males) whose tone is dominated by 'banter, irony and veiled hints' (p. 5). Some of the features of this discourse reappear in local PCI branch meetings, though here we begin to encounter a different type of discourse which becomes increasingly dominant as the location of the meeting (and the status of the speaker) move up the party's organisational hierarchy. The speeches of the major party figures are characterised by extensive 'preparation' (and by their length). 'Preparation' is signalled, among other things, by a lengthy passage which places the topic in context, 'framing it', *inquadrare*. If a speaker wishes to divert from his/her announced framework they will say 'And here I open a parenthesis' (p. 16), clearly indicating the formal literary mode that is employed.

Pratt himself specifically says that while rank-and-file speech resembles that produced via a restricted code, leadership discourse shows 'many of the characteristics of an elaborated code' (p. 18). On the other hand, the latter also resembles the formal oratory of traditional societies which Bloch assimilates to the restricted code in that its speakers operate with a limited vocabulary, style, range of illustrations and syntax (Bloch 1975a:13). My own view is that the discourse of PCI leaders (and that of Marxists generally) corresponds closely to the principles of the elaborated-formal discourse. The irony in the Italian case is that, in adopting this discourse, the PCI leadership reinforces an organisational cleavage between cadres and rank-and-file which resembles that prevailing in the wider, class-based, society. Authoritative becomes authoritarian.

The second example comes from Olivia Smith's account (1984) of the 'hegemonic' discourse of language of eighteenth-century England found characteristically in the work of Johnson. Drawing a firm distinction between 'barbarous' and 'cultivated' language, it assumed that rationality resided within the latter and its users. 'Grammar, virtue and class' were closely connected (Smith 1984:9). By their syntax, vocabulary, style and topic, some kinds of speech or writing were in this discourse defined as legitimate, others dismissed as simply unworthy of recognition. These judgements were not confined to 'literature', for instance determining what could and could not be printed and how the material that was published would be reviewed, but pervaded the world of politics in the ordinary sense of the term. They influenced, for example, the debate about the extension of (male) suffrage (Smith 1984:29 ff.), and, says Smith, 'Between 1797 and 1818 . . . Parliament dismissively refused to admit petitions because of the language in which they were written' (p. 30). She comments: 'the disenfranchised could not write in a language which merited attention' (p. 34). The discourse constituted a language of the powerful which defined and legitimated their power.

Smith's book is in large part concerned with attempts to break that hegemony and create what she calls an 'intellectual vernacular discourse' (p. x). She places a number of writers from Thomas Paine to William Cobbett in this tradition. Thus, '[The] *Rights of Man* demonstrated that a language could be neither vulgar nor refined, neither primitive nor civilized . . . [Paine] stressed the intellectual and moral capabilities of his audience and wrote in a language that was alleged not to exist, an intellectual vernacular prose' (Smith 1984: 35–6). This he did partly through a style in which he united 'vernacular diction' (vocabulary, rhythm) with formal syntax (see Smith, pp. 47–8). Cobbett, too, especially in his *Grammar of the English language* (1818) which was written for 'soldiers, sailors, apprentices and plough-boys' (Smith 1984:233), encouraged those outside the traditional literate classes to take hold of their language and employ it as part of their political armoury. (His grammar employed political phrases such as 'Sidmouth *imprisoned* Benbow' to illustrate points of syntax (Smith, p. 246).)

Another late eighteenth-/early nineteenth-century writer in this vernacular vein was William Hone whose pamphlets sometimes adopted 'an extreme demotic form' (Smith 1984:168) and who was eventually tried for blasphemy. But another element is apparent in some of Hone's writing and speech, for example in the evidence he gave in one of his later trials, in which Smith notes 'the stark simplicity of Hone's vocabulary, its concreteness, an abundance of metaphor, the frequent biblical references, and a dependence on sincerity for rhetorical power' (p. 190). Through this language Hone aligned himself with an older vernacular tradition, of the Bible, of *Foxe's Book of Martyrs*, of Bunyan's *Pilgrim's Progress* and of the Levellers, thus placing himself on a 'terrain where vernacular language had achieved its greatest freedom and power' (p. 201).

Hone and others such as John Horne Tooke (who was tried for treason in 1794) made the assumption, basic to modern linguistics, that all languages were equal, and all equally appropriate for political discourse – though Cobbett later argued that 'refined language' was in fact 'corrupt language', language to be abjured (Smith 1984:243). In line with this conception of a basic equality of tongues, which of course ran counter to the prevailing philosophy of language, was the proliferation of radical vernacular tracts and pamphlets, the creation of a 'popular' political literature. Some of the authors of these, however, betray a hesitation, an unwillingness to go the whole way. Smith cites from an article in the journal *Politics for the People* (edited by Daniel Isaac Eaton) in which it is admitted: 'the greater part of the poor know hardly any more of their native language than is just sufficient to express their wants' (in Smith 1984:87). The authors were, all too often, 'unwilling to claim the audience's language as their own' (p. 88). At the same time there was a *conservative* pamphlet literature, such as the tracts produced by the 'Association for Preserving Liberty and Property against Republicans and Levellers', which also in some instances employed the vernacular to counter the radical ideas then beginning to circulate: 'Do not leave the plain wholesome ROAST BEEF of OLD ENGLAND for the meagre unsubstantial diet of these political *French* cooks' (in Smith, p. 75).

If there was, under pressure of circumstances, a conservative movement towards the vernacular, those who espoused the rights of the latter did not entirely abandon the principles of the cultivated language. Cobbett, after all, emphasised grammatical accuracy and clarity: 'consider well what you *mean*; what you *wish* to say' (in Smith, p. 247). For Cobbett, 'clarity is the essential virtue of language because it is the only democratic means of exchanging ideas . . . enabling oneself to negotiate in a society that was apt to interfere with one's meaning' (*ibid.*). In a sense this is 'Republican' English, parallel to the 'Republican' French identified by Balibar.

Similarly, and in a way which reminds me of Grégoire, the Kingman Report (p. 7) argues that 'People need expertise in language to be able to participate effectively in a democracy . . . A democratic society needs people who have the linguistic abilities which will enable them to discuss, evaluate and make sense of what they are told, as well as to take effective action on the basis of their understanding.'

Smith's comments on Cobbett's ideas also suggest a parallel with George Orwell, in particular his essay *Politics and the English language*. This is to do with 'language as an instrument for expressing and not for concealing or preventing thought' (1970:169). It is a guide to using the language with clarity. Orwell himself was a past master at this, offering the following rules (Orwell 1970:169):

i Never use a metaphor, simile or other figure of speech which you are used to seeing in print.
ii Never use a long word where a short one will do.
iii If it is possible to cut a word out, always cut it out.
iv Never use the passive where you can use the active.
v Never use a foreign phrase, a scientific word or a jargon word if you can think of an everyday equivalent.
vi Break any of these rules sooner than say anything outright barbarous.

Note 'barbarous'. This is clear, rational, propositional language – the sort of language cultivated/refined discourse hoped to produce, but from which 'refinement', 'cultivation' (= 'corruption') have been stripped. It is what Gower (1977) aptly termed *Plain words* – simple, correct, accurate, unpretentious, entirely apt, its proponents would claim, for 'conveying ideas from one mind to another' (1977:14).

The Milroys (1985) also draw attention to Orwell, locating him in one of two 'complaint traditions' that have characterised debates about English. The first of these they term 'legalistic' (p. 37 ff.). It includes writers from Swift and Johnson through to their modern successors who have been concerned with maintaining 'correctness' of usage, convinced of the superiority of Standard English over any other variety (p. 40). The second tradition they call 'moralistic'. It includes those such as Orwell who are 'concerned with the usage of standard English in public, formal and written documents, and the effects of such usage on society and human behaviour' (p. 40). They differ from the legalists in that, like Orwell, they are engaged in opposing certain ways of practising the standard language: 'The linguistic abuses (Orwell) is criticising are not primarily found in the colloquial speech of ordinary people: they are found in centralised and official speeches and documents, and they are uttered or written in "standard English". He is criticising authority in language and some aspects of language use that are consequences of standardisation' (p. 45).

The third example goes much further by 'counter-proclaiming' the virtues of vernacular language against those of the language of the elaborated-formal discourse.

A feature of Romanticism was opposition to the traditional languages of literature and state, and a search for authenticity in the vernacular. In Britain of the 1950s, as part of a wider movement for the revaluation of working-class culture, a number of writers directly and indirectly addressed the question of the dominance of the standard language. Raymond Williams's *Culture and society 1780–1850* (1958), and Richard Hoggart's *The uses of literacy* (1957), and films and novels which appeared at that time – most emblematically perhaps Alan Sillitoe's *Saturday night and Sunday morning* – had a profound effect on the thinking of what was then called the 'New Left'.

These developments also had an important influence on thinking about language in education and on English sociolinguistics, though the relationship remains to be documented (cf. Gordon 1981:107). Certainly sociolinguists such as Trudgill emphasised the importance of studying the vernacular English of 'ordinary people', and sometimes at their peril asserted its communicative equality with the standard language. For example, *On dialect* (1983:198–9) records some reactions to Trudgill's earlier book *Accent, dialect and the school*, which had been interpreted as rejecting Standard English in the school curriculum. 'Poor children . . . are now threatened with a rash of Trudgills who won't correct their grammar', said the Sunday Telegraph (28 November 1975), and the Daily Mail (3 December 1985) recorded: 'He appeared looking sloppy and unattractive on television. He implied – fairly inarticulately – that if a child wanted to say "I don't want none of that", it would be acceptable because, Crikey, we know what he means, don't we' (cited in Trudgill 1983:198).

Fifty years earlier, the French linguist Henri Bauche encountered similar hostility, though couched in somewhat different terms. In the preface to the 2nd edition of *Le langage populaire* (which first appeared in 1920), Bauche reviewed what his critics had said:

I was surprised to read that I was a 'Bolshevik', a 'demophile', 'a populist', an 'arsonist', a 'shipwrecker'. Along with many others I had simply recalled that the popular language always, in the end, triumphed over the language of educated people and overturned the barriers set before it. For that I was accused of employing 'the style of the 1st of May' . . . My critics convinced themselves that when I devoted an entire volume to a popular phenomenon without declaring everything I observed to be offensive and detestable I must be a 'man of the left', even of the extreme left – as if there were a left and right in linguistics. In a spirit of religious reaction they wanted to excommunicate me, anathematise me.

(BAUCHE 1928:10–11)

In similar vein, perhaps, John Honey cites Ken Livingstone alongside Trudgill, Crystal, Lyons, Stubbs, Viv Edwards, Sutcliffe and other linguists as providing 'an interesting illustration of how a pseudo-scientific theory [i.e. of the equality of languages] is handed down by incautious academics first to school teachers and their like, ultimately to become the stock-in-trade of lightly educated politicians' (1983:4).

It is not only sociolinguists, however, who proclaim the vernacular. As we saw in chapter 8 non-standard dialects or styles may have what has been called 'covert prestige'. Drawing on the work in the USA of William Labov (1966a, 1966b, 1973), Trudgill and others have examined the 'hidden values associated with non-standard speech' in Britain (Trudgill 1983:172). Evidence for this comes from surveys in Norwich which tested actual usage of certain phonetic forms as against informants' believed usage (see Trudgill 1983:172–85, 1984a:89–95). Trudgill identified among his respondents a group of what he termed 'under-reporters', i.e. those who believed they employed non-RP more often than they did. In one test, half the men under-recorded their use of standard forms, suggesting that 'male Norwich speakers, at a subconscious level, are very favourably disposed towards non-standard, low status speech forms . . . For Norwich men . . . working-class speech is statusful and prestigious' (Trudgill 1984a:91–2, cf. 1983:177).

Trudgill treats this principally as an aspect of gender differentiation in language use. For though the percentage of male under-reporters was the same among both working-class and middle-class informants, women tended to *over-report* their use of standard forms. Age is also a factor, and thus Trudgill concludes that 'covert prestige reflects the value system of our society and of the different sub-cultures within this society, and takes the following form: for male speakers, and for female speakers under 30, non-standard speech forms are highly valued, although these values are not usually overtly expressed' (1983:184–5). Cheshire, too, in her Reading study, detected a greater use of non-standard forms by boys (1982a:87 ff.). As we saw earlier, she also found that such usage varied with the boys' involvement in the 'vernacular' culture of the playground gangs, in which activities such as fighting, swearing, and other signs of 'toughness' were accorded what was in this case fairly overt prestige.

Whether or not women, generally, are more likely to use standard forms, and if so, under what conditions, and for what reasons, are not issues which can be tackled here (see Coates 1986). What is interesting is the fact that frequently Standard English and RP are regarded symbolically as 'feminine'. Trudgill (1984:95) refers to a Caribbean study in which it was reported that young female Creole speakers acquired Standard English at school more rapidly than did the boys, who however mimicked 'in girlish voices, some of the standard forms they had learnt'. Many English speakers will have encountered instances where speakers of Standard English with RP were described as 'cissies' or 'pansies'. In wireless, and in British films of the 1930s and 1940s, the association was employed to represent 'silly ass' characters – Claude Hulbert did this with great success – or effete personalities such as 'Claude and Cecil' of the programme 'ITMA'.

Trudgill's (and to a lesser extent Cheshire's) analysis of the phenomenon in terms of gender – in both Trudgill 1983 and 1984 he deals with it in chapters entitled respectively 'Language and Sex', and 'Sex and Covert Prestige' – misses the point. The association of Standard English and RP with femininity is only indirectly concerned with a male/female distinction. That simply provides, for working-class men, and for those who, for whatever reason, wish to be associated with them, a metaphor through which to handle what are essentially class-based identifications. The covert prestige of working-class speech is, surely, to do with the covert prestige of working-class norms and values. A heightened emphasis on *masculinity* is only one component of that. The idea of (supposed) male/female *superiority* becomes an idiom through which the dominant view of vernacular/standard *inferiority* is reversed.

None of this is to deny a significant degree of sexism in male working-class language (and that of other classes too). Rereading *Saturday night and Sunday morning* after a gap of twenty-five years I was struck by the sexist values (and speech) of the culture it supposedly portrayed. 'What's nice about it?' The point here, however, is that such usage may also signify the covert prestige of the vernacular. The vernacular may therefore become an 'anti-language' (Halliday 1978:164ff.), as may happen also with Creole among Black English speakers, and thus represent a challenge to the elaborated-formal discourse which the opposed dialect (Standard English) actualises.

But rejection is not really a challenge. Subordinate languages may be powerful in their own domains, and indeed may create 'no-go' areas for the dominant culture. They may even, as with counter-cultures and anti-languages, offer satisfying alternative versions of reality and thus have an appearance of autonomy. But it is autonomy of a limited kind. Confined to their private domains, cultures may be turned in on themselves and thus face away from where real power is located. From the point of view of those holding that power this may be a reasonable outcome – 'reserved areas' of language may be tolerated, not everyone need be incorporated.

In fact it is possible that we are moving towards a new phase of society which will in a curious way bear a greater linguistic resemblance to an agro-literate system than to the techno-literate one with which we have become familiar. Few will care what a significant proportion of the population speaks because it will not matter, just as now, for many young people, it matters little what education they receive for there is nothing they can do with it.

Like all bleak prospects this too has another, more positive, side. Alternatives can and do emerge within the interstices of such a system. Many people are now much more aware of the significance of the authoritative–cum–authoritarian modes of discourse (for example in gender relations), which surround and in many respects actualise the core of our system. Haltingly, painfully, there is a great deal of experiment with 'alternatives' (much used and abused word). There is much opposition and there are many setbacks, and these experiments do not challenge the system directly. Nonetheless through an indirect approach they open up the real possibility, in the long term at any rate, of bypassing, isolating, and eventually replacing the dominant system of communicative practice.

REFERENCES

ABADAN-UNAT, N. 1975. 'Educational problems of Turkish migrants' children', pp. 311–22 of Willke, I. ed. *Education for children of migrant workers*, Special Number of International Review of Education, 21 (3)

ABSE, D. ED. 1971. *Corgi modern poets in focus I*. London: Corgi Books

ACTON, LORD J. 1909. *The history of freedom and other essays*. London: Macmillan

ADLAM, D. S. 1976. *Code in context*. London: Routledge and Kegan Paul

AITKEN, A. J. 1981. 'The good old Scots Tongue: does Scots have an identity?', pp. 72–90 of Haugen, E. *et al.* eds. *Minority languages today*. Edinburgh University Press

1984. 'Scots and English in Scotland', pp. 517–32 of Trudgill, P. ed. *Language in the British Isles*. Cambridge University Press

ALBERT, E. 1972. 'Culture patterning of speech behaviour in Burundi', pp. 72–105 of Gumperz, J. J. and Hymes, D. eds. *Directions in sociolinguistics: the ethnography of communication*. New York: Holt, Rinehart and Winston

ALDINGTON, R. 1956. *Introduction to Mistral*. London: William Heinemann Ltd

ANCEL, A. 1973. *L'intégration des migrants*. Lyons: Service des Migrants, cyclostyled

ANDERSON, B. 1983. *Imagined communities*. London: Verso

ARDENER, E. ED. 1971. *Social anthropology and language*, ASA Monographs in Social Anthropology No. 10, London: Tavistock Publications

1975. 'Belief and the problem of women', pp. 1–27 of Ardener, S. ed. *Perceiving women*. London: Dent

ARENSBERG, C. 1937 [1959]. *The Irish countryman*. Gloucester. Mass.: Peter Smith

ARENSBERG, C. AND KIMBALL, S. T. 1940 [1968]. *Family and community in Ireland*. Cambridge, Mass: Harvard University Press

ARMENGAUD, A. 1977. 'Enseignement et langues régionales au XIXe siècle. L'exemple du Sud-Ouest toulousain', pp. 265–72 of Gras, C. and Livet, G. eds. *Régions et régionalisme en France*. Paris: Presses Universitaires de France

ARMENGAUD, A. AND LAFONT, R. EDS. 1979. *Histoire d'Occitanie*. Paris: Hachette

ATKINSON, P. 1985. *Language, structure and reproduction: an introduction to the sociology of Basil Bernstein*. London: Methuen.

BAKHTIN, M. 1981. *The dialogic imagination*. Austin: University of Texas Press

BALIBAR, R. 1974. *Les français fictifs*. Paris: Librairie Hachette

BALIBAR, R. AND LAPORTE, D. 1974. *Le français national: politique et pratique de la langue nationale sous la Révolution*. Paris: Librairie Hachette

BANKS, J. 1984. 'Multiethnic education in the USA: practices and promises', pp. 68–95 of Corner, T. ed. *Education in multicultural societies*. London: Croom Helm

BARIC, L. 1979. 'Dominant languages and cultural participation'. Paper prepared for SSRC 'European Seminar', Sussex, September 1979, cyclostyled

BARKER, ERNEST 1939. *National character and the factors in its formation*. 3rd ed. London: Methuen

BARNARD, F. M. 1965. *Herder's social and political thought: from enlightenment to nationalism*. Oxford: Clarendon Press

1969. *J. G. Herder on social and political culture*. Cambridge University Press

BARNES, D., BRITTON J. AND ROSEN, H. 1971. *Language, the learner and the school*. London: Penguin Books

BASTID, PAUL. 1970. *Sieyès et sa pensée*. Paris: Hachette

BAUCHE, H. 1928. *Le langage populaire*. Paris: Payot

BAUGH, A. C. 1957. *A history of the English language*. 2nd edn. London: Routledge and Kegan Paul

BAUGH, A. C. AND CABLE, T. 1983. *A history of the English language*. 3rd edn. London: Routledge and Kegan Paul

BAUTIER-CASTAING, E. 1980. 'Pratiques linguistiques, discursives, pédagogiques: cause ou conséquence de l'échec scolaire?' *Langages*, 59:9–24

BEC, P. 1979. 'Protohistoire et typologie de l'Occitan', pp. 110–38 of Armengaud, A. and Lafont, R. eds. *Histoire d'Occitanie*. Paris: Hachette

BECKETT, J. C. 1966. *The making of modern Ireland, 1603–1923*. London: Faber and Faber

BELL, R. T. 1976. *Sociolinguistics: goals, approaches, problems*. London: B. T. Batsford

BELLIN, W. 1984. 'Welsh and English in Wales', pp. 449–79 of Trudgill, P. ed. 1984, *Language in the British Isles*. Cambridge University Press

BERNSTEIN, B. 1958. 'Some sociological determinants of perception: an enquiry into subcultural differences.' *British Journal of Sociology*, 9:159–74

1959. 'A public language: some sociological implications of a linguistic form.' *British Journal of Sociology*, 10:311–26

1964a. 'Aspects of language learning in the genesis of the social process', pp. 251–63 of Hymes, D. ed. *Language in culture and society*. New York: Harper and Row [originally *Journal of Child Psychology and Psychiatry*, 1961. 1:323–4]

1964b. 'Elaborated and restricted codes: their social origins and some consequences', pp. 55–69 of Gumperz and Hymes, ed. *The ethnography of*

References

communication. American Anthropologist Special Publication: vol. 66, no. 6, Pt. 2

1972a. 'A sociolinguistic approach to socialization; with some reference to educability', pp. 472–97 of Gumperz, J. J. and Hymes, D. eds. *Directions in sociolinguistics: the ethnography of communication*. New York: Holt, Rinehart and Winston

1972b. 'Social class, language and socialization', pp. 157–78 of Giglioli, P. ed. *Language and social context*. London: Penguin Books

ED. 1973. *Class, codes and control*, vol. 2. London: Routledge and Kegan Paul

1974. *Class, codes and control*, vol. 1. 2nd ed. London: Routledge and Kegan Paul

1975. *Class, codes and control*, vol. 3. London: Routledge and Kegan Paul

1981. 'Codes, modalities, and the process of cultural reproduction: a model'. *Language in Society*, 10:327–63

1985a. 'On pedagogic discourse', pp. 205–40 of Richardson, J. ed. *Handbook of theory and research in the sociology of education*. Westport, Conn.: Greenwood Press.

1985b. 'Elaborated and restricted codes: an overview 1958–1985.' Cyclostyled

BETTS, CLIVE 1976. *Culture in crisis: the future of the Welsh language*. Wirral, Merseyside: The Ffynnon Press

BHATNAGAR, J. ED. 1981. *Educating immigrants*. London: Croom Helm

BLACKALL, E. A. 1978. *The emergence of German as a literary language 1700–1775*. 2nd edn. Ithaca and London: Cornell University Press

BLOCH, M. 1975a. 'Introduction', pp. 1–27 of Bloch ed. *Political language and oratory in traditional societies*. London: Academic Press

ED. 1975b. *Political language and oratory in traditional societies*. London: Academic Press

BLOM, J. P. AND GUMPERZ, J. J. 1972. 'Social meaning in linguistic structures: code-switching in Norway', pp. 409–434 of Gumperz, J. J. and Hymes, D. eds. *Directions in sociolinguistics: the ethnography of communication*. New York: Holt, Rinehart and Winston

BLOOMFIELD, M. W. AND NEWMARK, L. 1963. *A linguistic introduction to the history of English*. New York: Alfred A. Knopf

BOISSIER, G. 1909. *L'Académie Française sous l'Ancien Régime*. Paris: Librairie Hachette

BOLTON, W. F. ED. 1975. *The English language*. Vol. 10 of *History of Literature in the English language*. London: Barrie and Jenkins Ltd.

BOURDIEU, P. 1977. 'L'économie des échanges linguistiques'. *Langue Française*, 34:17–34

1982. *Ce que parler veut dire*. Paris: Fayard

BOURDIEU, P. AND PASSERON, J-C. 1977. *Reproduction in education, society and culture*. London: Sage Publications

BRAZIL, D. C. 1983. 'Kinds of English: spoken, written, literary', pp. 149–66 of Stubbs, M. and Hillier, H. eds. 1983. *Readings on language, schools and classrooms*. London: Methuen

BRIGGS, A. 1960. 'The language of "class" in early nineteenth-century England', pp. 43–73 of Briggs, A. and Saville, J. eds. *Essays in labour history*, vol. I. London: Macmillan

BRITTON, J. ED. 1967. *Talking and writing*. London: Methuen

BRODY, H. 1974. *Inishkillane: change and decline in the West of Ireland*. London: Harmondsworth

BROOKS, D. AND SINGH, K. 1979. 'Pivots and presents: Asian brokers in British foundries', pp. 93–112 of Wallman, S. ed. *Ethnicity at work*. London: Macmillan

BROWN, G. 1982. 'The spoken language', pp. 75–87 of Carter, R. ed. *Linguistics and the teacher*. London: Routledge and Kegan Paul

1983. 'Understanding spoken English', pp. 167–84 of Stubbs, M. and Hillier, H. eds. 1983. *Readings on language, schools and classrooms*. London: Methuen

BROWN, G. AND YULE, G. 1983. *Discourse analysis*. Cambridge University Press

BRUN, A. 1927 [1972]. *La langue française en Provence de Louis XIV au Félibrige*. Geneva: Slatkin Reprints

1931. *Le français de Marseille*. Marseilles: Institut Historique de Provence

BRUNOT, F. 1927. *Histoire de la langue française des origines à nos jours*, vol. II. 'Le seizième.' Paris: Armand Colin

1930. *Histoire de la langue française des origines à nos jours*, vol. III. 'La formation de la langue classique.' Paris: Armand Colin

1932. *Observations sur la grammaire de l'Académie Française*. Paris: Librairie Droz

1947. *Histoire de la langue française des origines à nos jours*, vol. V. 'Le français en France et hors de France au XVIIème siècle.' Paris: Armand Colin

1967. *Histoire de la langue française des origines à nos jours*, vol. IX. 'La Révolution et l'Empire.' Paris: Armand Colin

BULLOCK REPORT 1975. *A language for life*. Report of the Committee of Inquiry under the chairmanship of Sir Alan Bullock. London: Dept. of Education and Science

BURKE, P. 1987. 'Introduction', pp. 1–21 of Burke, P. and Porter, R. eds. *The social history of language*. Cambridge University Press

BURKE, P. AND PORTER, R. EDS. 1987. *The social history of language*. Cambridge University Press

BURTON, D. 1983. 'I think they know that: aspects of English language work in primary classrooms', pp. 246–62 of Stubbs, M. and Hillier, H. eds. 1983. *Readings on language, schools and classrooms*. London: Methuen

CALVET, L. J. 1974. *Linguistique et colonialisme: petit traité de glottophagie*. Paris: Payot

CAMERON, D. 1985. *Feminism and linguistic theory*. London: Macmillan

CAMPANI, G. 1983. 'Identité et représentation dans l'analyse du contenu', pp. 31–46 of Dabène, L., Flasaquier, M., and Lyons, J. eds. *Status of migrants' mother tongues*. Strasbourg: European Science Foundation

References

CASTLES, S., BOOTH, H. AND WALLACE, T. 1984. *Here for good: Western Europe's new ethnic minorities*. London: Pluto Press

CASTLES, S. AND KOSACK, G. 1973. *Immigrant workers and class structure in Western Europe*. London: Oxford University Press/Institute of Race Relations

CATANI, M. 1973. *L'alphabétisation des travailleurs étrangers: une relation dominant–dominé*. Paris: TEMA Editione

CAZDEN, C. B. 1970 [1972]. 'The situation: a neglected source of social class differences in language use', pp. 294–313 of Pride, J. B. and Holmes, J. 1972. *Sociolinguistics*. London: Penguin Books

CAZDEN, C. B. AND DICKINSON, D. K. 1981. 'Language in education: standardization versus cultural pluralism', pp. 446–68 of Ferguson, C. A. and Heath, S. B. eds. 1981. *Language in the USA*. Cambridge University Press

DE CERTEAU, M., JULIA, D., AND REVEL, J. 1975. *Une politique de la langue: la Révolution française et les patois, l'enquête de Grégoire*. Paris: Gallimard

CHAMBERS, J. K. AND TRUDGILL, P. 1980. *Dialectology*. Cambridge University Press

CHAMBERS, W. W. 1946. 'Language and nationality in German pre-Romantic and Romantic thought.' *Modern Language Review*, 41: 382–92

CHAPMAN, M. 1978. *The Gaelic vision in Scottish culture*. London: Croom Helm/Montreal: McGill–Queen's University Press

CHARLOT, M. 1981. 'The education of immigrant children in France', pp. 96–112 of Bhatnagar, J. ed. 1981. *Educating immigrants*. London: Croom Helm

CHERVEL, A. 1977. . . . *et il fallut apprendre à écrire à tous les petits français*. Paris: Payot

CHESHIRE, J. 1982a. *Variation in an English dialect*. Cambridge University Press
1982b. 'Dialect features and linguistic conflict in school.' *Educational Review*, 341: 53–67

CHOMSKY, N. 1972. *Language and mind*. New York: Harcourt Brace Jovanovich
1979. *Language and responsibility*. Sussex: Harvester Press

CICOUREL, A. 1982. *Living in two cultures: the socio-cultural situation of migrant workers and their families*. Paris: Gower UNESCO Press

CITRINE, LORD W. 1952. *ABC of chairmanship*. Tillicoutry, Scotland: National Council for Civil Liberties Publishing Society Ltd.

CLARK, R. T. 1955. *Herder: his life and thought*. Berkeley/Los Angeles: California University Press

CLAYTON P. 1978. 'Domain and register in the use of Welsh', pp. 206–18 of Williams, Glyn ed. *Social and cultural change in contemporary Wales*. London: Routledge and Kegan Paul

CLYNE, M. 1984. *Language and society in the German speaking countries*. Cambridge University Press

COARD, B. 1971. *How the West Indian child is made ESN in the British school system*. London: New Beacon Books

COATES, J. 1986. *Women, men and language*. London: Longman

COHEN, A. P. ED. 1982. *Belonging: identity and social organisation in British rural cultures.* Manchester University Press

COHEN, G. 1980. *The controversy over bilingual education in California and the implications for Britain.* Civil Service College Working Paper No. 24

1984. 'The politics of bilingual education.' *Oxford Review of Education,* 10(2):225–41

COHLER, A. M. 1970. *Rousseau and nationalism.* New York: Basic Books

COLIN, R. 1976. 'Introduction à une analyse des migrations en relation avec les problèmes d'éducation interculturelle.' Lyons: CEFISEM, cyclostyled

COMMITTEE ON IRISH LANGUAGE ATTITUDES RESEARCH 1975. *Main Report.* Dublin: Stationery Office

CONSTANTINIDES, P. 1977. 'The Greek Cypriots: factors in the maintenance of ethnic identity', pp. 269–300 of Watson, J. L. ed. *Between two cultures.* Oxford: Basil Blackwell

COOK-GUMPERZ, JENNY 1972. *Social control and socialization.* London: Routledge and Kegan Paul

COOPER, D. 1958. *Talleyrand.* London: Arrow Books

CORNER, T. ED. 1984. *Education in multicultural societies.* London: Croom Helm

COTTLE, BASIL 1969. *The triumph of English, 1350–1400.* London: Blandford Press

COULTHARD, M. 1977. *An introduction to discourse analysis.* London: Longman

COUNCIL OF THE EUROPEAN COMMUNITIES 1983. *European educational policy statements, 1974–1983.* Brussels–Luxembourg: Office for Official Publications of the European Communities

COWARD, R. AND ELLIS, J. 1977. *Language and materialism.* London: Routledge and Kegan Paul

DABÈNE, L., FLASAQUIER, M. AND LYONS, J. EDS. 1983. *Status of migrants' mother tongues.* Strasbourg: European Science Foundation

DAMOURETTE, J. AND PICHON, E. 1968. *Des mots à la pensée: essai de grammaire de la langue française, 1911–1927,* vol. I. Paris: Editions d'Artrey

DAUZAT, A. 1930. *Histoire de la langue française.* Paris: Payot

1946. *Etudes de linguistique française.* 2nd edn. Paris: Editions d'Artrey

DAVIES, C. 1983. 'Ysgolion Cymraeg', pp. 82–92 of Stubbs, M. and Hillier, H. eds. 1983. *Readings on language, schools and classrooms.* London: Methuen

DAVIES, E. AND REES, A. D. EDS. 1962. *Welsh rural communities.* 2nd edn. Cardiff: University of Wales Press

DAVIS, H. ED. 1939. *The prose works of Jonathan Swift.* Oxford: Basil Blackwell

ED. 1948. *Jonathan Swift: Irish tracts 1720–1723 and sermons.* Oxford: Basil Blackwell

DE FREINE, S. 1977. 'The dominance of the English language in the nineteenth century', pp. 70–87 of O Muirthe, D. ed. *The English language in Ireland.* Dublin: Mercier Press

1978. *The great silence.* Cork: Mercier Press

DELAMONT, S. 1976. *Interaction in the classroom.* London: Methuen

References

DELPLA, CL. 1979. 'L'évolution politique', pp. 689–764 of Armengaud, A. and Lafont, R. eds. *Histoire d' Occitanie*. Paris: Hachette.

DELRIEU, J. 1983. 'Scolarisation des enfants de migrants et enseignement des langues d'origine', pp. 23–9 of Dabène, L., Flasaquier, M. and Lyons, J. eds. *Status of migrants' mother tongues*. Strasbourg: European Science Foundation

DENIEL, ALAIN 1976. *Le mouvement breton 1919–1945*. Paris: Maspero

DÍAZ LÓPEZ, CÉSAR E. 1982. 'The politicization of Galician cleavages', pp. 389–424 of Rokkan, S. and Urwin, D. eds. *The politics of territorial identity: studies in European regionalism*. London: Sage Publications

DIJOUD, P. 1976. 'La politique d'immigration.' *Droit Social*, 5:3–5

DITTMAR, N. 1976. *Sociolinguistics: a critical survey of theory and application*. London: Edward Arnold

DITTMAR, N., AND VON STUTTERHEIM, C. 1983. 'Communication strategies of migrants in interethnic interaction.' Cyclostyled

DOBSON, J. E. 1956. 'Early modern standard English.' *Transactions of the Philological Society 1955*, pp. 25–54
1968. *English pronunciation, 1500–1700*. Oxford: Clarendon Press

DORIAN, N. 1981. *Language death: the life cycle of a Scottish Gaelic dialect* Philadelphia: University of Pennsylvania Press

DOWLING, P. J. 1935. *The hedge schools of Ireland*. Dublin: The Talbot Press

DOWNER, C. A. 1901 [1966]. *Frédéric Mistral: poet and leader of Provence*. New York: Ams Press

DRIVER, G. 1979. 'Classroom stress and social achievement: West Indian adolescents and their teachers', pp. 131–41 of Saifullah Khan ed. *Minority families in Britain*. London: Macmillan

DUMONT, L. 1979. 'L'Allemagne réponds à la France: le peuple et la nation chez Herder et Fichte.' *Libre*, 79–6: 233–50. Paris: Payot

DURKACZ, V. E. 1983. *The decline of the Celtic languages*. Edinburgh: John Donald

EDWARDS, A. D. 1976. *Language in culture and class: the sociology of language and education*. London: Heinemann

EDWARDS, A. D. AND WESTGATE, D. P. G. 1987. *Investigating classroom talk*. London: Falmer Press

EDWARDS, J. R. 1979. *Language and disadvantage*. London: Edward Arnold
1984a. 'Irish and English in Ireland', pp. 480–98 of Trudgill, P. ed. *Language in the British Isles*. Cambridge University Press
ED. 1984b. *Linguistic minorities, policies and pluralism*. London: Academic Press
1985. *Language, society and identity*. Oxford: Basil Blackwell

EDWARDS, O. D. 1968. 'Ireland', pp. 1–209 of Edwards, O. D. *et al. Celtic nationalism*. London: Routledge and Kegan Paul

EDWARDS, O. D. *et al*. 1968. *Celtic nationalism*. London: Routledge and Kegan Paul

EDWARDS, T. 1964. *The Lion of Arles: a portrait of Mistral and his circle*. New York: Fordham University Press

References

EDWARDS, V. 1976. *West Indian language: attitudes and the school*. London: National Association for Multiracial Education

    1979. *The West Indian language issue in British schools*. London: Routledge and Kegan Paul

    1983. *Language in multicultural classrooms*. London: Batsford Academic and Educational Ltd.

    1984a. 'Language policy in multicultural Britain', pp. 49–80 of Edwards, J. R. ed. *Linguistic minorities, policies and pluralism*. London: Academic Press

    1984b. 'British black English and education', pp. 559–72 of Trudgill, P. ed. *Language in the British Isles*. Cambridge University Press

    1986. *Language in a Black community*. Clevedon, Avon: Multilingual Matters

EMMETT, I. 1964. *A North Wales parish*. London: Routledge and Kegan Paul

    1978. 'Blaenau boys in the mid-1960s', pp. 87–101 of Williams, Glyn ed. *Social and cultural change in contemporary Wales*. London: Routledge and Kegan Paul

    1982a. 'Fe godwn ni eto: stasis and change in a Welsh industrial town', pp. 165–97 of Cohen, A. P. ed. *Belonging: identity and social organisation in British rural cultures*. Manchester University Press

    1982b. 'Place, community and bilingualism in Blaenau Ffestiniog', pp. 202–21 of Cohen, A. P. ed. *Belonging: identity and social organisation in British rural cultures*. Manchester University Press

ENGELBRECHT, H. C. 1968. *Johann Gottlieb Fichte*. New York: Ams Press

ENNEW, J. 1980. *The Western Isles today*. Cambridge University Press

ERVIN-TRIPP, S. 1976. 'Sociolinguistics', pp. 15–91 of Fishman, J. A. ed. *Advances in the sociology of language*, vol. 1, 2nd edn. The Hague: Mouton

ESTIENNE, HENRI 1896. *La précellence du langage française*. Edition of 1579 reprinted with notes by Edmond Huguet. Paris: Armand Colin

EVANS, G. AND RHYS, I. 1968. 'Wales', pp. 211–98 of Edwards, O. D. *et al. Celtic nationalism*. London: Routledge and Kegan Paul

EVANS, L. W. 1974. *Studies in Welsh education*. Cardiff: University of Wales Press

FABRE, C. 1983. 'De quelques usages non standard dans des écrits d'écolier', pp. 36–67 of François, F. ed. *J'cause français, non?* Paris: La Découverte/Maspero

FENNELL, D. 1981. 'Can a shrinking linguistic minority be saved? Lessons from the Irish experience', pp. 32–9 of Haugen, E. *et al.* eds. *Minority languages today*. Edinburgh University Press

FERGUSON, C. A. 1959. 'Diglossia'. *Word*, 15: 325–40

FERGUSON, C. A. AND HEATH, S. B. EDS. 1981. *Language in the USA*. Cambridge University Press

FISHER, J. H. 1977. 'Chancery and the emergence of standard written English in the fifteenth century.' *Speculum* 52:870–99

FISHMAN, I. AND LEVY, H. 1964. 'Jewish education in Great Britain', pp. 67–85 of Gould, J. and Esh, S. eds. *Jewish life in modern Britain*. London: Routledge and Kegan Paul

236

References

FISHMAN, J. A. 1972a. 'Domains and the relationship between micro- and macrosociolinguistics', pp. 437–53 of Gumperz, J. J. and Hymes, D. eds. *Directions in sociolinguistics: the ethnography of communication*. New York: Holt, Rinehart and Winston

ED. 1972b. *Advances in the sociology of language: vol. II Selected studies and applications*. the Hague: Mouton

1973. *Language and nationalism: two integrative essays*. Rowley, Mass: Newbury House

1976a. 'The sociology of language: an interdisciplinary social sciences approach to language in society', pp. 217–404 of Fishman, J. A. ed. *Advances in the sociology of language: vol. I: Basic concepts, theories and problems: alternative approaches*

ED. 1976b. *Advances in the sociology of language: vol. I: Basic concepts, theories and problems: alternative approaches*. 2nd edn. The Hague: Mouton

FISHMAN, J. A. AND NAHIRNY, V. C. 1966. 'The ethnic group school and mother tongue maintenance', pp. 92–126 of Fishman, J. A. ed. *Language loyalty in the United States*. The Hague: Mouton

FOUCAULT, M. 1972. *The archaeology of knowledge*. Trans. A. M. Sheridan Smith. London: Tavistock Publications

FOWLER, R., HODGE, B., KRESS, G. AND TREW, T. 1979. *Language and control*. London: Routledge and Kegan Paul

FOWLER, R. AND KRESS, G. 1979. 'Critical linguistics', pp. 185–213 of Fowler R. *et al. Language and control*. London: Routledge and Kegan Paul

FRANÇOIS, A. 1959. *Histoire de la langue française cultivée des origines à nos jours*. 2 vols. Geneva: Alexandre Jullien

FRANÇOIS, F. 1980a. 'Analyse linguistique, normes scolaires et différentiation socio-culturelles.' *Langages* 59: 25–52

1980b. *Conduites langagières et sociolinguistique scolaire*. Special Issue, no. 59 of *Langages*

1983a. 'Bien parler? Bien écrire? Qu'est-ce que c'est?', pp. 11–36 of François F. ed. *J'cause français, non?*. Paris: La Découverte/Maspero

1983b. 'Examples de maniement "complexe" du langage: définir–résumer', pp. 127–47 of François, F. ed. *J'cause français, non?*. Paris: La Découverte/Maspero

1983c. *J'cause français, non?*. Paris: La Découverte/Maspero

FRANKENBERG, R. 1957. *Village on the border*. London: Cohen and West

FRED, M. A. 1983. *Managing culture contact: the organization of Swedish immigration policy*. EIFO English Series no. 6. Stockholm: Commission for Immigrant Research

FRIEL, BRIAN 1981. *Translations*. London: Faber and Faber

FURET, F. AND OZOUF, J. 1982. *Reading and writing: literacy in France from Calvin to Jules Ferry*. Cambridge University Press

FURST, L. R. 1969. *Romanticism in perspective*. London/New York: Macmillan/St Martin's Press

References

GAZIER, A. ED. 1969. *Lettres à Grégoire sur les patois de France 1790–1794*. Edited with an introduction by A. Gazier. Reprint of 1880 edition. Geneva: Slatkine Reprints

GEERTZ, C. 1964. 'Ideology as a cultural system', pp. 47–76 of D. Apter ed. *Ideology and discontent*. New York: Free Press

GELLNER, E. 1964. *Thought and change*. London: Weidenfeld and Nicolson 1983. *Nations and nationalism*. Oxford: Basil Blackwell

GERSHOY, LEO 1962. *Bertrand Barère: a reluctant terrorist*. Princeton University Press

GIBSON, A. 1986. *The unequal struggle*. London: Centre for Caribbean Studies

GIGLIOLI, P. P. ED. 1972. *Language and social context*. London: Penguin Books

GILES, H. AND POWESLAND, P. F. 1975. *Speech style and social evaluation*. London/New York: Academic Press

GILES, H. AND SAINT-JACQUES, B. EDS. 1979. *Language and ethnic relations*. Oxford: Pergamon Press

GIMSON, A. C. 1980. *An introduction to the pronunciation of English*. 3rd edn. London: Arnold

GIORDAN, H. 1975. 'L'enseignement d'Occitan', pp. 84–103 of Marcellesi, J. B. ed. *L'enseignement des 'langues regionales'*. *Langue Française*, no. 25. Paris: Larousse

GITTINS REPORT 1968. *Primary education in Wales*. Chairman, Prof. C. E. Gittins. London: Dept. of Education and Science

GODECHOT, JACQUES. 1968. *Les institutions de la France sous la Révolution et l'Empire*. 2nd ed. Paris: Presses Universitaires de France

GORDON, D. C. 1978. *The French language and national identity 1930–1975*. The Hague: Mouton

GORDON, J. C. B. 1981. *Verbal deficit: a critique*. London: Croom Helm

GOULD, J. AND ESH, S. EDS. 1964. *Jewish life in modern Britain*. London: Routledge and Kegan Paul

GOWER, E. 1977. *The complete plain words*. London: Penguin Books

GRAMSCI, A. 1957. *The Modern Prince and other writings*. New York: International Publishers
    1971 . *Selections from the prison notebooks of Antonio Gramsci*. Edited and translated by Quentin Hoare and Geoffrey Nowell-Smith. London: Lawrence and Wishart

GRANGE, P. AND CHEREL, P. 1975. *Les enfants de partout et l'école française*. Paris: Hommes et Migrations Etudes no. 123

GRAS, C. AND LIVET, G. EDS. 1977. *Régions et régionalisme en France*. Paris: Presses Universitaires de France

GRECO 13. 1981. *Les travailleurs étrangers et la langue*. Paris: Groupement de Recherches Coordonnées sur les Migrations Internationales

GREEN, P. A. 1985. 'Multi-ethnic teaching and the pupils; self-concepts', pp. 46–56 of *Education for all. Report of the Committee of Inquiry into the education of children from ethnic minority groups*. Chairman, Lord M. Swann. Cmnd. 9453. London: HMSO

References

GREENE, D. 1972. 'The founding of the Gaelic League', pp. 9–19 of O Tuama, S. ed. *The Gaelic League idea*. Cork/Dublin: Mercier Press

GREGORY OF TOURS 1974. *The history of the Franks*. Trans. Lewis Thorpe, London: Penguin Books

GRILLO, R. D. ED. 1980. *Nation and State in Europe: anthropological perspectives*. London: Academic Press

1982. 'Alternative perceptions of language training in France: a case study from Lyon', *Journal of Multilingual and Multicultural Development*, 33:233–46

1985. *Ideologies and institutions in urban France: the representation of immigrants*. Cambridge University Press

1987. 'The power of words'. Unpublished ms.

1989. 'Anthropology, language, politics' in Grillo, R. D. ed. *Social anthropology and the politics of language*. Sociological Review Monographs No. 36

GRILLO, R. D., PRATT, J., AND STREET, B. V. 1987. 'Anthropology, linguistics and language', pp. 268–95 of Lyons, J., Coates, R., Deuchar, M. Gazdar, G. eds. *New horizons in linguistics 2*. London: Penguin Books

GUIOMAR, JEAN-YVES 1974. *L'idéologie nationale*. Paris: Champ Libre

GUIRARD, P. 1973. *Le français populaire*. Paris: Presses Universitaires de France

GUMPERZ, J. J. 1971. *Language in social groups: essays selected and introduced by Anwar S. Dil*. Stanford University Press

1982a. *Discourse strategies*. Cambridge University Press

ED. 1982b. *Language and social identity*. Cambridge University Press

GUMPERZ, J. J. AND COOK-GUMPERZ, J. 1981. 'Ethnic differences in communicative style', pp. 430–45 of Ferguson, C. A. and Heath, S. B. eds. 1981. *Language in the USA*. Cambridge University Press

1982. 'Introduction: language and the communication of social identity', pp. 1–21 of Gumperz, J. J. ed. *Language and social identity*. Cambridge University Press

GUMPERZ, J. J. AND HYMES, D. EDS. 1964. *The ethnography of communication*. American Anthropologist Special Publication, vol. 66, no. 6, pt. 2

EDS. 1972. *Directions in sociolinguistics: the ethnography of communication*. New York: Holt, Rinehart and Winston

HALLIDAY, M. A. K. 1973. 'The functional basis of language', pp. 343–66 of B. Bernstein ed. *Class, codes and control*, vol. 2. London: Routledge and Kegan Paul

1978. *Language as social semiotic: the social interpretation of language and meaning*. Baltimore: University Park Press

HALLIDAY, M. et al. 1964. *Linguistic sciences and language teaching*. London: Longman

HASAN, R. 1973. 'Code, register and social dialect', pp. 253–92 of B. Bernstein ed. *Class, codes and control*, vol. 2. London: Routledge and Kegan Paul

HAUGEN, EINAR 1972. *The ecology of language*. Stanford University Press

1977. 'Linguistic relativity: myths and methods', pp. 11–28 of McCormack, W. C. and Wurm, S. A. eds. *Language and thought: anthropological crises*. The Hague: Mouton

References

1981. 'Language fragmentation in Scandinavia', pp. 100–19 of Haugen, E., McClure, J. D. and Thomson, D. eds. *Minority languages today*. Edinburgh University Press

HAUGEN, E., MCCLURE, J. D. AND THOMSON, D. EDS. 1981. *Minority languages today*. Edinburgh University Press

HAWKINS, P. 1977. *Social class, the nominal group and verbal strategies*. London: Routledge and Kegan Paul

HECHTER, M. 1975. *Internal colonialism: the Celtic fringe in British national development 1536–1966*. London: Routledge and Kegan Paul

HEIBERG, M. 1975. 'Insiders/outsiders: Basque nationalism'. *European Journal of Sociology*, 16:169–93

1980. 'Basques, anti-Basques and the moral community', pp. 45–60 of Grillo, R. D. ed. *Nation and State in Europe: anthropological perspectives*. London: Academic Press

HEIDELBERGER FORSCHUNGSPROJEKT 'PIDGIN-DEUTSCH'. 1978. *The unguided learning of German by Spanish and Italian workers. A sociolinguistic study*. Paris: UNESCO

DE HEREDIA, C. 1983. 'Les parlers français des migrants', pp. 95–126 of François, F. ed. *J'cause français, non?*. Paris: La Découverte/Maspero

HESSEL, S. 1976. 'Une politique culturelle avec les immigrés'. *Droit Social*, 5:178–80

HEWITT, R., 1982. 'White adolescent creole users and the politics of friendship'. *Journal of Multilingual and Multicultural Development*, 3 (3):217–32

1986. *White talk, black talk: interracial friendship and communication amongst adolescents*. Cambridge University Press

HIGONNET, P. L. R. 1980. 'The politics of linguistic terrorism and grammatical hegemony during the French Revolution.' *Social History*, 51:41–69

HILL, JANE H. AND KENNETH C. 1986. *Speaking Mexicano: dynamics of syncretic language in Central Mexico*. Tucson: University of Arizona Press

HOBSBAWM, E. AND RANGER, T. 1983. *The invention of tradition*. Cambridge University Press

HODGE, B., KRESS, G., AND JONES, G. 1979. 'The ideology of middle management', pp. 81–93 of Fowler, R. *et al. Language and Control*. London: Routledge and Kegan Paul

HOGGART, R. 1957. *The uses of literacy*. London: Chatto and Windus

HONEY, J. 1983. *The language trap*. Kay-Shuttleworth Papers on Education, no. 3. Kenton, Middx.: National Council for Educational Standards

HONEYFORD, R. 1984. 'Education and race: an alternative view'. *Salisbury Review*, Winter 1984:30–2

HUDSON, R. A. 1980. *Sociolinguistics*. Cambridge University Press

HUGHES, A. AND TRUDGILL, P. 1979. *English accents and dialects*. London: Edward Arnold

HUGHES, E. C. 1972. 'The linguistic division of labour', pp. 269–309 of Fishman,

References

J. A. ed. *Advances in the sociology of language*, vol. 2. The Hague: Mouton

HYDE, DOUGLAS 1967 [1899] . *A literary history of Ireland*. London: Ernest Benn Ltd

HYMES, D. 1971a. 'Social anthropology, sociolinguistics and the ethnography of speaking', pp. 47–93 of Ardener, E. ed. *Social anthropology and language*, ASA Monographs in Social Anthropology no 10. London: Tavistock Publications

  1971b. 'On communicative competence', pp. 269–93 of Pride, J. B. and Holmes, J. 1972. *Sociolinguistics*. London: Penguin Books

  1972. 'Models of the interaction of language and social life', pp. 38–71 of Gumperz, J. J. and Hymes, D. eds. *Directions in sociolinguistics: the ethnography of communication*. New York: Holt, Rinehart and Winston

  1975. 'Speech and language: on the origins and foundations of inequality among speakers', pp. 45–71 of Bloomfield, M., and Haugen, E. eds. *Languages as a human problem*. Guildford/London: Lutterworth Press

  1977. *Foundations in sociolinguistics: an ethnographic approach*. London: Tavistock Publications

HYSLOP, B. 1934. *French nationalism in 1789 according to the General Cahiers*. New York: Columbia University Press

HYWEL DAVIES, D. 1983. *The Welsh Nationalist Party 1925–1945: a call to nationhood*. Cardiff: University of Wales Press

INSTITUT NATIONAL D'ETUDES DEMOGRAPHIQUES 1954. *Français et immigrés*. Travaux et Documents, Cahier no. 20. Paris: Presses Universitaires de France.

JACKSON, L. A. 1974. 'The myth of elaborated and restricted code.' *Higher Education Review*, 6(2): 65–81

JACKSON, B. AND MARSDEN, D. 1962. *Education and the working class*. London: Penguin Books

JEFFCOATE, R. 1984. *Ethnic minorities and education*. London: Harper and Row

JENKINS, D. 1962. 'Aber-porth: a study of a coastal village in South Cardiganshire', pp. 1–63 of Davies and Rees eds. *Welsh rural communities*. 2nd edn. Cardiff: University of Wales Press

JENKINS, P. 1983. *The making of a ruling class: the Glamorgan gentry 1640–1790*. Cambridge University Press

JOHNSON, SAMUEL. 1971. *A journey to the Western Islands of Scotland*. New Haven and London: Yale University Press

JONES, A. R. AND THOMAS, G. EDS. 1973. *Presenting Saunders Lewis*. Cardiff: University of Wales Press

JONES, D. 1958. *The pronunciation of English*. Cambridge University Press

  1960 [1917]. *Everyman's pronouncing dictionary*. London: J. M. Dent

  1969 [1918]. *An outline of English phonetics*. Cambridge: W. Heffer and Sons

JONES, D. G. 1973. 'His politics', pp. 23–78 of Jones, A. R. and Thomas, G. eds. *Presenting Saunders Lewis*. Cardiff: University of Wales Press

References

JONES, E. 1962. 'Tregarm: the sociology of a market town in Central Cardiganshire', pp. 65–117 of Davies and Rees eds. *Welsh rural communities.* 2nd edn. Cardiff: University of Wales Press

JONES, R. AND POUDER, M-C. 1980. 'Les échanges adulte–enfant en situation scolaire.' *Langages,* 59: 79–86

JONES, R. M. 1979. 'Welsh bilingualism: four documents', pp. 231–43 of Mackey, W. F. and Ornstein, J. eds. *Sociolinguistic studies in language contact: methods and cases.* The Hague: Mouton

JUPP, T. C., ROBERTS, C. AND COOK-GUMPERZ, J. 1982. 'Language and disadvantage: the hidden process', pp. 232–56 of Gumperz, J. J. ed. *Language and social identity.* Cambridge University Press

KAY-SHUTTLEWORTH, J. P. 1847. *Report of the Commissioners on the state of education in Wales.* British Parliamentary Papers, vol. 27

KEDOURIE, E. 1960. *Nationalism.* London: Hutchinson

KEENAN, E. 1975. 'A sliding sense of obligatoriness: the polystructure of Malagasy oratory', pp. 93–122 of Bloch ed. *Political language and oratory in traditional society.* London: Academic Press

KELLY, G. P. 1981. 'Contemporary American policies and practices in the education of immigrant children', pp. 214–32 of Bhatnagar, J. ed. 1981. *Educating immigrants.* London: Croom Helm

KELMAN, H. C. 1972. 'Language as aid and barrier to involvement in the national system', pp. 184–212 of Fishman, J. A. ed. *Advances in the sociology of language,* vol. 2. The Hague: Mouton

KHLEIF, BUD B. 1980. *Language, ethnicity and education in Wales.* Contributions to the Sociology of Language, 28. The Hague: Mouton

KINGMAN REPORT 1988. *Report of the committee of inquiry into the teaching of English language.* Chairman, Sir John Kingman. London: HMSO

KLEIN, W. AND DITTMAR, N. 1979. *Developing grammars: the acquisition of German syntax by foreign workers.* Berlin: Springer-Verlag

KOHN, H. 1944. *The idea of nationalism: a study in its origins and background.* New York: Macmillan

  1946. *Prophets and people: studies in nineteenth-century nationalism.* New York: Macmillan

  1967. *Prelude to nation-states: the French and German experience, 1789–1815.* Princeton: D. Van Nostrand Comp. Inc.

KRAMERAE, C., SCHULTZ, M. AND O'BARR, W. EDS. 1984. *Language and power.* London: Sage

KRESS, G. 1979. 'The social values of speech and writing', pp. 46–62 of Fowler, R. et al. *Language and control.* London: Routledge and Kegan Paul

KRESS, G. AND HODGE, R. 1979. *Language as ideology.* London: Routledge and Kegan Paul

KROCH, A. 1978. 'Toward a theory of social dialect variation.' *Language in Society,* 7: 17–36

KUHN, T. S. 1970. *The structure of scientific revolutions.* 2nd enlarged edn.

References

Chicago/London: University of Chicago Press

LABOV, W. 1966a. *The social stratification of English in New York City.* Washington: Center for Applied Linguistics

1966b. 'Hypercorrection by the lower middle class as a factor in linguistic change', pp. 84–113 of Bright, W. ed. *Sociolinguistics.* The Hague: Mouton

1972a. 'The logic of non-standard English', pp. 179–215 of Giglioli, P. P. ed. *Language and social context.* London: Penguin Books

1972b. *Sociolinguistic patterns.* Philadelphia: University of Pennsylvania Press

1973. 'The linguistic consequences of being a "lame"'. *Language in Society,* 21:81–115

1976. 'The study of language in its social context', pp. 152–216 of Fishman, J. A. ed. 1976. *Advances in the study of language, vol. 1: Basic concepts, theories and problems: alternative approaches.* 2nd edn. The Hague: Mouton

1982. 'Objectivity and commitment in linguistic science: the case of the Black English trial in Ann Arbor.' *Language in Society,* 22, August 1982:165–201

LAFONT, R. 1967. *La révolution régionaliste.* Paris: Gallimard

1968. *Sur la France.* Paris: Gallimard

1974. *La revendication occitane.* Paris: Flammarion

LAFONT, R. *et al.* 1982. *Langue dominante, langues dominées.* Paris: Edilig

LAWTON, D. 1968. *Social class, language and education.* London: Routledge and Kegan Paul

LEECH, G. N., DEUCHAR, M. AND HOOGENRAAD, R. 1982. *An English grammar for today.* London: Macmillan

LEFEBVRE, C. 1982. *La syntaxe comparée du français standard et populaire.* Quebec: Office de la langue française

LEONARD, S. S. 1962. *The doctrine of correctness in English usage, 1700–1800.* New York: Russell and Russell

LE PAGE, R. B. 1979. 'Review of Dell Hymes' *Foundations in sociolinguistics* and Norbert Dittmar's *Sociolinguistics'. Journal of Linguistics,* 15:168–79

LEPELLEY, R. 1973. 'Le vocabulaire des pommes dans le parler normand du Val de Saire (Manche)', pp. 42–64 of Lerond, A. ed. 1973. *Les parlers régionaux. Langue Française,* 18

LEROND, A. ED. 1973. *Les parlers régionaux. Language Français,* 18

LÉVI-STRAUSS, C. 1966. *The savage mind.* London: Weidenfeld and Nicolson

LEWIS, SAUNDERS. 1962. 'The fate of the language.' Reprinted in Jones, A. R. and Thomas, G. eds. 1973. *Presenting Saunders Lewis.* Cardiff: University of Wales Press

LINDENFIELD, J. 1972. 'The social conditioning of syntactic variation in French', pp. 77–90 of Fishman, J. A. ed. *Advances in the sociology of language,* vol. 2. The Hague: Mouton

LINGUISTIC MINORITIES PROJECT. 1985. *The other languages of England.* London: Routledge and Kegan Paul

LORWIN, V. R. 1972. 'Linguistic pluralism and political tension in modern Belgium', pp. 386–412 of Fishman, J. A. ed. *Advances in the sociology of language,* vol. 2. The Hague: Mouton

243

LOVEJOY, A. O. 1941. 'The meaning of Romanticism for the historian of ideas.' *Journal of the History of Ideas*, 11 June 1941: 257–78

LUKES, S. 1982. 'Relativism in its place', pp. 261–305 of Hollis, M. and Lukes, S. eds. *Rationality and relativism*. Oxford: Blackwell

LYLE, R. 1953. *Mistral*. Cambridge: Bowes and Bowes

MACAODHA, B. S. 1972. 'Was this a social revolution?', pp. 20–30 of O Tuama, S. ed. *The Gaelic League idea*. Cork/Dublin: Mercier Press

MACAULAY, R. K. S. 1977. *Language, social class and education: a Glasgow study*. Edinburgh University Press

  1978. 'Variation and consistency in Glasgow English', pp. 132–43 of Trudgill, P. ed. *Sociolinguistic patterns in British English*. London: Arnold

MACDIAIRMID, HUGH. 1968. 'Scotland', pp. 299–358 of Edwards, O. D. *et al*. *Celtic nationalism*. London: Routledge and Kegan Paul

MACDONAGH, O. 1983. *States of mind: a study of Anglo-Irish conflict 1780–1980*. London: Allen and Unwin

MACDONALD, M. 1986. 'Celtic ethnic nationalism and the problem of being English.' *Current Anthropology*, 27(4):333–41

MACKEY, W. F. AND ORNSTEIN, J. EDS. 1979. *Sociolinguistic studies in language contact: methods and cases*. The Hague: Mouton

MACKINNON, K. 1977. *Language, education and social processes in a Gaelic community*. London: Routledge and Kegan Paul

  1984. 'Scottish Gaelic and English in the Highlands', pp. 499–516 of Trudgill, P. ed. *Language in the British Isles*. Cambridge University Press

MACNAMARA, J. 1966. *Bilingualism and primary education: a study of Irish experience*. Edinburgh University Press

MADGWICK, P. J. *et al*. 1973. *The politics of rural Wales*. London: Hutchinson

MARCELLESI, J. B. ED. 1971. *Linguistique et société*. Langue française, 9

  ED. 1975. *L'enseignement des 'langues régionales'*. Langue française, 25

  1979. 'Quelques problèmes de l'hégémonie culturelle en France: langue nationale et langues régionales' *International Journal of the Sociology of Language*, 21:63–80

MARCHAND, F. ED. 1972. *Le français à l'école élémentaire*. Langue française, 13

MARTEL, PH. 1979. 'Le XIIIe siècle', pp. 291–345, and 'L'Occitanie dans les crises du bas Moyen Age', pp. 345–88 of Armengaud, A. and Lafont, R. eds. *Histoire d'Occitanie*. Paris: Hachette

MARTIN, N. C. 1967. 'Stages of progress in language', pp. 64–71 of Britton, J. ed. *Talking and writing*. London: Methuen

MARTIN-JONES, M. 1984. 'The newer minorities: literacy and educational issues', pp. 425–48 of Trudgill, P. ed. *Language in the British Isles*. Cambridge University Press

MARTIN-JONES, M. AND ROMAINE, S. 1985. 'Semilingualism: a half-baked theory of communicative competence.' *Applied Linguistics*, 71:26–38

MARX, K. AND ENGELS, F. 1965. *The German ideology*. London: Lawrence and Wishart

MAURAND, G. 1981. 'Situation linguistique d'une communauté rurale en domain

References

occitan', pp. 99–119 of Tabouret-Keller, A. ed. 1981. *Regional languages in France*. Special issue no. 29 of *International Journal of the Sociology of Language*

MEEUS, B. 1979. 'A diglossic situation: standard vs. dialect', pp. 335–44 of Mackey, W. F. and Ornstein, J. eds. *Sociolinguistic studies in language contact: methods and cases*. The Hague: Mouton

MESSENGER, J. C. 1969. *Inis Beag, Isle of Ireland*. New York: Holt, Reinhart, and Winston

MEWETT, P. 1982. 'Associational categories and the social location of relationships in a Lewis crofting community', pp. 101–30 of Cohen, A. P. ed. *Belonging: identity and social organisation in British rural cultures*. Manchester University Press

MILROY, J. 1984. 'The history of English in the British Isles', pp. 5–31 of Trudgill, P. ed. *Language in the British Isles*. Cambridge University Press

MILROY, J. AND MILROY, L. 1978. 'Belfast: change and variation in an urban vernacular', pp. 19–36 of Trudgill, P. 1978. ed. *Sociolinguistic patterns in British English*. London: Edward Arnold

1985. *Authority in language: investigating language prescription and standardisation*. London: Routledge and Kegan Paul

MILROY, L. 1980. *Language and social networks*. Oxford: Blackwell

MISHRA, A. 1982. 'Discovering connections', pp. 57–71 of Gumperz, J. J. ed. *Language and social identity*. Cambridge University Press

MISTRAL, F. 1906. *Mès origines: mémoires et récits*. Paris: Librairie Plon

MORGAN, K. O. 1981. *Rebirth of a nation: Wales 1880–1980*. Oxford: Clarendon Press/Cardiff: University of Wales Press

MORGAN, P. 1983. 'From a death to a view: the hunt for the Welsh past in the Romantic period', pp. 43–100 of Hobsbawm, E. and Ranger, T. *The invention of tradition*. Cambridge University Press

MORNET, D. 1929. *Histoire de la clarté française*. Paris: Payot

MOSKOS, C. A. 1980. *Greek Americans: struggle and success*. Englewood Cliffs, New Jersey: Prentice-Hall

MUELLER, C. 1973. *The politics of communication*. New York: Oxford University Press

NAIRN, T. 1977. *The break-up of Britain: crisis and neo-nationalism*. London: New Left Books

NAMIER, L. B. 1952. 'Nationality and liberty', pp. 20–44 of *Avenues of history*. London: Hamish and Hamilton

NECHELES, RUTH F. 1971. *The Abbé Grégoire 1787–1831: the odyssey of an egalitarian*. Westport, Conn: Greenwood Publishing Corporation

NEWBOLT, SIR H. 1921. *The teaching of English in England: report on the position of English in the educational system of England*. London: HMSO

NGUYEN, V. 1977. 'Aperçus sur la conscience d'Oc autour des années 1900', pp. 241–55 of Gras, C. and Livet, G. eds. 1977. *Régions et régionalisme en France*. Paris: Presses Universitaires de France

NICOLAS, M. 1982. *Histoire du mouvement Breton*. Paris: Editions Syros

References

NICOLSON, A. 1866. *Report on the state of education in the Hebrides*. Edinburgh: HMSO

NORST, M. 1982. *Ethnic schools: report with recommendation*. Canberra: Commonwealth Schools Commission

NOWLAN, K. D. 1972. 'The Gaelic League and other national movements', pp. 41–51 of O Tuama, S. ed. *The Gaelic League idea*. Cork/Dublin: Mercier Press

O'BARR, W. M. 1976. 'The study of language and politics', pp. 1–27 of O'Barr, W. M. and O'Barr, J. F. eds. *Language and politics. Contributions to the sociology of language*, 10. The Hague: Mouton

1982. *Linguistic evidence: language, power and strategy in the courtroom*. New York: Academic Press

O'BARR, W. M. AND O'BARR, J. F. EDS. 1976. *Language and politics. Contributions to the sociology of language*, 10. The Hague: Mouton

O CUIV, B. O. ED. 1969. *A view of the Irish language*. Dublin: Government Stationery Office

O FIAICH, T. 1969. 'The language and political history', pp. 101–11 of O Cuiv ed. *A view of the Irish language*. Dublin: Government Stationery Office

1972. 'The great controversy', pp. 63–75 of O Tuama, S. ed. *The Gaelic League idea*. Cork/Dublin: Mercier Press

O' HAILIN, T. 1969. 'Irish revival movements', pp. 91–100 of O Cuiv ed. *A view of the Irish language*. Dublin: Government Stationery Office

O MUIRTHE, D. ED. 1977. *The English language in Ireland*. Dublin: Mercier Press

O MURCHU, M. 1970. *Language and community*. Dublin: Stationery Office Comhairle na Gaeilge, Occasional Paper no. 1

ONIONS, C. T. 1950. 'The English language', pp. 280–302 of Barker, E. ed. *The character of England*. London: Oxford University Press

ORWELL, G. 1970. 'Politics and the English language', pp. 156–70 of Orwell, S. and Angus, I. eds. *The collected essays, journalism and letters of George Orwell*, vol. 4. London: Penguin Books

O TUAMA, S. ED. 1972. *The Gaelic League idea*. Cork/Dublin: Mercier Press

OWEN, TREFOR 1962. 'Chapel and community in Glan-llyn, Merioneth', pp. 183–248 of Davies and Rees eds. *Welsh rural communities*. 2nd edn. Cardiff: University of Wales Press

PALMER, R. 1972. *Immigrants ignored: an appraisal of the Italians in Britain*. Unpublished M. A. thesis, University of Sussex

PAREKH, B. ED. 1974 . *Colour, culture and consciousness*. London: Allen and Unwin

PARKIN, D. J. 1975. 'The rhetoric of responsibility: bureaucratic communications in a Kenya farming area', pp. 113–39 of Bloch, M. ed. *Political language and oratory in traditional society*. London: Academic Press

1984. 'Political language.' *Annual Review of Anthropology*, 13:345–65

PATEMAN, T. 1980. *Language, truth and politics*. 2nd edn. Lewes: Jean Stroud

PATTERSON, S. 1977. 'The Poles: an exile community in Britain', pp. 214–41 of Watson, J. L. ed. *Between two cultures*. Oxford: Basil Blackwell

References

PAULSTON, C. B. 1981. 'Bilingualism and education', pp. 469–85 of Ferguson, C. A. and Heath, S. B. eds. 1981. *Language in the USA*. Cambridge University Press

PÊCHEUX, M. 1982. *Language, semantics and ideology*. London: Macmillan

PERKINS, J. B. 1908. *Richlieu and the growth of French power*. London: Putnam's

PEYRE, H. 1933. *La royauté et les langues provinciales*. Paris: Les Presses Modernes

PFAFF, C. W. 1981. 'Sociolinguistic problems of immigrants: foreign workers and their children in Germany', pp. 155–88 of *Language in Society*, 10

PHILLIPS, K. C. 1984. *Language and class in Victorian England*. Oxford: Basil Blackwell/André Deutsch

PRATT, J. 1979. 'Communists talking.' Paper prepared for SSRC 'European Seminar', Sussex, September 1979, cyclostyled

PRATTIS, J. I. 1981. 'Industrialisation and minority language loyalty: the example of Lewis', pp. 21–31 of Haugen, E. *et al.* eds. *Minority languages today*. Edinburgh University Press

PRICE, G. 1984. *The languages of Britain*. London: Edward Arnold

PRIDE, J. B. AND HOLMES, J. 1972. *Sociolinguistics*. London: Penguin Books

PYLES, T. 1971. *The origins and development of the England language*, 2nd edn. New York: Harcourt Brace Jovanovich

RAMPTON REPORT 1981. *West Indian children in our schools: interim report of the committee of inquiry into the education from ethnic minority groups.* Chairman, A. Rampton. Cmnd. 8273. London: HMSO

RAWKINS, P. M. 1987. 'The politics of benign neglect: education, public policy, and the mediation of linguistic conflict in Wales', pp. 27–48 of Williams, Glyn ed. 1987. *The sociology of Welsh. International Journal of the Sociology of Language*, vol. 66

REECE, J. E. 1977. *The Bretons against France: ethnic minority nationalism in twentieth century Brittany*. Chapel Hill: N. Carolina Press

REES, A. D. 1951. *Life in a Welsh countryside*. Cardiff: University of Wales Press

REID, E. 1984. 'The new minorities: spoken languages and varieties', pp. 408–24 of Trudgill, P. ed. *Language in the British Isles*. Cambridge University Press

REINHARD, M. 1961. *Etude de la population pendant la Révolution et l'Empire*. Paris: Gap

REY-VON ALLMEN, M. 1983. 'Le statut des langues dans les pays d'accueil', pp. 17–22 of Dabène, L., Flasaquier, M. and Lyons, J. eds. *Status of migrants' mother tongues*. Strasbourg: European Science Foundation

RICHELIEU, CARDINAL DE, 1947. *Testament politique*. Paris: Laffont

RICKARD, P. 1974. *A history of the French language*. London: Hutchinson University Library

RIST, R. C. 1978. *Guestworkers in Germany: the prospects for pluralism*. New York: Praeger

RIVAROL, A. 1930. *De l'universalité de la langue française*. Edition of text of 1784 with notes by Th. Suran. Paris/Toulouse: Didier/Privat

ROBERTS, C. 1986. 'Political conflict over bilingual initiatives: a case study.' Paper presented to Linguistics and Politics Symposium, University of Lancaster, April 1986, cyclostyled

ROBINSON, W. P. 1972. *Language and social behaviour*. Harmondsworth: Penguin

ROKKAN, S. AND URWIN, D. W. EDS. 1982. *The politics of territorial identity: studies in European regionalism*. London: Sage Publications

ROSEN, H. 1967. 'The language of textbooks', pp. 100–14 of Britton, J. ed. *Talking and writing*. London: Methuen

1971. 'Towards a language policy across the curriculum', pp. 117–59 of Barnes, D. *et al*. *Language, the learner and the school*. London: Penguin Books

1972. *Language and class: a critical look at the theories of Basil Bernstein*. London: Falling Wall Press

ROSEN, H. AND BURGESS, T. 1980. *Language and dialects of London schoolchildren*. London: Ward Lock Educational

ROSS, A. S. C. 1954. 'Linguistic class-indicators in present-day English'. *Neuphilologische Mitteilungen*, 55:20–56

ROSS, J. A. 1979. 'Language and the mobilization of ethnic identity', pp. 1–13 of Giles, H. and Saint-Jacques, B. eds. *Language and ethnic relations*. Oxford: Pergamon Press

ROUSSEAU, J. J. 1968. *The Social Contract and Discourses*. trans. G. D. H. Cole. Everyman's Library. London: Dent

RUNCIMAN, W. G. ED. 1978. *Max Weber: selections in translation*. Cambridge University Press

RUNDLE, S. 1946. *Language as a social and political factor in Europe*. London: Faber and Faber

SAIFULLAH KHAN, V. 1977. *Bilingualism and linguistic minorities in Britain: developments, perspectives*. London: The Runnymede Trust

1980. 'The "mother tongue" of linguistic minorities in multicultural England'. *Journal of Multilingual and Multicultural Development*, 11:71–88

1983. 'Mother tongue schools and classes: implications from the English context', pp. 189–95 of Dabène, L., Flasaquier, M. and Lyons, J. eds. *Status of migrants' mother tongues*. Strasbourg: European Science Foundation

SAINÉAN, L. 1920. *Le langage parisien au XIXe siècle*. Paris: Bocard

SALOUTOS, T. 1964. *The Greeks in the United States*. Cambridge, Mass.: Harvard University Press

SAMUELS, M. L. 1972. *Linguistic evolution with special reference to English*. Cambridge University Press

SAUVAGEOT, A. 1972. *Analyse du français parlé*. Paris: Hachette

SCHATZMAN, L. AND STRAUSS, A. 1955. 'Social class and modes of communication.' *American Journal of Sociology*, 60: 329–38

SCHENK, H. G. 1966. *The mind of the European Romantics*. London: Constable

SCHLIEBEN-LANGE, B. 1977. 'The language situation in Southern France.' *International Journal of the Sociology of Language*, 12: 101–8

SEBBA, M. 1986. 'London Jamaican and Black London English', pp. 149–67 of

Sutcliffe, D. and Wong, A. eds. *The language of the Black experience*. Oxford: Basil Blackwell

SEERS, D. *et al.* 1979. *Underdeveloped Europe: studies in core–periphery relations*. Hassocks, Sussex: Harvester Press

SEIDEL, G. 1975. 'Ambiguity in political discourse', pp. 205–26 of Bloch, M. ed. *Political language and oratory in traditional society*. London: Academic Press

1979. 'Dominant languages and structures of domination', paper presented to SSRC European Seminar, September 1979, cyclostyled

1986. 'Culture, nation and "race" in the British and French New Right', pp. 107–35 of Levitas, R. ed. *The ideology of the New Right*. Cambridge: Polity Press

SERANT, P. 1971. *La Bretagne et la France*. Paris: Fayard

SETON-WATSON, H. 1977. *Nations and states: an enquiry into the origins of nations and the politics of nationalism*. London: Methuen

SHAKLEE, M. 1980. 'The rise of standard English', pp. 33–62 of Shopen, T. and Williams, J. M. eds. *Standards and dialects in English*. Cambridge, Mass.: Winthrop Publishers Inc.

SHOPEN, T. AND WILLIAMS, J. M. EDS. 1980. *Standards and dialects in English*. Cambridge, Mass.: Winthrop Publishers Inc.

SIEYÈS, E. J. 1963. *What is the Third Estate?* trans. M. Blondel. London: Pall Mall Press

SINCLAIR, J. M. AND COULTHARD, R. M. 1975. *Towards an analysis of discourse: the English used by teachers and pupils*. Oxford University Press

SKUTNABB-KANGAS, T. 1978. 'Semilingualism and the education of migrant children as a means of reproducing the caste of assembly line workers', pp. 221–51 of Dittmar, N. *et al.* eds. *Papers for the First Scandinavian–German Symposium on the language of foreign workers and their children*. Roskilde

1981. 'Guest worker or immigrant – different ways of producing an underclass.' *Journal of Multilingual and Multicultural Development*, 22:89–115

1984. 'Children of guest workers and immigrants: linguistic and educational issues', pp. 17–48 of Edwards, J. R. ed. *Linguistic minorities, policies and pluralism*. London: Academic Press

SMITH, A. D. ED. 1976. *Nationalist movements*. London: The Macmillan Press Ltd

1981. *The ethnic revival in the modern world*. Cambridge University Press

1983. *Theories of nationalism*. 2nd ed. New York: Holmes and Meier

SMITH, O. 1984. *The politics of language 1791–1819*. Oxford: Clarendon Press

SMITHERMAN, G. 1980a. 'The contemporary merger of linguistics and the law.' Paper presented to the International Language and Power Conference, Bellagio, Italy, April 4–8, 1980

1980b. 'White English in Black face', pp. 158–68 of Michaels, L. and Ricks, C. eds. *The state of the language*. Berkeley: University of California Press

1984. 'Black power as language', pp. 101–15 of Kramerae *et al.* eds. *Language and power*. London: Sage

References

SNOW, C. *et al.* 1981. 'The international origins of foreigner talk: municipal employees and foreign workers.' *International Journal of the Sociology of Language*, 28:81–91

SOBOUL, A. 1977. 'De l'Ancien Régime à la Révolution. Problème régional et réalitès sociales', pp. 25–54 of Gras, C. and Livet, G. eds. *Régions et régionalisme en France*. Paris: Presses Universitaires de France

STEDMAN JONES, G. 1983. *Languages of class: studies in English working-class history 1832–1982*. Cambridge University Press

STEINBERG, J. 1987. 'The historian and the Questione della Lingua', pp. 198–209 of Burke, P. and Porter, R. eds. *The social history of language*. Cambridge University Press

STEPHENS, M. 1976. *Linguistic minorities in Western Europe*. Llandysul: Gomer Press

STONE, M. 1981. *The education of the black child in Britain: the myth of multiracial education*. London: Fontana

STRAKER-WELDS, M. 1984. *Education for a multicultural society: case studies in ILEA schools*. London: Bell and Hyman

STRATHERN, A. 1975. 'Veiled speech in Mount Hagen', pp. 185–203 of Bloch, M. ed. *Political language and oratory in traditional society*. London: Academic Press

STRAYER, J. R. 1963. 'The historical experience of nation-building in Europe', pp. 17–26 of Deutsch, K. W. and Foltz, W. J. eds. *Nation-building*. New York: Atherton Press

STREET, B. V. 1984. *Literacy in theory and practice*. Cambridge University Press

STUBBS, M. 1980. *Language and literacy*. London: Routledge and Kegan Paul
1983. *Language, schools and classrooms*. 2nd edn. London: Methuen

STUBBS, M. AND HILLIER, H. EDS. 1983. *Readings on language, schools and classrooms*. London: Methuen

SUTCLIFFE, D. 1982. *British Black English*. Oxford: Basil Blackwell

SUTCLIFFE, D. AND WONG, A. EDS. 1986. *The language of the Black experience*. Oxford: Basil Blackwell

SWANN REPORT. 1985. *Education for all. Report of the Committee of Inquiry into the education of children from ethnic minority groups*. Chairman, Lord M. Swann. Cmnd. 9453. London: HMSO

SWORD, K. R. 1982. *Ethnic identity and association among Polish émigrés in a British town*. Unpublished D. Phil., University of Sussex

SYDENHAM, M. J. 1961. *The Girondins*. London: Athlone Press

TABOURET-KELLER, A. ED. 1981. *Regional languages in France*. Special Issue no. 29 of *International Journal of the Sociology of Language*

TAESCHNER, T. 1983. *The sun is feminine: the study of language acquisition in bilingual children*. Berlin: Springer

TAPIÉ, V-L. 1974. *France in the age of Louis XIII and Richelieu*. London: Macmillan

TEULAT, J. 1979. 'Le problème de l'écrit occitan depuis 1914', pp. 883–98 of Armengaud and Lafont eds. *Histoire d' Occitanie*. Paris: Hachette

References

THOMPSON, J. B. 1984. *Studies in the theory of ideology*. Cambridge: Polity Press

THOMPSON, J. M. 1944. *The French Revolution*. 2nd edn. Oxford: Basil Blackwell

THOMSON, D. 1981. 'Gaelic in Scotland: assessment and prognosis', pp. 10–20 of Haugen, E. *et al.* eds. *Minority languages today*. Edinburgh University Press

THOMSON, R. L. 1984. 'The history of the Celtic languages in the British Isles', pp. 241–58 of Trudgill, P. ed. *Language in the British Isles*. Cambridge University Press

TIMM, L. A. 1980. 'Bilingualism, diglossia, and language shift in Brittany'. *International Journal of the Sociology of Language*, 25: 29–42

TOMLINSON, S. 1983. *Ethnic minorities in British schools*. London: Heinemann Educational Books

TÖNNIES, F. 1955. *Community and association*. London: Routledge and Kegan Paul

TOSI, A. 1984. *Immigration and bilingual education*. Oxford: Pergamon Press

TOURAINE, A. 1977. *The self-production of society*. Chicago/London: University of Chicago Press

TOURAINE, A., DUBET, F., HEGEDUS, Z., AND WIEVIORKA, M. 1981. *Le pays contre l'Etat: luttes Occitanes*. Paris: Editions de Seuil

TOUTAIN, J. C. 1963. *La population de la France de 1700 à 1959*. Paris: Cahiers de l'Institut de Science Economique Appliquée, Suppl. no. 133

TOWNSEND, H. E. R. 1971. *Immigrant pupils in England: the LEA response*. Slough: NFER (National Foundation for Educational Research in England and Wales)

TOWNSEND, H. E. R., AND BRITTAN, E. M. 1972. *Organization in multiracial schools*. Slough: NFER (National Foundation for Educational Research in England and Wales)

TREW, T. 1979a. 'Theory and ideology at work', pp. 94–116 of Fowler, R. *et al. Language and control*. London: Routledge and Kegan Paul

1979b. '"What the papers say": linguistic variation and ideological difference', pp. 117–56 of Fowler, R. *et al. Language and control*. London: Routledge and Kegan Paul

TRUDGILL, P. 1974. *The social differentiation of English in Norwich*. Cambridge University Press

1975. *Accent, dialect and the school*. London: Edward Arnold

ED. 1978. *Sociolinguistic patterns in British English*. London: Edward Arnold

1979a. 'Standard and non-standard dialects of English in the United Kingdom: problems and politics.' *International Journal of the Sociology of Language*, 21: 9–24

1983. *On dialect*. Oxford: Basil Blackwell

1984a. *Sociolinguistics*. 2nd edn. London: Penguin Books

ED. 1984b. *Language in the British Isles*. Cambridge University Press

VAN DEN BROECK, J. 1977. 'Cognitive code or situational style: class differences in syntactic complexity in the Flemish town of Masseik.' *Language in Society*, 6: 149–81

References

WAKELIN, M. 1984. 'Rural dialects in England', pp. 70–93 of Trudgill, P. ed. *Language in the British Isles.* Cambridge University Press

WARNANT, L. 1973. 'Dialects du français et français régionaux', pp. 100–25 of Lerond, A. ed. *Les pariers régionaux. Langue française,* 18

WARNER, W. L. AND SROLE, L. 1945. *The social system of American ethnic groups.* Yankee City Series, vol. 2. New Haven: Yale University Press

WATSON, J. L. ED. 1977. *Between two cultures.* Oxford: Basil Blackwell

WEBER, E. 1976. *Peasants into Frenchmen: the modernization of rural France 1870–1914.* London: Chatto and Windus

WEBER, M. 1964. *The theory of social and economic organisation.* New York: The Free Press

WEIL, D. 1972. 'Langage parlé à l'école et dans la famille.' *Langue française,* 13:71–94

WEINREICH, U. 1967. *Languages in contact.* The Hague: Mouton

WELLIVER, W. 1981. *Dante in Hell: the De Vulgari Eloquentia.* Ravenna: Longo Editore

WIGHT, J. 1983. 'The space between', pp. 226–37 of Stubbs, M. and Hillier, H. eds. 1983. *Readings on language, schools and classrooms.* London: Methuen

WILLIAMS, GLANMOR. 1979. *Religion, language and nationality in Wales.* Cardiff: University of Wales Press

WILLIAMS, GLYN. ED. 1978. *Social and cultural change in contemporary Wales.* London: Routledge and Kegan Paul

1987a. 'Bilingualism, class dialect and social reproduction', pp. 85–98 of Williams, Glyn ed. 1987. *The sociology of Welsh. International Journal of the Sociology of Language,* vol. 66

ED. 1987b. *The sociology of Welsh. International Journal of the Sociology of Language,* vol. 66

WILLIAMS, GWYN, A. 1982. 'When was Wales?', pp. 189–201 of *The Welsh in their history.* London: Croom Helm

1985. *When was Wales? A history of the Welsh.* London: Penguin Books

WILLIAMS, R. 1958. *Culture and society 1780–1950.* London: Chatto and Windus

1977. *Marxism and literature.* Oxford: Oxford University Press

WILLKE, I. ED. 1975. *Education for children of migrant workers.* Special Number of *International Review of Education,* 21 (3)

WODAK-ENGEL, R. 1984. 'Determination of guilt: discourse in the courtroom', pp. 89–100 of Kramerae *et al.* eds. *Language and power.* London: Sage

WOLFSON, N. AND MANES, J. EDS. 1985. *Language of inequality.* Berlin/New York/Amsterdam: Mouton

WYLD, H. C. 1921. *A history of modern colloquial English.* London: T. Fisher Unwin

INDEX

Index

Scotland (*cont.*)
  Lallans, 50, 90; language loyalty, 55;
  Lowlands, 50, 97; Scottish Nationalist
  Party (SNP), 90, 106; Sutherland, 50,
  51, 54, 86; Western Isles, 52, 59, 102,
  177
Seidel, G., 9, 10, 16
Sieyès, E. J., 23, 30
Sillitoe, A., 225
Sinclair, J. M. and Coulthard, R. M.,
  202–3, 214
Skutnabb-Kangas, T., 122, 123, 124
Smith, O., 7, 10, 176, 192, 193, 222, 224
Smitherman, G., 147
SNP, *see* Scotland
Soboul, A., 72
social linguistics, 11, 13–16, 152; discourse
  analysis, 12–13, 197, 202ff; ethnography
  of speaking, 184; social psychology,
  8–9; sociolinguistics, 14, 18, 44, 153–4,
  159, 165, 184, 193, 196, 226; sociology
  of language, 7
sociolinguistics, *see* social linguistics
SPCK, 98
speech, *see* language
Standard English, *see* English language
state, 2, 17, 28–9, 45, 60, 73, 88, 96, 155,
  191, 219–20, 225, 228; Act of Union of
  England and Wales, 84–5, 94, 96, 156;
  agro-literate, 2, 28; bureaucratic
  encounters, 135–7; language-of-state, 2,
  6, 156; mosaic state, 27; techno-literate,
  228; Villers Cotteret, Ordonnance of,
  28, 47, 67, 162; *see also* Ancien Régime,
  nations, and nation-states
status, *see* class and language
Statute of Pleading, 47
Statutes of Iona, 88
Statutes of Kilkenny, 84
Steinberg, J., 2–3
Strathern, A., 190
Strayer, J. R., 27
Street, B. V., 15, 219
Stubbs, M., 169, 194, 197, 200, 202–3,
  207
style and language, 1, 11, 167, 171, 183,
  185, 194
Sutcliffe, D., 226

Sutherland, *see* Scotland
Swann Report, 18, 107, 117, 121–3,
  125–7, 129, 131, 139, 141, 143, 144,
  147, 148, 150
Swansea, 56
Sweden, 116
Swift, Jonathan, 86–7, 156, 225
Sword, K., 115
Sydenham, M., 72

Talleyrand, 29, 30, 32, 36
tally sticks, etc., 62, 74
Tapié, V-L., 190
techno-literate societies, 228
Teulat, J., 74
Thompson, J. B., 13
Thompson, J. M., 34
Tomlinson, C., 140
Tönnies, F., 23, 187
Tooke, J. H., 223
Tosi, A., 121, 122
Touraine, A., 78
Townsend, H. E. R., 140–1, 142, 144,
  145
Tregaron, 58
Trew, T., 13
troubadours, *see* Provence
Trudgill, P., 157, 169, 170, 172, 176, 179,
  185, 188, 199, 207, 225, 226, 227;
  Trudgill's Triangle, 153–4
Turkish immigrants, 109, 134, 140, 149

underachievement, *see* education
underdevelopment, regional, and language,
  8, 17, 81–3; and migration, 109
United Kingdom, 60–1
urbanisation and language, 20, 61, 68–9
Urdu language, 15, 125, 134
USA, language in, 118, 122, 133, 141,
  146–7, 152, 180, 226

Vaugelas, C. F., 29, 163, 164, 189, 191
Vaughan Thomas, Wynford, 92
Veblen, T., 183
vernacular, *see* language
Victorian England, 160–2
Villers Cotteret, Ordonnance of, *see* state
vulgar, *see* language